Style, Mediation, and Change

OXFORD STUDIES IN SOCIOLINGUISTICS

General Editors:

Nikolas Coupland
University of Copenhagen and Cardiff
University

Adam Jaworski
University of Hong Kong

Recently Published in the Series:

Style, Mediation, and Change

SOCIOLINGUISTIC PERSPECTIVES ON TALKING MEDIA

Edited by Janus Mortensen
Nikolas Coupland
and
Jacob Thøgersen

OXFORD
UNIVERSITY PRESS

OXFORD
UNIVERSITY PRESS

Oxford University Press is a department of the University of Oxford. It furthers the University's objective of excellence in research, scholarship, and education by publishing worldwide. Oxford is a registered trade mark of Oxford University Press in the UK and certain other countries.

Published in the United States of America by Oxford University Press
198 Madison Avenue, New York, NY 10016, United States of America.

Library of Congress Cataloging-in-Publication Data
Names: Mortensen, Janus, editor. | Coupland, Nikolas, 1950- editor. | Thøgersen, Jacob, editor.
Title: Style, mediation, and change : sociolinguistic perspectives on talking media / edited by Janus Mortensen, Nikolas Coupland and Jacob Thøgersen.
Description: Oxford ; New York : Oxford University Press, [2017] |
"The present book is one of two edited collections to appear from a Round Table held at the University of Copenhagen in June 2014 on Sociolinguistics and the Talking Media: Style, Mediation and Change." | Includes bibliographical references and index.
Identifiers: LCCN 2016018909 | ISBN 9780190629489 (hardcover : alk. paper) | ISBN 9780190629496 (pbk. : alk. paper) | ISBN 9780190629502 (Updf) | ISBN 9780190641047 (Epub) | ISBN 9780190629519 (online)
Subjects: LCSH: Discourse analysis--Social aspects. | Radio broadcasting—Social aspects. | Television broadcasting—Social aspects. | Mass media and language. | Sociolinguistics.
Classification: LCC P302.84 .S79 2016 | DDC 401/.41—dc23
LC record available at https://lccn.loc.gov/2016018909

9 8 7 6 5 4 3 2 1
Paperback printed by WebCom, Inc., Canada
Hardback printed by Bridgeport National Bindery, Inc., United States of America

CONTENTS

PREFACE AND ACKNOWLEDGEMENTS

The present book is one of two edited collections to appear from a Round Table held at the University of Copenhagen in June 2014 on *Sociolinguistics and the Talking Media: Style, Mediation, and Change.** At the Round Table and in the two collections, a total of 30 researchers were invited to debate theoretical issues at the interface between language, change, and the 'talking media,' and to report new research with a shared focus on the notions of style, mediation, and sociolinguistic change.

The chapters in the current collection adopt a broad semiotic perspective on style, ranging from brand styling in advertising to styles of critical journalism, interviewing, news reading, reality television, sitcoms, and TV art, and in doing so contribute to new theoretical understandings of several central concepts in contemporary sociolinguistics. These include mediation and mediatization, the hybridizing and situated enactment of media genres and identities, sociolinguistic change, and—of course—style itself. Under the rubric of style we explore how media, across many of their most salient modes and activities, both exploit and reshape normative ways of speaking and ways of meaning. As a sociolinguistic concept, style orients both to stability/continuity—media as repositories of culturally familiar personas, relational designs in interaction, speech genres, and semiotic configurations—and also to change/renewal—media designers, presenters, and consumers engaged in more or less focused projects that create new orders of signification. The present book therefore opens up perspectives on change that are fundamentally sociolinguistic: not necessarily change in forms and patterns of language itself, but change in relationships between language and society, mediated into sociocultural salience.

The book's chapters show how a style perspective is sufficiently nuanced to capture the complex laminations of mediated representation and performance, when stances are built or subverted in humorous or parodic frames. The much-vaunted 'authority of the media,' and new sources and constructions of authority, can also be scrutinized in sophisticated ways through the analytical lens of style. In the spirit of critical sociolinguistic inquiry, several chapters address diverse sociopolitical concerns particular to local contexts and conditions of language use, where change (or resistance to change) is in the air.

For the present volume we have selected studies that relate to various different national media contexts and to a wide range of sociolinguistic changes—the construction of new sociolinguistic norms and ideologies—in which media are implicated. Furthermore, the chapters all share a methodological commitment to closely contextualized interactional analysis, bringing the insights of Critical Discourse Analysis and Interactional Sociolinguistics to bear on particular sets of data.

As organizers of the Copenhagen Round Table we would like to express our gratitude to the participants for devoting their time and energy to the event, also to the Department of Nordic Research at the University of Copenhagen for hosting it, and to the Department of Nordic Research and the LANCHART Research Centre for providing financial support. As editors of the book, we would like to thank all authors for their remarkable patience and never-ending willingness to engage in discussions about their contributions.

The project would not have been possible without the general framework, inspiration and funding provided by the research endeavor known as SLICE, headed by Tore Kristiansen at the University of Copenhagen. SLICE, an acronym for Standard Language Ideology in Contemporary Europe, is a collective research network and an evolving project which promotes pioneering approaches to the investigation of sociolinguistic change, and we hope the book will contribute to that general aim.

Nikolas Coupland's contribution to the book would not have been possible without the support provided through his affiliations to both the University of Copenhagen and University of Technology Sydney throughout the period when this book was conceived, planned, and developed. Similarly, Janus Mortensen's work on the book would not have been possible without his successive appointments at Roskilde University and the University of Copenhagen.

*The partner volume from the Round Table, *Style, Media, and Language Ideologies* (Thøgersen, Coupland, and Mortensen, eds.), will appear as the third volume in the SLICE series published by Novus. This collection draws together studies that focus on media-led dialect variation and change in different contexts.

JM, NC, and JT
Cardiff and Copenhagen
December 2015

CONTRIBUTORS

Jannis Androutsopoulos, Professor of German Linguistics and Media Linguistics, Universität Hamburg, Germany

Monika Bednarek, Senior Lecturer, Department of Linguistics, The University of Sydney, Australia

Nikolas Coupland, Emeritus Professor, Centre for Language and Communication Research, Cardiff University, Wales; Honorary Professor, Department of Nordic Research, University of Copenhagen University, Denmark

Adam Jaworski, Professor, School of English, The University of Hong Kong

Helen Kelly-Holmes, Professor, School of Modern Languages and Applied Linguistics, University of Limerick, Ireland

Nuria Lorenzo-Dus, Professor, English Language and Literature, College of Arts and Humanities, Swansea University, Wales

Martin Montgomery, Professor, Department of English, Faculty of Arts and Humanities, University of Macau

Janus Mortensen, Associate Professor, Centre for Internationalisation and Parallel Language Use, University of Copenhagen, Denmark

Tereza Spilioti, Lecturer, Centre for Language and Communication Research, Cardiff University, Wales

Joanna Thornborrow, Professor, UFR Lettres et Sciences Humaines, Université de Bretagne Occidentale, France

Jacob Thøgersen, Associate Professor, Department of Nordic Studies and Linguistics, University of Copenhagen, Denmark

Theo Van Leeuwen, Professor, Department of Language and Communication, University of Southern Denmark

style →media →change (handwritten)

1

Introduction: Conceptualizing style, mediation, and change
Janus Mortensen, Nikolas Coupland, and Jacob Thøgersen

the relationship b/w style, media, change (handwritten)

Although their histories are unique and still evolving, *style, mediation*, and *change* are all central concepts in contemporary sociolinguistics, and each of them merits (and has been accorded) book-length studies in its own right. We refer to some of these sources below. Yet, with this introduction—and indeed with this book as a whole—our aim is to provide a perspective that allows us to interrogate the *interconnections* between style, media, and change. We argue that style holds the potential to provide a unifying perspective for contemporary sociolinguistics (a theme we will take up again in the book's final chapter), including sociolinguistic approaches to media and change—arenas where theoretical and empirical developments are, we suggest, now required.

style definition (handwritten)

In its barest outline, our argument is as follows. Style orients to what is conventional in any context of language use but also to what is dynamically constructed in particular acts of contextualization; sociolinguistics in general needs to focus on the dialectical relationship between normativity and creativity. Style always presupposes mediation, but technological media have unique styling resources to shape how meanings are made and interpreted through linguistic and semiotic performance; 'media' (however we precisely interpret this term) are integral parts of how 'the social' is nowadays experienced. The rapid reconfiguration of media engagement in the current era is a key locus for change—it is a key social change in its own right; but what we refer to as sociolinguistic change points to the more specific, more localized dimension of change in relations between language and society in which stylistic innovation is consequential.

media (handwritten)

change (handwritten)

1

In order to substantiate these stark and compressed claims, this introduction first provides a brief discussion of the concepts of style, media, and change, where we hope to explain their interrelations, as we see them, in a cumulative fashion. We then point to the sociolinguistic issues that this integrated theoretical perspective allows us to explore, and which the following chapters pursue in detail, in specific regards. At the end of the chapter we briefly introduce the main themes of the analytic chapters that follow and explain how we have structured them into sections.

Style as a theoretical perspective in sociolinguistics

Tracing the route by which style came to be a key concept in sociolinguistics is complex, and some of the foundational approaches seem particularly narrow from today's perspective (see Coupland 2007 for a review). It is well known that Labov (1972) formalized style as a dimension of sociolinguistic variation in the earliest accounts of variationist method—so-called stylistic variation, referring to 'intra-individual' variability in speech across social contexts of speaking. Styles of speech could, for example, be called 'casual' versus 'formal' in this approach, leaving some ambiguity over whether these were categories of speech *per se* (different frequencies in the use of particular variable dialect features) or categories of social context. Style in this sense was, in any event, quickly elaborated in various emerging paradigms, including Bell's (1984, 2001) audience design perspective, where speech styles (once again established on the basis of quantitative distributions of features) could be shown to vary in response to characteristics of addressees—different styles for different audiences. A parallel perspective, inspired by Giles's accommodation theory (e.g. Giles 1973; Giles and Powesland 1975; Giles, Coupland, and Coupland 1991), emphasized the sociopsychological bases of speech style convergence and divergence. In this approach speech was once again conceived as being styled for audiences, but this time in relation to speakers' particular motivations vis-à-vis their addressees, whether they wanted to symbolize higher or lower degrees of interpersonal alignment and achieve particular relational outcomes. A third extrapolation from Labov's perspective in early sociolinguistics was sometimes referred to as 'speaker design,' where style was viewed as 'persona management,' the shaping of a speaker's own projected identities in interactional situations (e.g. Coupland 1985). This perspective drew its inspiration from Goffman's (1959) early accounts of the presentation of self, as well as from related psychological theorizing of impression management. Along with Giles's idea of accommodation, this represented an early view of style as a dynamic resource for identity performance—style as a locus for agentive social action.

Style also has its own distinctive pedigree in applied linguistics under the name of stylistics, which could at one stage be split into 'literary stylistics,' representing early incursions of linguistic analysis into literary criticism, and 'general stylistics,' following the recognition that language use in any specific genre was a stylistically rich field of activity, for example in using the expressive resources of intonation, stress, and voice quality (Crystal and Davy 1969). Style was often theorized as 'register' in this tradition—language tailored to the demands of particular functional priorities in different contexts of usage. Stylistic analyses were sometimes couched in terms of 'norm and deviation,' orienting to the idea that creative uses of language could be seen as deviating from a pattern of usage that could be considered normative in a given context of use. Style in this general sense was amply represented in the field of (ethno)poetics (e.g. Bauman and Briggs 1990; Hymes 2004), which has continued to unite aspects of anthropological and literary enquiry (cf. Johnstone and Marcellino 2011; Stockwell 2015; see also the Poetics and Linguistics Association[1]). Many of the affordances we attribute to style in this volume could also be attributed to poetics as a whole, and particularly to Hymes's career-long defense of both poetics and the ethnography of speaking, the latter being a defining paradigm for sociolinguistics (e.g. Hymes 1974, 1996). Bauman's research on performance and verbal art (e.g. Bauman 1977, 2004) has been another agenda-setting contribution to the sociolinguistics of style.

Yet in current sociolinguistics, building on the extensive foundations sketched above, style has assumed still further importance, through the merging of two other broad currents of thought. The first is the systematic reworking of semiotic theory and the wholesale reconsideration of the interface between semiotic processes and the sociolinguistic concepts of linguistic variation and differentiation. The second is the perennially important 'critical' agenda of discourse analysis and discursive sociolinguistics. The first of these currents, once again (as in the case of research inspired by Hymes, Bauman, and others), emerged largely in the North American context of linguistic anthropology, and the second largely emerged from European initiatives in discourse studies and critical theory, although both are highly influential across the full range of subfields that we take to constitute sociolinguistics.

Semiotic reinterpretations of linguistic variation have helped to theorize style as the complex of interactional processes by which indexical meanings are brought into play in speech events. A speech style carries social meaning relative to normative (or at least culturally conventional) patterns of association between linguistic and contextual categories. Silverstein elaborated this simple idea in arguing that social meaning could be seen as a metapragmatic dimension of language use—a social penumbra existing outside or alongside the most immediate pragmatic effects of an utterance. The metapragmatic interpretation amounts to a 'cultural construal' of that utterance, which can then itself be reinterpreted at increasingly abstract levels, constituting a system of ordered indexicalities (Silverstein 2003). Eckert identifies a 'Third Wave' of variation research, explicitly centered on style, which picks up on a similar view, that linguistic variation is "a system of signs, whose meanings emerge in their role in styles that enact social personae or types. These types, in turn, are both constrained by, and contribute to, macro-social patterns" (Eckert 2016: 69). As we noted earlier, the view of style as persona management entered sociolinguistics several decades ago, although at first it struggled to challenge a dominant structuralist version of variationist sociolinguistics that emphasized large-scale patterns of linguistic differentiation and change. More recent accounts of sociolinguistic differentiation (notably by Gal 2016; see also Irvine and Gal 2000) emphasize how difference is *achieved*, and what ideological work is involved in specific instances, just as Agha (e.g. 2007) has explored Silverstein's concept of orders of indexicality in theorizing how styles or registers[2] come to gain cultural recognition, through the process of enregisterment.

Critical Discourse Analysis (CDA, cf. Fairclough 1992, 1995; van Leeuwen 2008) has generally used the concept of style to refer to the 'identity' functions of discourse working across 'genres'; discourse, style, and genre therefore provide a theoretical architecture for some important CDA models. This line of analysis has a very long interdisciplinary history, including seminal contributions from Bakhtin, Foucault, and Habermas. Critical Linguistics (e.g. Hodge and Kress 1988) came to represent one coherent version of critical research where the notion of style was prominent, treated as the semiotic expression of ideology. Since then, of course, ideology has been promoted into general circulation in sociolinguistics from several different sources, particularly in the theorizing of language ideologies—ideologies of or about language and language use (e.g. Blommaert 1999; Schieffelin et al. 1998). In the context of the present book, it is also relevant to note the close connection, in diverse respects, between language and change in 'critical' approaches. Not only was social change a regular concern in critical linguistics, but emancipatory change through critical analysis was also a fundamental ambition of critical research in its own right. Similarly, contemporary sociolinguistic engagement with multimodal style and meaning (a theme we return to in the next section) can also be traced to initiatives within CDA (Kress and van Leeuwen 2006), and such initiatives have themselves adopted a critical perspective.

Affordances of style

We are unable to offer a full review of the complex historical movements and confluences around the concept of style here. But we need to overview what we see as the contemporary affordances of a style perspective, particularly as it relates to the remit of this book. What are these affordances? First, the concept of style has the advantage of drawing together more static and more dynamic aspects of language use and social interaction in particular social contexts. Style, when used as a countable noun, points to a configuration of linguistic and semiotic usage that has a certain stability and durability. It points to a way of meaning that is sufficiently stable to be identified as such by at least some members of a society. In its most rudimentary sense, a style is a 'way of doing,' perhaps also a 'way of being,' and social styles are woven into the fabric of how any society functions, linguistically and otherwise. A style in this sense is therefore a cultural category, a way of meaning that has achieved a degree of cultural recognition, even if it is necessarily idealized and 'rounded out' in this process of being recognized. As Agha (2007) similarly suggests in defining his concepts of register and enregisterment, and as Silverstein has also emphasized, a style is also therefore a metacommunicative concept—it gives us a way of referring to a mode of communicative practice, and to that extent styles are also metacultural entities. Named styles are concepts that allow people to discuss how their culture is organized and differentiated, how it is and was, how it might be, and perhaps even how it ought to be.

But we immediately have to recognize that styles can never, in practice, live up to their metapragmatic billing as stable categories. After all, a style—what is construed to be a distinctive mode of social action—has to be *enacted*. It has to be 'carried off' and performed, worked into a social environment which it thereby shapes and colors, just as normative understandings of particular contexts shape and color the actions through which they are partly constituted. Style-in-action, or 'styling' in a verbal sense, therefore needs to be seen as a dynamic practice of constructing social meanings of diverse sorts, as the meaning potential associated with a given style or styles is creatively worked into a new social environment ('new' in the sense that each and every sociolinguistic episode, however routinized in other respects, is unique in its local enactment). The concept of style therefore forces us to pay attention to the sociolinguistic processes through which social meanings are continually made (stabilized, known, and metacommunicatively consolidated) and unmade (performed, reshaped, and reinterpreted) across serial episodes of communicative interchange. This already gives us one justification for saying that style is theoretically well-attuned to the study of sociolinguistic change (which we discuss below in the section on *Style, mediation, and change*).

A second affordance of style is that it points to the creation and negotiation of social meaning across multiple levels of linguistic organization and across linguistic and other semiotic modes. Style is a holistic concept, and styles are typically configured across multiple communicative modes simultaneously. Classic instances are the postwar British, popular music-associated subcultural styles analyzed by Hebdige (1979), such as teddy boy, mod, rocker, skinhead, and punk styles. Each of these styles was a fusion of visual self-presentation (e.g. clothes, shoes, and hair), discourse (e.g. ways of talking and singing), demeanor, and taste (e.g. modes of transport, patterns of social congregation, and musical preferences). More recent sociolinguistic accounts of youth styles (e.g. Madsen 2015; Madsen, Karrebæk and Møller 2015) are similarly multimodal, many of them taking inspiration from Eckert's research into identity stylings of Jocks and Burnouts at Belten High (Eckert 2000). This multimodal emphasis is particularly salient in the analysis of how 'style groups' enact and perform their distinctiveness, as well as in how they are metacommunicatively distinguished and represented. We might say that style groups primarily exist in their mediated representations, because to enact a particular group style is to mediate it into salient contexts of social action. Again, style groups of the Hebdige sort are often relatively ephemeral, existing in dynamic processes of stylistic innovation, competition, and change.

Third, as Irvine (2001), Gal (2016), and others have pointed out, style is fundamentally involved in the establishment of distinctiveness, and distinctiveness of personal and social identity or persona as a key instance. But style implicates differences of many sorts, not only those that distinguish subcultural or other groups (and individuals who construct their own identities with reference to such groups) within and across communities of practice. We also need to construe *relational* styling, where the relevant social meaning of style and styling attaches to how people relate to others in interactional terms. To some extent this extends Labov's original suggestion that speech style could be invoked to explain degrees of formality in social interaction, as well as defining social group categories such as those based around social class designations. In other words, style is a quality of interpersonal relations as well as a quality of social identities themselves. The idea of stance, for instance, as conceptualized by Du Bois (2007) and empirically elaborated by Jaffe (2009), is able to capture much of the relational dimension of style, when the distinctiveness of a way of speaking relates to the design of interpersonal relations (e.g. the aggressiveness of a political interviewer's stance, the feigned sociability of a salesperson in sales encounters, or the polite form of address in a foreign dignitary's interaction with the Danish Queen).

Style is also a distinctive quality of social context itself. Wee (2015), for example, focuses on how organizations are styled and style themselves, in terms of how they manage their public faces. It would be possible to theorize this as an extrapolation from the styling of individuals and groups, organizations being anthropomorphized into beings with human-like properties (such as approachability and dependability). But the more general point is that any configuration of social action itself can be said to constitute a distinctive style, which makes salient the relationship between style and genre. Genre is generally said to refer to culturally recognized modes of purposive social action in specific domains (Swales 1990), so that we can talk of genres of written text (e.g. novels, poetry, or journalism), of popular music (e.g. country, rock, or hip-hop) or of spoken exchange (e.g. narrating, joking, or advice-giving). But any genre can be styled in distinctive ways. Certainly, particular styles are normatively associated with particular genres, but social meaning is made in the detailed styling of any given genre performance (cf. Coupland 2011 on vocal styling in popular music). But just as identities can be stylistically reshaped over time on the basis of stylistic innovations, so can genres themselves. What it means in any particular cultural environment to 'read the news' or to 'do stand-up comedy' can change, incrementally or more suddenly, on the basis of salient stylistic innovations.

Style and mediation

As we have already suggested, all forms of communication can be said to be mediated in the sense of being produced through a medium. Speech may be deemed to be the primordial case as the medium that facilitates communication through verbal exchanges. Following from this, mediation can be defined as the set of processes by which meaning-making practices such as talk (where 'talk' entails semiosis which includes symbolic activity that goes beyond speech itself, and the collaborative construction of relationships and events) are designed and contextualized into social settings and interactional encounters. On many occasions, mediation occurs through particular technologies and through mediational systems and institutions that have arisen around them, including radio, TV, film, and—more recently—various forms of digital 'participatory' media. With inspiration from Scollon and Scollon (2004) and others, we can refer to this type of second-order mediation as 'technological mediation' and thus distinguish, for example, technologically mediated (TM) talk from other types of talk. While face-to-face interaction was the starting point of early sociolinguistic enquiry, technological mediation is becoming an increasingly pressing concern for sociolinguistics today, and it is our claim that style and styling (in the senses we have introduced earlier) are of central importance if we want to theorize the reflexive processes of meaning making that occur under conditions of technological mediation. The corollary of this point is that TM talk and interaction themselves need to be seen as quintessentially 'styled' phenomena.

Jaffe (2011) refers to this second-order mediation by the term *mediatization*, focusing on the resources and devices that particular technological media systems make available and exploit in the construction of TM products and discourse. These would include scripting and rehearsal, camera work and acoustic manipulation, manipulation of audience perspectives, editing, and so on. Agha, on the other hand, uses the term *mediatization* to refer to acts of mediation (by which he mainly means linkages between people) which are distinctive by being associated with commoditization. This is when the production and dissemination of mediated acts incur costs, and when whatever is communicated itself has some specific market value, or is treated as having such a value (Agha 2011a, b). However, we prefer to use the term *mediatization* to refer more broadly to what may be conceptualized as ongoing historical processes of *increasing* technological mediation—that is, the experience that more and more aspects of social life are located in mediated forms and practices (Hjarvard 2013). We may think of this as a gradual and ongoing movement into the late-modern cultural condition that Livingstone (2009, cited and discussed by Androutsopoulos 2014a: 10ff) evocatively refers to as 'the mediation of everything.' With this increased degree of technological mediation comes new potential for style, both as an analytical concept and as a resource for media producers, performers and consumers.

The term *media* and especially the problematically reified concept of 'the media,' whose shortcomings are well reviewed by Androutsopoulos (2014a), points to a huge and fast-evolving set of technologies, platforms, and communication practices. So-called new media, including interactive/participatory platforms such as Facebook and Twitter, have been quite extensively researched in recent years by sociolinguists and by communication researchers whose approaches overlap with those of sociolinguists (see e.g. Crystal 2011; Page et al. 2014; Thurlow and Mroczek 2011). Partly for this reason, 'new media' are not the exclusive or even central focus of this book. They are certainly not excluded from view either, but we take a particular and deliberate interest in 'talking media,' by which we mean media formats that predominantly represent spoken language, talk, and interaction, particularly television and radio, either broadcast in the traditional sense or available online through web services such as *YouTube*. One specific reason for this choice is that the chapters of the book, through this focus, are able to draw on the coherent theoretical and analytic traditions associated with Interactional Sociolinguistics and its cognate approaches, including CDA, media discourse analysis, or broadcast talk (cf. the section below on *Style as a theoretical perspective in sociolinguistics*).

What we call the talking media are sometimes framed as 'old media,' to set them apart from 'new media,' but we do not accept the 'oldness' of 'old media' (or, actually, the newness of 'new media'), particularly if 'old media' is taken to imply a lesser research priority. The presence and importance of the talking media have not diminished, even though media universes are of course far more complex today than they have previously been. Talking media demand renewed sociolinguistic investigation because they continue to constitute rich points of sociolinguistic practice, because they are metalinguistically and metaculturally salient (Androutsopoulos 2011, 2014a; Coupland 2009, 2010), and because they are a primary means by which cultural norms and boundaries, and language ideologies in particular, are reflexively represented, held up for scrutiny, and enacted. Talking media put ways of speaking on display and imbue them with social meaning and cultural value—very differently across different genres and contexts, and differently over time. Sociolinguists have sometimes sought to distance themselves from TM data and processes, on the assumption that 'the everyday world of talk' is where the 'real stuff' of language in use happens, specifically *because* 'ordinary talk' (as has been controversially argued, or often simply assumed) is 'unmediated' and, by implication, unsullied or more natural. Issues of authenticity and inauthenticity lurk behind such stances of TM discourse avoidance, which we will postpone discussing in detail at this point. But we would stress the cogency of the contrary stance—that large-scale engagement with the talking media is very much a part of 'ordinary' sociolinguistic experience in contemporary societies around the globe. Indeed, sociolinguistic diversity, normativity and (as we argue in the next section) change are at issue both in how various systems and institutions mediate language and in how the ensuing stylistic constructions do—or do not—survive subsequent movement out of technological mediation.

A style perspective is particularly sensitive to the analysis of semiotic chains and overlays, which are characteristic of technologically mediated (and remediated) materials of various sorts. The data that contributors examine in the book are, therefore, only rarely data exclusive to primary broadcasting media themselves. Personas, styles, set expressions, captioned images, narratives, or whole episodes that might originally have been broadcast in the manner of 'old media' can find new existence, often intertextually modified or recontextualized, in 'new media' circulations. Correspondingly, trending 'new media' features and texts can form the basis of TV commentaries and even news. Non-speech-based interactive media (e.g. texting or tweeting) can themselves enact 'talk' and 'voice' exchanges, e.g. using the stylistic resources of typed text to perform gossip (cf. Jones et al. 2011), but the phonological-to-visual repertoire of talking media, in the classical sense of 'talk,' remains distinctive.

In any event, technological mediation has complicated the indexical landscapes within which meanings are made, introducing various significant relativities. Historical mediatization has not simply amounted to 'more media' and more media consumption. When, as we have already done, we emphasize the reflexivity of TM processes, we are referring to how talking media have accelerated and intensified the metalinguistic and metapragmatic potential of all situated language use. TM talk can be called 'insistent,' because there has been a massive proliferation of the means by which most people access (and in some cases cannot avoid accessing) audio or audiovisual representations of language in use—e.g. accumulating instances of what TV or radio broadcasting deems to be authoritative styles of talk and demeanor, or styling what is conventionally humorous or politically permissible and nonpermissible, or representing diverse community-saturated dialect styles (e.g. in soap operas or stand-up comedy), or in styling different modes and contexts of desire or revulsion. But TM talk can also be called 'ephemeral,' in the sense that the news, soap operas, advertisements, and so on in traditional flow-TV all typically run to pre-established schedules, so that any particular mediated moment has temporally limited vitality. Even with increased options for audiences to customize their media consumption through video on-demand services and through various recording and playback technologies, most talking media formats generally maintain their status of being potential ephemera, as they are at all times liable to be truncated at the press of a button. All the same, these ephemera can be given 'second lives,' through re-mediation, and even one-off events can have strong cultural impact, through mass exposure.

These simple and obvious qualities of audiences' experiences impose a reflexive awareness that the realities of mediated experience 'can be otherwise,' and shortly *will* be otherwise, unless uptake is managed in particular ways. With increasing sophistication among audiences about 'how media work' and about 'what we should expect' from talking media, producers and their agents (perhaps with advertisers being the most obvious constituency) have sharpened their own reflexive resources in order to allow their products to maintain interest and entertainment value, to heighten their persuasive function, or generally to justify their place in increasingly cluttered media spaces. As one of the most recent trends, various forms of direct audience engagement, for instance through so-called second-screen technology, have recently become very popular, adding new potential for meaning-making processes.[3]

This dynamically evolving mediascape needs to be matched by analytic perspectives that transcend flat and linear accounts of meaning making and reception. The general analytic apparatus needed to analyze mediated performance and interpretation along these lines has been available for several decades, e.g. in Goffman's ideas of frame and footing, and in Bakhtin's accounts of voice and heteroglossia, but there is a need for these concepts to be applied in nuanced ways—and perhaps expanded—in light of the new conditions of style and styling brought about by historical mediatization. This is a condition under which, again following Bakhtin (cf. Coupland 2001a, b; Rampton 2006), it becomes particularly necessary to distinguish styling (the routine enactment and reshaping of styles in social interaction) from stylization. Stylization is the knowing deployment of socially familiar semiotic material where the speaker strategically complicates and ambiguates her or his relationship with that material. Stylization is 'as if' styling, which is inferably associated with the performer having specific communicative goals or enacting certain stances, although the nature of these goals and stances is likely to be opaque to immediate participants (some or all) and to analysts alike.

For this reason, style research, not least in the context of TM discourse, needs to be informed both by CDA's approach to the political and ideological contexts in which communicative acts function, and to Gumperz's (1982) inferential approach to social meaning. Style is a dynamic construct in this further sense—that it rejects the view that social meanings inhere in utterances, or for that matter in consolidated styles themselves. Styles are resources that become meaningful under specific conditions of use. This is why terminology like *deployment* (of a style, or a stance, or a persona) can be helpful, in cases where strategic social action is in evidence.

Correspondingly, caution is necessary to avoid overgeneralizing about the uptake of social meanings. In complex, multiparty social environments, and certainly in TM data where there is often a mix of participants who are active in the mediated frame and others ('audience members') who stand outside that frame, there may be only partial uptake by selective subgroups of recipients. This is often the case with humorous or parodic styling, where the communicative design may be to play off predictable meaning uptakes from one segment of an audience against predictably failed uptakes from other segments. Again, then, styling can be functional in the creation of social difference, as well in the exploitation of differentiated sociolinguistic norms.

We believe it is important to confront this problem of complexity and potential indeterminacy at both theoretical and methodological levels. TM products are undoubtedly still 'interested,' in the sense of serving specific interests and priorities, usually economic. Particular interests may be visible—for example, in anxieties over the reach and audience share achieved by particular television channels and programs. But TM styling is often adept at concealing the sources of interest that have shaped it. TM output from any given institution will typically be massively diverse, as to styles that are deployed and as to ideologies in relation to them, even though general trends might also be discernable (cf. Turner 2016). Some of the most attention-grabbing mediated events are those that *do not* pattern with historical convention, or that show creativity in other regards. Because of its ability to capture stability as well as change, style as a sociolinguistic perspective will be entertained just as much in relation to complex, multilayered, and opaque stylistic constructions as to constructions that can be securely interpreted as confirming societal norms. Because of its holistic nature, a style perspective will also potentially be able to capture the complexity—and perhaps identify specific contradictions—in the variable ways meanings are generated, taken up, and renegotiated across semiotic modes. But the rapid proliferation of TM formats also generates considerable semiotic complexity, variability, and unpredictability (e.g. in the blurring of familiar genres and the ever-increasing quest for more creative ways of framing social context). In the general manner of poetic analysis, then, we need to expect analyses of media styling to be, on occasions, challenging and incomplete, rather than definitively conclusive. However, we should also emphasize that inconclusiveness and interpretive modesty do not discredit critical inquiry.

Style, mediation, and change

Change has already been implicit in our discussion of style and mediation. In relation to each of these concepts we have emphasized agentivity and process, alongside normativity and stability. These dialectical relations imply that even normativity and stability should be viewed as matters of local achievement, in the context of potential change. Mediatization, in its historical sense, is clearly a process of change, and few would dispute that 'the mediatization of social life' has been a defining feature of sociocultural change over recent decades. The question is therefore not *whether* change is relevant to the sociolinguistics of talking media, but *how* its relevance should be theorized. There are clearly different understandings of what constitutes change, and how sociolinguistics should orient to change in the context of style and media.

Let us consider three broad alternatives, where we take the last of the three to define our principal orientation to change in this book. The first dimension of change is *social change* in which media practices, media institutions, and media consumption (and therefore language, discourse, and semiosis) are implicated. Turner (2016) considers 'the media' (including how academic research interprets 'the media') to be undergoing substantial change, which he summarizes as a process of 're-invention.' Some of Turner's arguments echo points we have already made in this chapter, such as the fact that 'the media' can no longer be treated as a unified field of 'mass communication.' As the digital era has progressed, the distinction between 'broadcast' and 'connective' (i.e. 'social') media has become less clear. 'Broadcasting' includes the targeting of consumer niches—'narrowcasting,' therefore—and the dissemination of content via various digital platforms, just as online 'user-generated content' includes the circulation of audiovisual material sourced from TV and TV-like systems (e.g. advertising and other promotional initiatives). As Turner says, "the 'massness' of the media is no longer the common element in the industries, practices and technologies we examine" (2016: 2). These points, we think, support our decision here to focus on talking media as a fully contemporary facet of technologically mediated circulation.

Other important sociological changes include the declining importance of state-led, ideologically centripetal 'national broadcasting' in favor of more obviously commercially based, more deregulated and often transnational corporate networks. Linked to these changes, Turner also identifies a continuing shift toward entertainment as the primary rationale for program making of all sorts, further displacing the centrality and authority bases of national news organizations (with blogs, for example, tending to fill this void). Turner follows Couldry (2012) and Rojek (2001) in identifying an increasing demand for (what Couldry calls) 'presencing'—the need to project celebrity or celebrity-like statuses and personas, and to do this in all contexts of technological mediation.

Social change of course encompasses wider processes that can be summarized under labels such as globalization, transnationalization, detraditionalization, and marketization, and technological media are quite obviously implicated in these seismic shifts. (In fact, the media-internal changes that Turner explores are quite direct reflexes of such wider social changes). This is not the place to elaborate on the different dimensions of social change or on the research that has investigated it. But we should note that language and discourse, whether or not in the context of technological mediation, are of considerable relevance in social change, and that social change is partly *constituted in* changes relating to language and discourse. Set against this general vision of social change, which has dominated international research in the social sciences in recent decades, it is remarkable that the dominant change-focused paradigm in sociolinguistics, the second broad orientation to change we need to discuss, has continued to be the much narrower research program referred to as *language change*, carried forward by the variationist sociolinguistic program pioneered by Labov (e.g. Labov 1972, 2001).

The language change program has featured quite limited forms of social engagement, and it has had no systematic engagement with language in the context of mediatization. As we noted earlier, the language change paradigm has positively resisted engaging with TM data, because the dimensions of change that it seeks to model relate to community-bound vernacular speech norms, particularly as regards phonological systems (so-called sound change). In order to track changes of this sort, variationists have had to locate speakers and speech styles that conform to pre-established criteria of locality (speakers deemed to be local to a specific place) and vernacularity (speech styles deemed to be natural and unmediated), and to compare them over time (in real time or in apparent time, by comparing data from speakers of different ages), under controlled conditions. Whether TM speech plays any part in language change has become a controversial area of research (see e.g. Sayers 2014; Stuart-Smith and Ota 2014), the details of which, once again, we do not need to explore here. Language change research plays into the enduring concerns of both traditional dialectology and historical linguistics, where the structural composition of linguistic systems is principally at issue. To that extent we can see that the style perspective we have set out in this chapter—particularly its critical orientation, its focus on the local construction of social meaning and its holistic concern with multidimensional and multilayered indexicality—could easily be seen as a distraction for language change research. Conversely, seen from a contemporary style perspective, language change research risks ignoring many of the aspects of change that are most salient in contemporary social life.

We therefore need to establish a third broad orientation to change in sociolinguistics, one that is fully sensitive to and critically engaged with social change, and one that might even provide a theoretical architecture within which instances of language change can be reinterpreted. Following earlier accounts (Androutsopoulos 2014a; Coupland 2009, 2014), we can label this *sociolinguistic change*. Its ambition is to establish, when relevant, a case for changing relationships between 'language' and 'society' (as opposed to social change and language change, which privilege one 'side' of the sociolinguistic enterprise at the expense of the other). Sociolinguistic change therefore establishes a broad research agenda within which shifting sociocultural priorities as well as changing norms for language use need to be entertained. From this perspective, whether linguistic forms and systems themselves change over time is not necessarily at issue; linguistic forms and systems may persist intact, but language-ideological values and orders of indexicality may change around them (see e.g. Fabricius and Mortensen 2013). Researching sociolinguistic change is not a descriptivist activity; it needs to be driven by a critical agenda asking what sorts of language-related changes are *consequential*, for who and under what conditions.

The style agenda brings specific foci to the study of sociolinguistic change. Sociolinguistics has always recognized that ways of speaking and ways of being exist in complex but often tacit normative frameworks; frameworks that determine what is possible, necessary, legitimate, desirable, or proscribed for particular constituencies of people in particular circumstances. These issues have tended to coalesce in critical accounts of the politics of language use, where *voice* has been given new status as a focal concept, but generally in static rather than change-sensitive accounts. Historically, technologically mediated discourse is recognized to have played some part in legitimizing some voices—particular ways of speaking associated with specific groups and speaking positions—and discrediting others, not least in relation to 'standard' and 'vernacular' dialects (cf. Mugglestone 2003 on the history of 'talking proper' in the United Kingdom). What evidence exists is disputed and there has arguably been an overemphasis on whether media models do or do not 'affect' 'everyday' practices (e.g. in the diffusion of pronunciation features). Yet TM discourse is *continually* proposing new metapragmatic norms around styles and genres, and subtly editing and reconfiguring the profiles of existing stylistic and generic norms. The analytic challenge is to identify the normative pressure points to which TM innovations apply, and the conditions under which they may trigger or contribute to consequential change.

Sociolinguistic change will be consequential if, in some particular regard, people's autonomy and freedom to act are altered, for better or for worse, if people's social relations are more, or less, constrained, if lives are more, or less, enriched, if diversity comes to command more, or less, respect, and so on. These are the classical motivating concerns of sociolinguistics, in all its traditions, when language, discourse, and meaning can be shown to be implicated in these political and moral issues. A fully *socio*linguistic conception of change will be one where these considerations can command due attention, particularly in relation to linguistic and discursive dimensions of the large-scale social changes that are impacting on social life.

The reflexivity entailed in style, and particularly in TM styling, is again key to its potential in respect of sociolinguistic change. It seems unlikely that any form of density theory could account for most sociolinguistic changes—that is, a presumption that whatever is most densely represented in TM discourse will somehow disseminate into 'unmediated' practice. The sheer diversity, and also the ephemerality, of TM stylistic representations and performances suggest that, on the whole, there can be no clearly dominant exemplary models that might function this way. As we noted earlier, however, TM representations and performances can be insistent and intense, and these qualities potentiate change, even on the basis of very limited exposure. They can reflexively expose and sometimes subvert normative structures—for example, in moments of stylization (which is styling at its most reflexive). With digital social media's propensity to extract audiovisual fragments and sequences and to circulate them widely in recontextualized forms, even single instances of talking media stylized performance can rapidly come to media consumers' critical attention and become a basis for reflexive sociolinguistic change.

The main chapters of the book, which will be introduced in the following section, shed light on local instances of actual or potential sociolinguistic change across a wide range of national, linguistic, institutional, and mediational contexts. They show how processes of styling and stylization (1) play with or against sociocultural norms, including norms for media performance, (2) impinge consequentially on political and commercial practices, (3) reshape nationally established contexts for language use, (4) negotiate elite and vernacular identities, and (5) model modes of participation in the public sphere.

Content and structure of the book

In addition to this Introduction, the book contains 11 chapters, distributed across five thematic sections. In the following, we introduce the chapters and outline their central themes and common points of interest.

The three chapters in Part I, *Sociopolitical Change and the Emergence of New Styles and Genres*, all focus on the emergence of particular styles of talk and media genres, and place them in the context of ongoing sociopolitical change. The studies originate in three different European countries, *viz.* Spain, Greece, and Wales, but the chapters all illustrate how innovation in otherwise familiar styles of mediated talk and the creative manipulation of established media genres hold the potential to challenge—or at least to some extent unsettle—prevailing social/societal and linguistic norms by holding them up for reflexive scrutiny.

In Chapter 2, *Style, sociolinguistic change, and political broadcasting: The case of the Spanish news show* Salvados, Nuria Lorenzo-Dus analyses what she sees as an emerging form of critical journalism in Spain, personified by the TV news program *Salvados* and its anchor Jordie Évole. In the program, Évole adopts a soft-spoken, naïve style of interviewing that allows him to question perceived injustices in a seemingly innocent manner, thereby catching his interview victims unawares (not entirely unlike Peter Falk in the well-known role of Inspector Columbo). Despite the fact that his style does not conform to established conventions of critical/confrontational journalism, Lorenzo-Dus is able to show, through analyses of audience uptake on Twitter, that Évole is perceived by many as an important 'incisive' critical voice, exposing the wrongdoings of people in power, expanding the critical remit of political journalism in Spain in the process. As such, Évole may, Lorenzo-Dus suggests, be seen as a 'metacultural entrepreneur' (Urban 2001) with the potential to facilitate sociocultural change through the generation of metacultural and metadiscursive reflexivity.

In Chapter 3, *Radio talk, pranks, and multilingualism: Styling Greek identities at a time of crisis*, Tereza Spilioti also addresses new modes of styling and stylization in broadcast media, and discusses their interaction with processes of social change. Her data are taken from a political satire radio show called *Ελληνοφρένεια* ('Greekophrenia'), in which the host *Apostolis* deploys stylized performances of Greek and English in conversation with callers who are unaware that they have been framed as the 'dupes' (Bauman 1986) of on-air telephone pranks. Following the so-called Greek debt crisis, tensions have arisen between Greece and the rest of the European Union. In this context, ideological conceptions of different languages (*in casu* Greek and English) and different ways of speaking come to the fore as indexes of different sociopolitical stances and identities. In his seemingly haphazard use of English, often intertwined with distinctly different styles of Greek, *Apostolis* is activating a complex and ambiguous network of social meanings. Following Woolard, Bencomo, and Soler-Carbonell (2013), Spilioti argues that these acts of broadcast talk 'refract' speech practices of the wider community and therefore point to on-going change in the ideological alignment between Greek and English in Greece, where the preference for either language is perceived as indexical of particular sociopolitical positions.

To date, most sociolinguistic approaches to style and styling have focused on 'within-code' operations such as stylistic processes at the level of accent and dialect. But as Chapter 3 by Spilioti and Chapter 4 by Coupland (introduced below) show, the holism of the style perspective allows sociolinguistics to transcend the classical distinction between within-code (formerly referred to as style-shifting) and between-code (formally referred to as code-switching) processes, and see them as essentially similar semiotic processes (under the right contextual conditions). Ways of using 'languages'—in combination or in isolation, through single or multiple registers (in the sense of Agha)—are in themselves matters of style.

In Chapter 4, *Styling syncretic bilingualism on Welsh-language TV*: Madamrygbi, Nikolas Coupland introduces readers to the case of *Madamrygbi*, a comedian-cum-rugby reporter persona of the Welsh actor Eirlys Bellin. With a name that translates ambiguously as either 'Madam Rugby' or 'mad about rugby,' Madamrygbi's interviews are a regular tongue-in-cheek feature of a popular rugby-related entertainment show on S4C, the Welsh-language television channel in Wales. Bellin uses this high-profile platform to playfully subvert a number of Welsh national icons. Her syncretic (mixed) and playful use of English and Welsh challenges the perceived 'purity' of the Welsh language, and her mildly sexually transgressive approach to rugby reporting challenges the sacredness of the national sport. As in the case of Évole and *Apostolis, Madamrygbi*'s styling arguably serves to challenge the established boundaries of the media genre within which she performs, though it is also in part the cultural stability of the conventions of that genre (and similar genres) that enables her performances to acquire meaning in the first place. Like the protagonists in the chapters by Lorenzo-Dus and Spilioti, Eirlys Bellin/*Madamrygbi* can be seen as a potential catalyst for sociocultural change. Yet the trouble (for the analyst, at least) is, as Urban (2001) reminds us, that cultural change can only truly be recognized retrospectively when change is *evaluated* to have happened, and when the awareness of it has acquired metadiscursive salience. There is fragmentary evidence in the chapter that this is in fact being achieved.

The two chapters in Part II of the book, *The Business of Style: The Style of Business*, turn the focus away from individual media personas and onto that of large corporations and consumer products. Focusing on two different kinds of corporate media product—a TV commercial for an alcoholic beverage and an American sitcom with international reach, respectively—the chapters explore the commodification of style, and show how businesses, including media corporations, may seek to exploit recognizable styles and styled fragments and particular indexical values associated with these in their marketing. The chapters also show, however, how media audiences, given the affordances of contemporary media platforms, may actively 'buy into' the styles of the products and through this contribute to the process of value and meaning creation, for instance by recycling salient phrases from the media products as a way of performing group identity.

In Chapter 5, *Brand styling, enregisterment, and change: The case of* C'est Cidre, Helen Kelly-Holmes looks at a commercial for the (historically) Belgian brand *Stella Artois*, targeted at the British market, promoting a cider that is 'really,' according to the commercial, a *cidre*—pronounced in mock French as part of the phrase *c'est cidre*. The lamination of languages and styles deployed in the commercial—that is, the sparing use of 'fake' French in an otherwise French-accented English-language commercial for an ostensibly Belgian (Flemish) product—gives rise to complicated questions of indexical meaning which Kelly-Holmes investigates through audience uptake on *YouTube*. An interesting point emerging from the analyses is that the use of French may be said to help establish a metaparodic frame (Coupland 2012) in which the brewery is at one and the same time asserting and parodying stylized 'fake' French. The crucial point is that consumers need to actively co-construct this metaparody in order for it to work. In this sense the commercial constitutes an interesting case of relational styling, making quite particular demands on its audience as a *knowing* audience. Not entirely unlike *Madamrygbi* and *Apostolis, Stella Artois*—anthropomorphized through styling—seems to be drawing on recognizable indexical/stereotypical meanings—in this case meanings attaching to mock French—while at the same time also challenging these very meanings by taking an ambiguous stance on the process of exploiting linguistic stereotypes for particular purposes.

Whereas most chapters in the book find their data in broadcast media such as television and radio, Monika Bednarek's contribution, Chapter 6, *(Re)circulating popular television: Audience engagement and corporate practices*, focuses on the remediation, recontextualization, or, in her own term, *recirculation*, of broadcast texts, partly through printed T-shirts and partly through online platforms like Twitter and Facebook. In general, recirculation of this kind can be described as processes of audience engagement whereby fans appropriate commercial products for identity purposes, keeping the style of the original products busy, as it were. Yet Bednarek shows that it also works in the opposite direction when corporations appropriate the stylistic practices of fans through a process she refers to as 'corporate mimicry.' Building on Richardson (2010), Bednarek offers a four-part typology of (re)circulation and uses this to show how complex the opportunities for styling and stylization are in remediated texts in 'analogue' as well as digital media. Interestingly, while there is undeniably a considerable amount of creativity involved in audience engagement of the type described by Bednarek, it is not immediately apparent that these practices hold the potential for sociocultural reflexivity of the sort discussed in other chapters. What seems to be at stake here is language innovation and play, achieved, for instance, through the wide circulation of catchphrases like 'Bazinga!' (originating in the American sitcom *The Big Bang Theory*, Bednarek's main case). However, developments in media and media usage in themselves obviously constitute a changing relationship in the language-society nexus simply by the introduction of new forms of public engagement.

Public engagement is also a central issue for the two chapters in Part III, *The Art of Mediated Style: Blurring the Boundaries between 'Ordinary' and 'Elite'*. Chapters 7 and 8 take their data from very different television formats, one from the seemingly mundane world of reality TV and the other from a series of ostensibly high-brow programs on 21st-century art. In Harvey Sacks's (1984) famous dictum, people invest a lot of work in 'doing being ordinary,' but in Chapter 7, *Styling the 'ordinary': Tele-factual genres and participant identities*, Joanna Thornborrow tells a somewhat different story of how careful effort goes into presenting so-called ordinary people as rather extraordinary on reality TV. In the most naïve understanding of its genre label, reality TV purports to show us reality as it really is, but through her analyses of data from two different formats, *WifeSwap* (United States/United Kingdom) and *Come Dine with Me* (United Kingdom), Thornborrow shows how this supposed 'reality' is in fact a carefully orchestrated universe where participants essentially acquire their 'identities' through being different from the other participants and, to some extent, by being presented as being *extreme*. The differentiating potential of style is clearly in evidence here, but what makes the analysis particularly interesting is that Thornborrow is able to show how the construction of difference occurs—or is being occasioned—through the mediated representation of participant lifestyles, relying crucially on affordances of the TV medium, editing choices in particular, and the recurrent deployment of template-like performance styles. In *Come Dine with Me*, for example, participant monologues are interspersed with sarcastic voice-over commentary. The commentary voice enters into a series of pseudo dialogues that effectively position participants as members of typological (and stereotyped) social groups, in a device that amounts to an advanced form of mediated relational styling.

The processes of styling and stylization dealt with in Part I may all be said to have more or less explicit critical ramifications, but what is the critical potential of the programs investigated by Thornborrow? Reality programs may invite audiences to engage in reflexive practices about different ways of life, but through their mocking display of otherness, the program producers can hardly, on the one hand, be seen as 'metacultural entrepreneurs.' If anything, they are more like cultural consolidators, implicitly—through the process of othering that the programs embody—reaffirming the normality of 'genuinely ordinary' ways of life, which we may, by implication, take to be those millions of lifestyles that are never deemed worthy of this form of mediated display. On the other hand, it is striking to note how shows of this type do in some ways seem to undermine 'normal' hierarchies of class and taste. Participants can be styled as 'posh' *and* tasteless as well as 'common' *and* tasteless. For that reason, the shows may carry potential for unsettling traditional assumptions about ways of speaking (e.g. 'posh' vs. 'vernacular') and their perceived social value and therefore, through the insistent nature of the talking media (discussed in the two previous sections), come to be instrumental in furthering sociolinguistic change.

Adam Jaworski in Chapter 8, *Art on television: Television as art*, also explores notions of (extra)ordinariness, but whereas Thornborrow's case concerns the ordinary-turned-extraordinary, Jaworski explores a case where an 'elite' practice, namely, contemporary art, is rendered if not 'ordinary' than at least *accessible* through the medium of TV. The data come from *Art in the Twenty-first Century*, a program series produced and broadcast by Public Broadcasting Service (PBS) in the United States. By making parallels to the notion of style as it is employed in art history and art theory, Jaworski argues that the vignettes used to introduce the programs, produced by prominent contemporary artists, constitute works of (video) art that are capable of catering to novices in the world of art as well as an acculturated audience of connoisseurs. This is achieved, at least in part, through the deployment of richly laminated multimodal styles that have an immediate appeal as show-rather-than-tell introductions to the work of the individual artists, while at the same time incorporating intertextual references galore which add further layers of meaning for viewers who are already 'in the know.' In this way, Jaworski argues, the programs negotiate the tension that may be said to exist between television as a 'mass medium' and the perception of contemporary art as 'elitist.' Interestingly, though, whatever the inherent elitism of art itself, the participants in Jaworski's data are quite clearly involved in 'doing celebrity' (as discussed earlier), in much the same way as the participants in Thornborrow's data are, or if not 'doing celebrity,' then at least to some extent 'being celebritized.' This could suggest that celebrity status, as part of a shift toward entertainment as the main rationale for program making, is becoming a new, hybrid, mediatized social identity category which might function as a replacement category for increasingly defunct traditional class-based categories like 'posh' (as discussed above in relation to Thornborrow's chapter).

Part IV, *Styles of Technologically Mediated Talk: What's New Anyway?*, focuses on the relationship between stability/continuity and change/renewal in broadcast style. In Chapter 9, *Talking for fun and talking in earnest: Two styles of mediated broadcast talk*, Martin Montgomery takes the notion of 'dead air' as his starting point and argues that, while silence is generally avoided in radio talk (because it is only through the consistent transmission of sound that the successful operation of the communicative channel can be affirmed), silence has found its distinct place in certain forms of broadcast talk. Through the analysis of a selection of examples from various US and UK television interviews, he shows that longer silences can be seen as co-constructed 'hearable properties' of a particular style of broadcast talk which he refers to as talking 'in earnest.' Interestingly, this style—and the deployment of ambiguous silences that partly construct it—depend not only on the interaction of participants for its realization but also on the affordances of technological mediation as well as the (implicit) contrast with other mediated styles which are more lively and upbeat, upholding the traditional imperative of avoiding dead air. Again, we see how stylistic difference is *achieved*, and how the achievement of difference has important implications for the construction of meaning in particular contexts.

In the last data analysis chapter, Chapter 10, *The meaning of manner: Change and continuity in the vocal style of news reading*, Theo van Leeuwen looks at what may be the most recognizable of all media speaking styles—perhaps even the quintessential case of talking media—namely, news reading. Comparing his own earlier studies of radio news reading on Australian radio (e.g. van Leeuwen 1983) to more recent examples from several different contexts, van Leeuwen argues that the vocal style of news reading, at least insofar as patterns of intonation and rhythm are concerned, exhibits considerable—and perhaps surprising—stability over time, both transnationally (in Australia, the United States, Netherlands, and the United

Kingdom) as well as cross-linguistically (in English as well as Dutch). Part of the reason for this stability may be related to the historical process underlying the establishment of news reading as a culturally salient style or *manner* in van Leeuwen's own term. Through extensive metapragmatic processes, much like the processes of enregisterment described by Agha, the manner of news reading has gradually moved from its 'genesis' in the late 1920s into a 'consolidation' phase where the style has taken on particular sociocultural salience and significance and subsequently become the object of prescription, handbook-writing and formalized teaching. In fact, van Leeuwen argues that there are signs that the manner of news reading is now reaching the third and final stage of 'automatization' in which the style is spreading to new domains where there is a perceived need for voices, including synthesized voices in public spaces, that can draw parasitically from the supposed authoritativeness and neutrality that, in van Leeuwen's analysis, have come to be indexed by the manner of news reading.

The book concludes with Part V, *Postscripts and Prospects*, which comprises two chapters offering commentaries on themes raised in the main analytical chapters in the book, as well as linking them to wider theoretical concerns. In Chapter 11, *Style, change, and media: A postscript*, Jannis Androutsopoulos constructively reviews the contributions made by the main chapters in light of his substantial earlier work on a wide range of sociolinguistic issues in different media contexts (e.g. Androutsopoulos 2014a, b, 2016), while Nikolas Coupland and Janus Mortensen, in Chapter 12, return to the notion of *Style as a unifying perspective for the sociolinguistics of talking media*, which we introduced at the beginning of this Introduction, making further connections to the main chapters.

Notes

1. http://www.pala.ac.uk/.

2. 'Style' and 'register' can often appear to be synonymous; both terms provide short-form reference to culturally recognizable modes of language use and to the sociolinguistic processes through which they are consolidated and then exploited and reshaped in usage. Style is arguably the more open concept, more easily reconciled with multilevel, socially meaningful semiotic action. It is also more readily transposed into a verbal, agentive concept—'styling.' Register also suffers from having collapsed the long-recognized distinction between 'dialect' and 'register,' which Halliday (e.g. 1978) used at a relatively abstract level to distinguish between 'user-related' styles ('dialects') and use-related styles ('registers').

3. This may happen with or without the explicit intention on the part of TV producers through Twitter, WhatsApp, or a number of similar third-party platforms, some of them purpose-made for comments on TV, such as the now discontinued tvtag (formerly GetGlue). However, second-screen interaction may also be integrated more closely into the program design by TV producers through custom-made smart phone/tablet applications. Thus, in several of its localized instantiations, the official app for *The X Factor* not only offers viewers the option of interacting with live shows by voting for their favorite participants but also provides opportunity for interaction with other viewers.

References

Agha, Asif. 2007. *Language and Social Relations*. Cambridge: Cambridge University Press.
Agha, Asif. 2011a. Meet mediatization. *Language & Communication* 31: 163–170.
Agha, Asif. 2011b. Large and small scale forms of personhood. *Language & Communication* 31: 171–180.
Androutsopoulos, Jannis. 2011. Language change and digital media: A review of conceptions and evidence. In Tore Kristiansen and Nikolas Coupland (eds.) *Standard Languages and Language Standards in a Changing Europe*. Oslo: Novus. 145–161.
Androutsopoulos, Jannis (ed.). 2014a. *Mediatization and Sociolinguistic Change*. Berlin: De Gruyter.
Androutsopoulos, Jannis. 2014b. Mediatization and sociolinguistic change: Key concepts, research traditions, open issues. In Jannis Androutsopoulos (ed.) *Mediatization and Sociolinguistic Change*. Berlin: De Gruyter. 3–48.
Androutsopoulos, Jannis. 2016. Theorizing media, mediation, and mediatization. In Nikolas Coupland (ed.) *Sociolinguistics: Theoretical Debates*. Cambridge: Cambridge University Press. 282–302.
Bauman, Richard. 1977. *Verbal Art as Performance*. Rowley: Newbury House.
Bauman, Richard. 1986. *Story, Performance, and Event: Contextual Stories of Oral Narrative*. Cambridge: Cambridge University Press.
Bauman, Richard. 2004. *A World of Others' Words: Cross-cultural Perspectives on Intertextuality*. Oxford: Blackwell Publishing.
Bauman, Richard and Charles L. Briggs. 1990. Poetics and performance as critical perspectives on language and social life. *Annual Review of Anthropology* 19: 59–88.
Bell, Allan. 1984. Language style as audience design. *Language in Society* 13: 145–204.
Bell, Allan. 2001. Back in style: Reworking audience design. In Penelope Eckert and John R. Rickford (eds.) *Style and Sociolinguistic Variation*. Cambridge: Cambridge University Press. 139–169.
Blommaert, Jan (ed.). 1999. *Language Ideological Debates*. Berlin: De Gruyter.
Couldry, Nick. 2012. *Media, Society, World: Social Theory and Digital Media Practice*. Malden: Polity Press.
Coupland, Nikolas. 1985. "Hark, hark the lark": Social motivations for phonological style-shifting. *Language & Communication* 5, 3: 153–172.
Coupland, Nikolas. 2001a. Dialect stylisation in radio talk. *Language in Society* 30, 3: 345–375.
Coupland, Nikolas. 2001b. Stylisation, authenticity and TV news review. *Discourse Studies* 3, 4: 413–442.
Coupland, Nikolas. 2007. *Style: Language Variation and Identity*. Cambridge: Cambridge University Press.
Coupland, Nikolas. 2009. Dialects, standards and social change. In Marie Maegaard, Frans Gregersen, Pia Quist and Jens Normann Jørgensen (eds.) *Language Attitudes, Standardization and Language Change*. Oslo: Novus. 27–50.
Coupland, Nikolas. 2010. Language, ideology, media and social change. In Karen Junod and Didier Maillat (eds.) *Performing the Self*. Tübingen: Gunter Narr Verlag (*Swiss Papers in English Language and Literature*). 127–151.
Coupland, Nikolas. 2011. Voice, place and genre in popular music performance. *Journal of Sociolinguistics* 15, 5: 573–602.

Coupland, Nikolas. 2012. Bilingualism on display: The framing of Welsh and English in Welsh public space. *Language in Society* 41: 1–27.

Coupland, Nikolas. 2014. Sociolinguistic change, vernacularization and broadcast British media. In Jannis Androutsopoulos (ed.) *Mediatization and Sociolinguistic Change*. Berlin: De Gruyter. 67–96.

Crystal, David. 2011. *Internet Linguistics*. London: Routledge.

Crystal, David and Derek Davy. 1969. *Investigating English Style*. London: Longmans.

Du Bois, John W. 2007. The stance triangle. In Robert Englebretson (ed.) *Stancetaking in Discourse: Subjectivity, Evaluation, Interaction*. Amsterdam: John Benjamins. 139–182.

Eckert, Penelope. 2000. *Linguistic Variation as Social Practice: The Linguistic Construction of Identity in Belten High*. Malden: Blackwell.

Eckert, Penelope. 2016. Variation, meaning and social change. In Nikolas Coupland (ed.) *Sociolinguistics: Theoretical Debates*. Cambridge: Cambridge University Press. 68–85.

Fabricius, Anne and Janus Mortensen. 2013. Language ideology and the notion of construct resources: A case study of modern RP. In Tore Kristiansen and Stef Grondelaars (eds.) *Language (De)standardisation in Late Modern Europe*. Oslo: Novus. 375–402.

Fairclough, Norman. 1992. *Discourse and Social Change*. Cambridge: Polity Press.

Fairclough, Norman. 1995. *Critical Discourse Analysis*. Boston: Addison Wesley.

Gal, Susan. 2016. Sociolinguistic differentiation. In Nikolas Coupland (ed.) *Sociolinguistics: Theoretical Debates*. Cambridge: Cambridge University Press. 113–135.

Giles, Howard. 1973. Accent mobility: A model and some data. *Anthropological Linguistics* 15: 87–105.

Giles, Howard and Peter Powesland. 1975. *Speech Style and Social Evaluation*. London: Academic Press.

Giles, Howard, Justine Coupland and Nikolas Coupland (eds.). 1991. *Contexts of Accommodation: Developments in Applied Sociolinguistics*. Cambridge: Cambridge University Press.

Goffman, Erving. 1959. *The Presentation of Self in Everyday Life*. New York: Doubleday.

Gumperz, John J. 1982. *Discourse Strategies*. Cambridge: Cambridge University Press.

Halliday, M. A. K. (1978) *Language as Social Semiotic*. London: Edward Arnold.

Hebdige, Dick. 1979. *Subculture: The Meaning of Style*. London: Routledge.

Hjarvard, Stig. 2013. *The Mediatization of Culture and Society*. New York: Routledge.

Hodge, Robert and Gunther Kress. *Social Semiotics*. Ithaca: Cornell University Press.

Hymes, Dell H. 1974. *Foundations in Sociolinguistics: An Ethnographic Approach*. Philadelphia: University of Pennsylvania Press.

Hymes, Dell H. 1996. *Ethnography, Linguistics, Narrative Inequality: Toward an Understanding of Voice*. London: Taylor & Francis.

Hymes, Dell H. 2004. *"In vain I tried to tell you": Essays in Native American Ethnopoetics*. Lincoln: University of Nebraska Press.

Irvine, Judith. 2001. "Style" as distinctiveness: The culture and ideology of linguistic differentiation. In Penelope Eckert and John R. Rickford (eds.) *Style and Sociolinguistic Variation*. Cambridge: Cambridge University Press. 21–43.

Irvine, Judith and Susan Gal. 2000. Language ideology and linguistic differentiation. In Paul V. Kroskrity (ed.) *Regimes of Language: Ideologies, Politics, and Identities*. Santa Fe, NM: School of American Research Press. 35–83.

Jaffe, Alexandra (ed.). 2009. *Stance: Sociolinguistic Perspectives*. New York: Oxford University Press.

Jaffe, Alexandra. 2011. Sociolinguistic diversity in mainstream media: Authenticity, authority and processes of mediation and mediatisation. *Journal of Language and Politics* 10, 4: 562–586.

Johnstone, Barbara and William M. Marcellino. 2011. Dell Hymes and the ethnography of communication. In Ruth Wodak, Barbara Johnstone and Paul Kerswill (eds.) *The Sage Handbook of Sociolinguistics*. London: Sage. 57–66.

Jones, Graham M., Bambi B. Schieffelin and Rachel E. Smith. 2011. When friends who talk together stalk together: Online gossip as metacommunication. In Crispin Thurlow and Kristine Mroczek (eds.) *Digital Discourse: Language in the New Media*. Oxford: Oxford University Press. 26–47.

Kress, Gunther and Theo van Leeuwen. 2006. *Reading Images: The Grammar of Visual Design* (2nd ed.). London: Routledge.

Labov, William. 1972. *Sociolinguistic Patterns*. Philadelphia: University of Pennsylvania Press.

Labov, William. 2001 *Principles of Linguistic Change: Social Factors*. Malden: Blackwell.

Livingstone, Sonia. 2009. On the mediation of everything. *Journal of Communication* 59, 1: 1–18.

Madsen, Lian Malai. 2015. *Fighters, Girls and Other Identities: Sociolinguistics in a Martial Arts Club*. Bristol: Multilingual Matters.

Madsen, Lian Malai, Martha Sif Karrebæk and Janus Spindler Møller (eds.). 2015. *Everyday Languaging: Collaborative Research on the Language Use of Children and Youth*. Berlin: De Gruyter.

Mugglestone, Lynda. 2003. *Talking Proper: The Rise of Accent as Social Symbol*. Oxford: Oxford University Press.

Page, Ruth, David Barton, Johann Unger and Michele Zappavigna. 2014. *Researching Language and Social Media*. London: Routledge.

Rampton, Ben. 2006. *Language in Late Modernity: Interaction in an Urban School*. Cambridge: Cambridge University Press.

Richardson, Kay. 2010. *Television Dramatic Dialogue: A Sociolinguistic Study*. Oxford: Oxford University Press.

Rojek, Chris. 2001. *Celebrity*. London: Reaktion.

Sacks, Harvey. 1984. On doing 'being ordinary.' In J. Maxwell Atkinson and John Heritage (eds.) *Structures of Social Action: Studies in Conversation Analysis*. Cambridge: Cambridge University Press. 413–429.

Sayers, Dave. 2014. The mediated innovation model: A framework for researching media influence in language change. *Journal of Sociolinguistics* 18, 2: 185–212.

Schieffelin, Bambi B., Kathryn A. Woolard and Paul V. Kroskrity. 1998. *Language Ideologies: Practice and Theory*. New York: Oxford University Press.

Scollon, Ron and Suzie Wong Scollon. 2004. *Nexus Analysis: Discourse and the Emerging Internet*. London: Routledge.

Silverstein, Michael. 2003. Indexical order and the dialectics of sociolinguistic life. *Language & Communication* 23: 193–229.

Stockwell, Peter. 2015. Poetics. In Eva Dabrowska and Dagmar Divjak (eds.) *Handbook of Cognitive Linguistics*. Berlin: De Gruyter. 432–452.

Stuart-Smith, Jane and Ichiro Ota. 2014. Media models, "the shelf," and stylistic variation in East and West: Rethinking the influence of the media on language variation and change. In Jannis Androutsopoulos (ed.) *Mediatization and Sociolinguistic Change*. Berlin: De Gruyter. 127–170.

Swales, John. 1990. *Genre Analysis: English in Academic and Research Settings*. Cambridge: Cambridge University Press.

Thurlow, Crispin and Kristine Mroczek (eds.). 2011. *Digital Discourse: Language in the New Media*. Oxford: Oxford University Press.

Turner, Graeme. 2016. *Re-inventing the Media*. London: Routledge.

Urban, Greg. 2001. *Metaculture: How Culture Moves Through the World*. Minneapolis: University of Minnesota Press.

van Leeuwen, Theo. 1983. The intonation of radio news readers. *Australian Journal of Cultural Studies* 2, 1: 84–98.

van Leeuwen, Theo. 2008. *Discourse and Practice: New Tools for Critical Analysis*. Oxford: Oxford University Press.

Wee, Lionel. 2015. *The Language of Organizational Styling*. Cambridge: Cambridge University Press.

Woolard, Kathryn, with Aida Ribot Bencomo and Josep Soler-Carbonell. 2013. What's so funny now? The strength of weak pronouns in Catalonia. *Journal of Linguistic Anthropology* 23, 3: 127–141.

PART I

Sociopolitical Change and the Emergence of New Styles and Genres

2

Style, sociolinguistic change, and political broadcasting: The case of the Spanish news show *Salvados*

Nuria Lorenzo-Dus

The motivating concern

On July 3, 2006, a railway carriage with 150 passengers on board derailed on a curve near a Valencia city underground station, killing 43 people and wounding a further 47. An inquiry was launched to determine possible criminal liability by the government-owned underground rail company, but the attempt was promptly dismissed on grounds of an alleged lack of evidence. Unsatisfied with the inquiry and in light of emerging evidence that a member of the regional parliament had sought to buy the silence of some of the victims' relatives with employment offers, the victims' relatives formed the *3 July Underground Accident Victims' Association*[1] (henceforth, 3J Association) to campaign for the re-opening of the investigation. On the third of each month, they began to hold a protest gathering in one of the city's main squares. The gatherings were poorly attended, making the association's Twitter hashtag *#olvidados* ('#forgotten') a largely accurate one.

Little else happened for the next few years until, on April 28, 2013, the news show *Salvados* ('Saved') broadcast an episode about the accident. Through a series of interviews with victims' relatives, rail company workers, and politicians, the show's director and anchor, Jordi Évole, revealed that the regional government had concealed evidence potentially indicative of criminal liability on the part of the rail company. Through Twitter, Évole called for citizens to show their support for the 3J Association's cause. Citizens responded: Twitter traffic around the *#olvidados* hashtag soared, and over 5,000 people literally filled the city square on May 3, 2013.

The April 28 *Salvados* show was awarded the prestigious *Ondas Prize* for the best Spanish news and current affairs broadcast in 2013. Évole's interviewing style in

Style, Mediation, and Change. Edited by Janus Mortensen, Nikolas Coupland, and Jacob Thøgersen
© Oxford University Press 2017. Published 2017 by Oxford University Press

the show received extensive media praise (inter)nationally. The French (*Libération*) and US (*New York Times*) press paid him tribute through nicknames such as, respectively, "the Spanish Tintin" and "the Spanish Michael Moore." Selected content from Évole's interviews during the broadcast was included in the evidence that led to the accident inquiry finally reopening in July 2013. Despite further regional government attempts to halt it, the inquiry is ongoing at the time of writing. The last protest gathering of the 3J Association was held on July 3, 2015. The reason given by the Association for discontinuing the gatherings was its belief that it had finally secured the necessary judicial support and an agreement from the majority of the regional government parties that the inquiry would be conducted "without vetoing and with full guarantee [of fairness and transparency]."[2]

Although the April 28 *Salvados* broadcast was key in promoting Évole's journalistic standing internationally, he had already received—and has since continued to receive—numerous national awards.[3] His journalistic style is branded as controversial, incisive, and instrumental in "renewing journalistic genres" and "establishing a politically independent and socially necessary journalistic agenda."[4] Évole is explicit about the need for a change in journalistic praxis, too. He publicly advocates freedom of speech within the profession by saying, for example, "in this profession, silence does not achieve anything," and he asks fellow journalists to sever long-established ties with the ruling classes since "the closer journalism is to political power, the further it gets from citizens."[5]

This chapter explores the notions of sociolinguistic change and style in relation to *Salvados* and Évole's journalistic persona and performances. In order to do so, the following section explains how these notions are used in my work. After this, I provide an overview of recent and contemporary political journalism in Spain before turning to two analytical sections that examine (1) Évole's style in the April 28 *Salvados* episode and (2) how this was evaluated by citizens across online/social media. The chapter concludes by placing the findings of this case study within a wider research agenda for furthering our understanding of style and sociolinguistic change.

Style and sociolinguistic change

In this chapter, style is understood to comprise the use of various semiotic resources—including linguistic ones—that contribute centrally to the enactment of identity in interaction (Coupland 2007; Jaffe 2009). This styling of identity is performed through processes of indirect indexicality (Bucholtz 2009); that is, certain semiotic resources become dynamically associated with (rather than being immediately linked to) particular social types. Association processes are ideologically patterned and often work "within a semiotic system in relation to other locally available—and often competing and contrasting—styles" (Bucholtz 2009: 148). For example, in the case of *Salvados*, Évole's style—the realization of his journalistic persona—emerges within the historical background of political journalism in Spain, as well as through how he relates to the public, politicians, and other journalists across contexts. These contexts, which are always unique, include his public appearances, where he might talk about the need for political journalism to change by becoming independent of political power (as discussed in the previous section), and his *Salvados* interviews (which are treated in detail below in the section on *Évole's style in* Salvados).

In this chapter I argue that Évole's interviewing style contributes to changing the genre of political broadcasting in Spain. Building on Swales (1990), Fairclough (2003) defines genres as ways of (inter)acting discursively, and positions them as in-between stages between ways of representing (discourses) and ways of identifying or being (styles). Although genres rely on a certain level of structural stability, variation is a *sine qua non* for their continuity. Genre change is related to social change in terms of potential "new functions [that] a genre is thought to fulfil within a community" (Luginbühl 2014: 307). This is because of the social dimension of genres: they offer resources to discourse communities, upon which their users draw in creative and multifaceted ways (Fairclough 2003). Discourse communities use genres to "establish, stabilize or change their common norms and values," which means that genres play a key role in how culture is transmitted and changed (Luginbühl 2014: 310).

In bringing together language and culture, Luginbühl's (2014) notion of genre change also prompts examination of the meaning of change at the crossroad between language and society. In his metacommentary to a special issue of the *Journal of Sociolinguistics* on language, change, and media, Coupland (2014a) reviews the contributions of the field of sociolinguistics to the concept of change before proposing, as a way forward for the field, a new conceptualization of sociolinguistic change that offers "more perspective on the social value of language change" and "open[s] a window on changing language-society relations that are not consequential on changes in linguistic forms, features and distributions" (2014a: 282).

For Coupland (2014a, b) sociolinguistic change implies the interplay of five theoretical dimensions, namely, discursive practice, language ideology, social normativity, cultural reflexivity and media(tiza)tion. An emphasis on discursive practice within a sociolinguistics of change is beneficial in three respects. First, it makes it possible to attend to "more elaborated contextualisation processes" beyond those typically addressed such as "speech" or "sound change" (2014b: 75). This is crucial when examining essentially multimodal media contexts such as television, as is the case in *Salvados*. Second, it allows simultaneous examination of value judgments about discourse that flow within different social structures, at different points in time, and for different language users. This is particularly relevant to the analysis of how Évole's interviewing style is evaluated by the members of different discourse communities across other media, as examined in the section below on audience engagement (*Engaging with Évole's style*). Third, it enables a dynamic reassessment of how social norms relate to both discursive practice norms and potential shifts in value structures (Coupland 2014a: 282–283). An integrated analysis of the discourse practices of both Évole's *Salvados* interviews and their uptake by professionals (journalists/politicians) and viewers contributes to identifying and better understanding some of the norms and values that may underpin sociolinguistic change in relation to the journalism profession in contemporary Spain.

The cultural reflexivity dimension has less of a tradition in sociolinguistics, yet it is crucial to sociolinguistic change. Coupland's (2014a, b) argument here draws upon Urban's (2001) theory of sociocultural change, whereby it is our reflexive awareness of culture that makes culture "move through the world." Similarly, acts of reflexivity about change at a meta level, especially when "metacultural brokers" or "entrepreneurs" become involved, can make certain changes salient to discourse communities. Évole's style of interviewing triggers considerable metacultural and metadiscursive reflexivity from citizens across different media platforms (as discussed in the section on *Engaging with Évole's style*, below), which reflects and contributes to his role of metacultural entrepreneur as regards sociolinguistic change.

Metaculturally reflexive sociolinguistic change may, or may not, coincide with technological change. Yet, technological change is a key component of the fifth interrelated dimension of sociolinguistic change in Coupland's (2014a, b) account: media(tiza)tion. A social-constructivist account of this/these notions (Hepp and Krotz 2014; Livingstone 2009) sees (1) all language as being mediated and (2) technologized mediation as a facet of sociocultural change that both enriches and complicates understanding of sociolinguistic meaning and diversity (Androutsopoulos 2011). A social-constructivist account, moreover, challenges technological determinism in the study of media discourse, including the study of sociolinguistic change. Media discourse is undeniably an important arena for sociolinguistic change, but the questions we should be asking ourselves regarding such change should concern the whole array of agentive and creative ways in which we engage with media language, rather than the assumed influence it has on us as sociolinguistic beings. This is why this case study focuses on some of the ways in which citizens involve themselves, through social and online news media, in broader socio-political and sociolinguistic debates around the recent past, present, and potential future of political journalism in Spain. It is to the latter that the chapter turns its attention to next.

Politics and television in Spain—crisis and transformation

Political journalism in Spain has a bad reputation. Public opinion is openly condemnatory: surveys by Spain's national Social Research Centre (*Centro de Investigaciones Sociales*) repeatedly show journalism to be among the professions least valued by Spanish citizens. Scholarship is generally critical, too, accusing Spanish journalism—especially political broadcasting—of failing to adhere to the professional standards of objectivity and neutrality evidenced in other Western democracies (e.g. Humanes Humanes et al. 2013).

In their seminal work on international media systems, Hallin and Mancini (2004) situate journalism in Spain within a "Mediterranean or Polarized Pluralist Model."[6] This is one of three "ideal" (in the sense of Weber) models of media-politics relations, all of which are modeled against four analytic dimensions: structure of media markets, political parallelism, professionalization of journalism, and the role of the state.[7] With reference to these analytic dimensions, Hallin and Mancini (2004) characterize the Polarized Pluralist Model as (1) having an elite, politically oriented press; (2) displaying high levels of political parallelism, being oriented to commentary rather than facts, adopting a politics-over-broadcasting system and being controlled by parliamentary policy; (3) experiencing weaker journalistic professionalization levels; and (4) operating under strong state intervention, periods of censorship, and "savage deregulation." Within the development of commercial broadcasting in Europe in the 1970s, savage deregulation refers to media corporations—as opposed to political systems—defining the regulations of broadcasting markets, whereby competition among broadcasters leads to a reduction of media content diversity (Musso and Pineau 1985; Traquina 1995).

A number of studies confirm Hallin and Mancini's (2004) placement of Spanish journalism within the Polarized Pluralist Model, especially with regard to low levels of professionalization among its journalists (Roca-Cuberes 2012) and strong state intervention, bordering on state paternalism (Papatheodorou and Machin 2003). Within this model, Spanish television is regarded as a particular area of concern—so ineffective has it been in holding the political class to account that it has been called "the weak point of Spanish democracy" (Bustamante 2006). For instance, in 2006, under *Socialist Party* rule, the Spanish Parliament passed an Act on "State-Owned Radio and Television" that adopted several measures to instil editorial independence in Spanish public broadcasting (*Radio Televisión Española,* or *RTVE*). This included a law whereby consensus between government and opposition was required for electing the heads of public corporations. Progress toward achieving these measures was very slow and received a further setback in 2012 when, with the right-wing *Partido Popular* in power, a law was approved that modified the 2006 Act for electing boards of directors of public broadcasting so that governments with a sufficient parliamentary majority, as was the case of the *Partido Popular* at the time, could appoint them unilaterally. The subsequent *RTVE* chairman was part of an editorial team previously found guilty of information manipulation—an appointment that drew considerable criticism from the Parliamentary Assembly of the Council of Europe in 2013 but no change in legislation.

Since the late 2000s, however, the Polarized Pluralist Model has come under some pressure in Spain. Dwindling ratings for *RTVE* provided clear signs of discontent with government attempts to control political broadcasting (Roca-Cuberes 2012), and a series of political broadcasting formats have emerged that are openly critical of the political class. They include political satire shows, such as *El Intermedio* (*La Sexta*) and *Mire Usted* (*Antena 3*), citizen interview shows, like

Tengo una Pregunta para Usted (*RTVE*), panel debates and news interviews shows, such as *Los Desayunos de la Primera* (*RTVE*) and *Al Rojo Vivo* (*La Sexta*), and news shows, like *El Objetivo* and *Salvados* (*La Sexta*).

While different in some respects, these shows all have a strong denouncement ethos in common, for which the current sociopolitical climate is arguably perfect. The 2008–2015 period marks the worst financial crisis in Spain for decades.[8] The period has been dubbed "the Great Spanish Depression" (Bentolila et al. 2012) and has led to major economic downturn in a country that has seen unemployment rise to a historical maximum of 27% and major companies go into bankruptcies throughout the period. It has also led to rapidly increasing citizen concern regarding widespread corrupt practices among the political and business sector (Web Forum Report, 2013–2014), as evident from the formation of the *Movimiento 15 M* ('15-M Movement'), also known as *Los Indignados* ('Indignants')—an anti-austerity measures movement that began as an impromptu revolt of thousands in the country's capital on May 15, 2011, and that has become a voice of resistance to Spain's *Partido Popular* and to political corruption in general.[9]

Expectedly, the unprecedented success of these new political broadcasting formats has faced strong opposition from the party in government: the *Partido Popular*. For example, in 2014 the *Partido Popular* accused *El Intermedio* of systematically undermining its policies and some of its members. The director of the media corporation that owns *El Intermedio* responded not only by publicly revealing government pressure for him to change the show's format and replace its host, *el gran Wyoming* ('the great Wyoming'),[10] but also by publicly announcing his decision to do neither: "no-one touches Wyoming."[11]

A further example concerns former presenter of *Los Desayunos de la Primera* (*RTVE*), Ana Pastor, who was allegedly fired in 2012 because of her antagonistic interviewing style[12] even though this arguably fitted squarely within the Anglo-Saxon tradition of "neutralistic interviewing" (Greatbatch 1998).[13] After a period of employment in the United States (*CNN News*), Pastor returned to Spanish political broadcasting in 2013, this time as lead presenter of *El Objetivo*. In its opening broadcast, Pastor characterized the show as belonging to a firmly established genre of political news broadcasting in the United States ("fact-checking news"), yet a new, much needed one in Spain—particularly given the need for social change in the country. Although *El Objetivo* has brought Pastor several journalistic awards, including one jointly with Évole for raising social awareness against political corruption,[14] it has also made her the target of political criticism. In 2013, for example, co-founder of the *Unión, Progreso y Democracia* Party, Gonzalo Martínez Gorrián, used Twitter to accuse Pastor of "shameful distortion of truth" in her interviews and of being "scum." Pastor challenged those accusations, also via Twitter. Their exchange became hotly debated across social, press and broadcast media.[15]

The two examples highlight the dialectic nature of the relationship between genre and social change. Genres do not change overnight; nor do societies: the processes involved entail moving across metacultures of continuity and change. Even when attempts at genre change cluster around a seemingly brief period of time, tradition and innovation coexist with different degrees of interpenetration. The style of journalists such as Pastor, Wyoming, and Évole results in professional recognition (e.g. journalistic awards), citizen support (see examples in the section on audience engagement below) and increasing viewer numbers. It also leads to political controversy and resistance. This makes the case study under consideration here all the more worthy of study since, as Coupland (2014b: 77) observes, sociolinguistic change is more likely to become part of our metacultural reflexivity when it focuses on "sociolinguistic norms and ideological assessments of 'what is meaningfully old' and 'what is meaningfully new.'"

Évole's style in *Salvados*

Salvados was first broadcast in 2008. After modest viewer ratings during the first couple of years, it has doubled its audience since 2010. The most recent statistics reveal that the show is three times more popular than its channel's average ratings every week, and the active tweeting of Évole's over 911,000 Twitter followers has resulted in *Salvados* broadcasts being crowdsourced as trending topics in Spain after virtually every show. The 60-minute Sunday evening program is constructed as a learning journey for Évole and, through him, his viewers, to understand and expose where responsibility vis-à-vis a given social problem lies. The *Salvados* journey resembles the narrative structure of fairy tales in its clear-cut portrayal of 'victims' and 'villains,' with Évole in the role of 'hero.' Unlike fairy tales, Évole's heroism is distinctively "post-modern" (Forster 2002), for it is premised upon a strong sense of ordinariness. Also unlike fairy tales, *Salvados* episodes lack narrative closure, let alone a happy ending. The show is structured around a series of seamless interviews of social actors that, on the whole, promote a sense of close proximity/identification between Évole and the show's viewers.

To examine Évole's journalistic style, my analysis draws upon multimodal transcripts of all the interviews conducted by him during the April 28 *Salvados* program. These interviews constitute a homogeneous corpus in that, in addition to exhibiting thematic coherence, they all share several broadcast talk features: they are scripted (rather than live) and have been edited post-filming. They are also performed with Évole 'in character' (interviewer) and produced with a wide though specific audience in mind: television audiences assumed to be dissatisfied with the ruling classes and with journalists' close ties to the political class. During the interviews Évole's style emerges out of repeated use of semiotic resources that index stance-taking choices in relation to morality, ordinariness, and mock naïvety. Although I analyze these aspects of his style separately here, they complement each other in his interviews.

CONSTRUCTING MORAL FRAMEWORKS

Évole constantly invites his interviewees to co-construct meaning during the interviews, not only by asking them questions (as expected within his interviewer role) but also by evaluating their answers, often on moral grounds. This he frequently does by asking them to confirm his uptake of their turns at talk. Metadiscursively framed by Évole as comprehension checks (e.g. "have I got this right? you're saying that …"), these uptakes enable him to progress his (viewers') learning journey and to evaluate actions and actors morally. They also enable him to create an extended interactional space in which interviewee and interviewer are seen to attend to a shared stance object about which they respectively generate a series of stance-lead and stance-follow acts (see Du Bois 2007). Évole's stance-taking acts may converge with or diverge from his interviewees' to different extents, but they are always distinctively non-neutralistic, as Extract 1 illustrates.

Extract 1[16] comes from an interview with Arturo Rocher (R), former head of security at the railway company that operated the crashed train. It is filmed in R's living room, with him and Évole (E) sitting near each other (see Figure 2.1a). R has just revealed that staff members were coached prior to their inquiry testimony. This included their being instructed not to use terms such as *deficiency, tragedy*, and, as he emphasizes in lines 1–2, *track beacon*, which was subsequently found not to be operative when the accident happened.

Extract 1

MCU—R nodding.	1 R	… the issue of the track beacon (.) that was <u>logically</u>
	2	one of the main taboo words
MS—E & R sitting.	3 E	and didn't it cross your[i] mind at any point to
	4	think what we're doing is fraudulent?
MCU—R then MS—E	5 R	(1.5) well (.) it probably crossed our mind that it
& R. CU—E scratches	6	was not ethically correct an::d (.) er well also we
his beard, as he frowns.	7	were under enormous pressure …
LS—E gesticulates with	8 E	let's see if I get th- it (.) didn't anyone complain
hands.	9	abou- ? didn't anyone say I'm <u>not</u> doing that?
MCU—R shakes head.	10 R	no-one dared (.) <u>absolutely</u> no-one (.) <u>no-one</u>
MS—E & R. E opens	11 E	and can one sleep at night when one attends a
up arms, palms face up,	12	parliamentary inquiry a:::nd realizes the group one
eyebrows	13	represents is not telling the truth?
rise in surprise.	14 R	(2.0) well I think if one has nothing to hide one sleeps
MCU—R.	15	at night … in that respect I had the advantage that
Combination of LS &	16	*… R explains why his area of responsibility in work*
MCU shots of E & R.	17	*was not directly involved in the accident …*

LS—E & R.	18	E	did you[ii] have the feeling you[ii] were lying
	19		to the inquiry panel?
MCU—R shakes head	20	R	no:: the conversation was diverted °if you like° to
in denial.	21		those areas that were convenient (.) not in my case =
LS—E & R.[iii]	22	E	= you[ii] mean you[ii] didn't lie but yo-[ii] you[ii] didn't
	23		quite say all you[ii] knew?
MCU—R nods in	24	R	correct
agreement.	25		*... R talks reveals that the train log book and all its*
	26		*copies were stolen ...*
MS—E gesticulates.	27	E	(2.0) it's <u>terribly</u> cruel all you[ii]'re telling me
MCU—R.	28	R	yes (.) really terrible (.) but that's what happened

[i] You = plural (vosotros; T form).

[ii] You = singular (tú; T form).

[iii] Text on screen: "Arturo Rocher—Former Head of Security at Valencian Government Rail"

Évole's questions progressively evaluate the initial shared stance object (giving false testimony before an inquiry) and the ensuing revelations regarding the alleged theft of the train log, as "<u>terribly</u> cruel" (line 58)—an evaluation with which his interviewee ends up aligning himself ("yes (.) really terrible" line 59). Getting R to this point takes Évole five, progressively more personal and accusatory questions that involve five shifts of footing, specifically of the production role of principal (Goffman 1981), as shown in Table 2.1.

TABLE 2.1

Évole's shift of footing (principal) in Extract 1

Question (line numbers)	Footing (principal)	Action/group evaluated
1 (3)	A group of testifying employees (plural 'you')	Thinking about the possibility of fraudulent behavior.
1 (4)	A group of testifying employees (a 'we,' performed through direct speech)	(continued)
2 (8)	A group of testifying employees (a generic 'anyone')	Complaining about being asked to behave unethically.
2 (9)	An individual testifying employee ('I,' performed through direct speech)	Voicing unwillingness to comply with instructions to lie.
3 (11–13)	Rocher as a member of the group of testifying employees (a generic 'one')	Having a clear conscience (being able to sleep at night) when realizing truth not being told.
4 (18–19)	Rocher as in individual testifying employee (singular 'you')	Having the feeling of lying.
5 (22–23)	Rocher as in individual testifying employee (singular 'you')	Concealing relevant information.

Within these shifts of footing, Évole introduces two comprehension checks: "let's see if I get th-" (line 8) and "=you mean you . . ." (line 22). Both are stance-follow acts that enable Évole to question R's stance-lead acts, where R has respectively reframed Évole's evaluations of his actions from being "fraudulent" (line 4) into "probably... not ethically correct" (lines 5–6) and from "lying" (line 18) into a case of "a conversation [being] diverted . . . towards those areas that were convenient" (lines 20–21). These comprehension checks also enable Évole to evaluate the morality of both the actions being described and the interviewee's character, because they make evident R's reluctance to disclose the truth in plain terms. Through comprehension checks and shifts of footing Évole is able to take the viewers along on his own learning journey—one that reveals new facts, evaluates the morality of those involved in such events, and makes explicit his stance vis-à-vis the shared stance object around which this part of the interview revolves.

ORDINARINESS AND THE POWER OF INDEXING IGNORANCE

Évole's repeated references to his desire to learn are complemented by use of minor self-deprecation around the social type of 'the ordinary guy' who struggles with complex, specialist explanations. Évole interrupts his interviewees with a softly uttered, perplexed sounding "I don't understand"—or a "let's see if I get it" (Extract 1, line 8)—which he utters as he signals difficulty in taking in the information his interviewee is providing. This is accentuated through scratching his beard and frowning (Extract 1, lines 6–7) and hand gesturing (Extract 1, lines 8–9). He may ask for arguments to be presented in concrete, simple terms that citizens—and he—may understand, such as "just so that I, and the viewers can follow, can you explain this in lay terms?" Ordinariness is also indexed through jargon-free lexis, both in his questions and in his reformulation of interviewees' technical terms. Frequent use of deictic elements (principally demonstrative pronouns), colloquialisms, and interjections (mainly showing surprise and containing mild taboo words—see Extract 2, line 1, for an example) are commonplace in his speech, too. They all contribute to styling the interviews as conversational, casual contexts, despite the far from casual topics being discussed.

Évole's dress style matches the linguistic indexing of this ordinariness stance, which across his *Salvados* and public appearances is distinctively casual and unassuming: distressed jeans, trainers, loose checked shirt or cotton T-shirt, a parka (see Figures 2.1a–2.1d). His choice of interview locations indexes a similar stance. In the *Salvados* show under analysis it includes the sitting room of interviewees (Figures 2.1a and 2.1c), and several streets in Valencia (e.g. Figures 2.1b and 2.1d). These semiotic and linguistic signifiers stand in marked contrast to the formal register, attire, and studio-based setting of many other high-profile journalists on Spanish television.

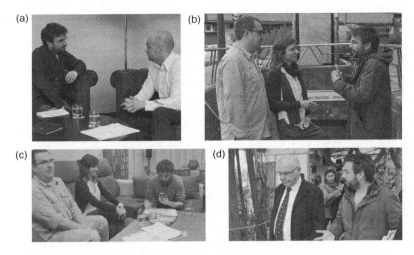

FIGURE 2.1 Évole's dress style. Top left (Figure 2.1a); top right (Figure 2.1b); bottom left (Figure 2.1c); bottom right (Figure 2.1d)[17]

MOCK NAÏVETY

In an interview with *Reuters* following the April 28 *Salvados* show, Évole explains the show's rationale as follows:

> Spain is going through a time when citizens are really questioning things. We are part of those people. We do the program to know what is going on and understand it. We ask really basic questions because we don't understand a lot of what's going on.[18]

The referential content of his explanation is supported by the semiotic and linguistic indexicalities of his interviewing style. Évole makes regular use of an epistemic stance that positions himself as a keen learner. Within his ordinariness, as we have seen, he refers to his ignorance (e.g. "I don't know anything about train machinery," "I'm no expert in . . ."). But he also uses epistemic expressions that call attention to the thought processes that he activates while trying to take in the information he is receiving (e.g. "I imagine," "I guess," "I can only assume"). Évole's body language co-indexes such a stance: his eyebrows are raised, his forehead creases slightly conveying quizzical concentration, the palms of his hands face upwards, and his arms open up in a gesture that signals a keen willingness to understand. Évole also goes to considerable lengths to align viewers to his stance. His epistemic expressions often entail strategic shifts of footing in which he alternates between first person singular and plural pronominal authoring choices, framing his eagerness to learn as being shared with Spaniards/specific social groups (e.g. "and I'm really wondering, as Spaniards do, we wonder, don't know, how come did . . .").

Importantly, Évole's 'not knowing' epistemic stance is keyed as ironic and draws upon hedging and stylistic dissonance. He often uses hedging to phrase accusatory questions, conveying an impression of innocence—for example, "maybe this is not what you/he intended"; "perhaps he genuinely wanted to help, not bribe . . . ." Yet hedging tends to follow details in the show that make it unnecessary from a referential point of view, such as hard-hitting factual evidence of wrongdoing on the interviewee's part. This renders the hedging as ironic and Évole's naïvety as mock, especially in the context of broadcast talk in Spain, where directness and assertiveness constitute the unmarked interactional style (Lorenzo-Dus 2007; Garcés-Conejos Blitvich, Lorenzo-Dus and Bou-Franch 2010).

Stylistic dissonance is realized via an overt clash between two or more semiotic modes within Évole's self-presentation. For example, the kind of hard-hitting factual evidence referred to previously, often including information from specialized fields of knowledge, may be semiotically presented via zoomed-in footage of his iPad with pre-highlighted statistical data or textual citations that he nevertheless verbally relays to his interviewee in low-affect, mockingly naïve prosody.

Évole's interviewing style does not make use of verbal aggression. As his questions become more direct and analytic, his use of emotional and/or colloquial language remains stable. He does not raise his voice. Nor does he quicken his tempo, gesticulate angrily, or convey any other verbal or nonverbal signals of loss of professional/personal control. The only change concerns his mock-naïve stylization: his quizzical frown may become more pronounced, his verbal references to not understanding his interviewees' answers more frequent, and his use of hedging and other negative politeness strategies that signal deference, but also distance, more marked. The stylistic dissonance that this creates does not go unnoticed by the wider journalistic community. For instance, in a feature on Évole on the occasion of his receiving his third *Ondas Prize* in 2013, *Vanity Fair* talks about the journalist receiving the prize "with the same half-smile with which he charges against a senior politician involved in a corruption case."[19] Nor does his use of stylistic dissonance fail to be detected by either segments of his show's audience (see Extracts 3–5) or, as in Extract 2, other social actors involved in the shows, whose positions he may wish to defend or promote.

In Extract 2 Évole and both the former president (FP) and the current president (P) of the 3J Association are sitting around a coffee table in P's living room (see Figure 2.1c). P has explained that, following the accident, regional government Minister Juan Cotino (C) tried to bribe family victims by offering them jobs if they decided against pursuing a judicial suit. P has also explained that Cotino gave his personal mobile phone number to those family victims. At that point in the interview, Évole asks P for Cotino's number and, when given it, calls him. He receives no answer and so he continues the interview. After a couple of minutes, Évole's mobile phone rings.

Extract 2

LS—E, P & FP. E [to	1	E	ooooh (.) blim-
FP/P]surprised.	2		Cotino's calling
[to E].	3	FP	he's returning your call? =
MCU- E [to FP & P]	4	E	= yep yep (.) Cotino's calling [to JC] Mr Cotino?
Looking down at phone	5	C	(.) speaking (.) who's calling?[iv]
and his hands.	6	E	Mr Cotino? (.) yes (.) I'm Jordi:: Évole (.)
	7		the director of the Sexta Channel Salvados show
MLS—E, P & FP.	8	C	no (.) not me
E shakes his	9	E	how come?
head, signalling	10	C	(2.0) no (.) not [me
puzzlement.	11	E	[how come? but you[v] just said
	12		you're Mr Cotino
MCU—E looks at FP	13	C	no (.) it's not [me
& P, mockingly	14	E	[what do you mean no?
confused;	15	C	I'm his brother
low-affect, smiling	16	E	ah you're <u>his</u> brother (.) well you do sound
voice.	17		very similar
LS—E, FP & P; FP	18	C	indeed (.) that's because we're brothers
sits back in mock	19	E	an::d isn't your brother with you now?
disbelief. E smiles as he	20	C	no (.) he left ten minutes ago
continues to listen,	21		. . . C explains that he answered
looking down towards	22		his brother's phone in case it was
his mobile phone.	23		his nephew calling . . .
MLS—E, smiling voice	24	E	you won't be deceiving me and you really are
quality, soft intonation.	25		Mr Cotino and don't want to talk to me now (.)
MCU—FP & P smiling.	26		will you?
C's voice conveys	27	C	no (.) I have no reason to lie to you (.) nor the
irritation.	28		pleasure to know you =
	29	E	= absolutely =
MCU—E still smiling	30	C	= I'm not in the business of deceiving anyone (.)
ironically. [line goes	31		goodbye
dead] MCU—E frowns.	32	E	(1.5) Mr Cotino?

[iv] From this point on, C's turns are transcribed as text on the screen.

[v] You = singular, formal (Usted) used throughout the conversation.

Most of Extract 2 is keyed as mock-naïve by Évole. The turns where C denies being himself (lines 8, 10, and 13) are verbally met by Évole with disbelief on two occasions (lines 11–12, line 14), though the second one is already accompanied by body language that indexes mock puzzlement. By the time C begins to impersonate his own brother (line 15), the stylistic dissonance between Évole's language and his body-/para-language becomes explicit to FP and P, who also align their body language to Évole's. FP sits back in disbelief, accompanying his movement with an exaggerated facial expression of disbelief as he looks 'knowingly' in the direction of one of the cameras (lines 18–19; Figure 2.1c). Also, FP and P are shot in medium close-up in line 26 smiling ironically as Évole, also smiling and with a soft intonation, challenges C's impersonation (lines 24–26). C's outright denials and brusque reactions in lines 27–28 and 30–31, including his suddenly ending the call, leave no doubt as to his interpreting Évole's question as face-threatening. Yet, Évole's questions make use of negative politeness, specifically hedging conveyed via a tag question ("you won't … will you?"). It is his para- and body-language that render his use of negative politeness as ironic and his stance of naïvety as mock.

The marked stylistic dissonance in Extract 2 is effective. His co-present audience, FP and P, find it amusing and actively contribute to the performance, as noted previously. His interviewee loses his cool—clearly a most undesirable outcome for a public political figure, especially of his seniority. Indeed, Évole followed up this telephone conversation during the last ten minutes of the April 28 broadcast with an unsolicited interview of Cotino at a public event in the city (see Figure 2.1d). During that interview, Cotino once again refused to speak to Évole. Both the telephone conversation and the 'street interview' subsequently went viral on Spanish-language social media. Viewers endorsed his style in those two interviews with a senior political figure across social and online media. Implicit references to Évole's mock naïvety were repeatedly made and positively appraised by viewers (see e.g. Extract 5a).

Engaging with Évole's style

Thus far, the analysis of Évole's style has revolved around his discursive performance during the April 28 *Salvados* show. In the current media ecology, where discourse communities engage with media texts across multiple media platforms, it is important to examine those other platforms too. How do members of these discourse communities 'read' Évole's stylistic constructions? Do all aspects of Évole's styling 'work' for all the discourse communities it reaches? If that is not the case, which aspects of his style are taken up by which discourse communities? And how can all this inform our understanding of sociolinguistic change?

In order to answer these questions, I examined viewers' uptake of the April 28 *Salvados* broadcast through the extensive coverage that it received across several media. This entailed collecting: all the #*olvidados* tweets between April 21 and May

29, 2013;[20] all the YouTube comments posted in response to two videos containing interviews from the show, and all the reader-generated online posts relating to articles about the broadcast featured by four national dailies (*El Mundo, El País, La Vanguardia, La Razón*) between April 29 and May 29, 2013. A content analysis of the corpus was conducted. This followed the Glaserian paradigm of Grounded Theory (Glaser 1992), where the researcher inductively and organically derives—through a multistage coding process—a set of themes from the data. Multiple coding was adopted throughout this process, so that the same stretch of text (i.e. the same part of a YouTube comment, tweet, or online newspaper post) could be coded under more than one of the emerging themes.

The results of the content analysis revealed that, thematically, the comments in the corpus mainly concerned the train accident, the Spanish political and economic crisis, and Spanish journalism. Within this last theme, most citizens referred to journalism being in a state of crisis; they blamed the government for controlling journalists and evaluated long-established styles of political journalism as "old" and "out-dated." There was also a significant amount of commentary about—and debate around—emerging journalistic formats, which *Salvados* was seen to epitomize. Some of these were negative evaluations, in which the show was accused of affiliation to the political left and hence of offering no actual change in journalistic practice. It goes without saying, too, that Évole's journalistic style was not without its detractors in these comments. But the majority of comments positively appraised the show and Évole's part in transforming Spanish journalism into a politically independent profession that would better serve citizens' right to know. The top 20 most re-tweeted tweets in the corpus, for instance, congratulated Évole and/or his show for acting as a catalyst of change: either change in judicial effectiveness, as in Extract 3a, or in social identity, as in 3b where change was seen to matter to an 'us' group, possibly Spain as a nation.

Extract 3a

@JordiEvole: You're going to achieve with one tv show more than the entire judicial system. Congratulations!!!

Extract 3b

The power of tv to change—and other people making such a vile use of it . . . @JordiEvole Congratulations.

Particularly noteworthy about the general public's uptake of the *Salvados* show was the salience of metacultural reflexivity in relation to sociolinguistic change. Citizens' comments across the social and online media environments examined acknowledged not only that Évole's style represented such change but also what it entailed and to whom it mattered. A sense of urgency to change Spanish journalism was explicitly and emotionally conveyed, too. Consider Extracts 4a–4c:

Extract 4a

[Twitter]: that's what we need now; quality, independent journalism; stop fooling citizens!

Extract 4b

> [Twitter]: 58 minutes without music or a single picture of the accident and its victims—let's no longer be fooled when they tell us that a different way of doing tv is not possible.

Extract 4c

> [*El País* online, comments section]: wow what an upheaval, Follonero![21] Here we have an example of what much-needed change and good journalism can achieve! CONGRATULATIONS!

In these three extracts citizens express their view that the change to journalistic practice that Évole's style is believed to bring about matters to a collective 'us' (Spanish citizens): it is "much-needed" change, and it is needed "now." They also illustrate the 'effects' of Évole's metacultural entrepreneurship and the meta*cultural* reflexivity regarding the "inertial and accelerative properties" (Urban 2001: 32) of culture, which is essential for cultural and sociolinguistic change (Urban 2001; Coupland 2014b).

Citizens' comments also displayed a level of meta*discursive* reflexivity. Admittedly, qualifiers like "independent" (Extract 4a) or "good" (Extract 4c) are rather vague metalinguistic labels for Évole's journalistic style. However, the corpus also included numerous instances of reflexive commentary about the specific semiotic resources that indexed such journalistic style. In Extract 4b, for example, a journalistic rhetoric of sensationalizing human suffering visually and acoustically ("58 minutes without music or a single picture of the accident and its victims") was explicitly rejected ("let's no longer be fooled when they tell us that a different way of doing tv is not possible"). All in all, there was clear ideological demarcation, if not outright polarization, between the *we group* (the citizens and Évole) and the *they group* (those within the Polarized Pluralist Model) in these comments, which revolved around reflecting on the need for change, and the forms that this should take.

Further evidence of the high level of meta-reflexivity triggered by the April 28 *Salvados* broadcast came from frequent instances of "other-stance attribution" (Coupland and Coupland 2009) toward Évole in the online/social media corpus. Stances attributed to Évole were on the whole congruent with those identified in the section on Évole's style above and positively appraised. His style appeared to be recognized as such in the corpus as a "knowing deployment of culturally familiar styles and identities," namely, moral evaluation, ordinariness, and irony, which were, however, marked as "deviating from those predictably associated with the current speaking context" (Coupland 2001: 345). Doing 'being ordinary,' for instance, is a widely adopted stance for media celebrities across western media (Lorenzo-Dus 2009; Tolson 2006; and cf. Thornborrow, this volume, Chapter 7), including Spanish broadcasting media (Lorenzo-Dus 2007). Yet, irony, and specifically mock naïvety, is not—as far as I have been able to ascertain—a common style among Spanish broadcast journalists. This may be part of the reason this stance was most frequently linked to change in my corpus, as Extracts 5a and 5b illustrate:

Extract 5a

> [*La Razón Online;* citizen comments' section]: Few journalists know how to fuck with those arseholes in such an 'innocent' way as Évole. The last 10 minutes leave no doubt whatsoever: http://www.youtube.com/watch?v=hQckavuirlQ.

Extract 5b

> [YouTube]: Unlike other journalists, Évole doesn't need to shout to challenge or be heard. One of his ironic looks and politicians shake in fear!! How refreshing for Spanish journalism, and what an opportunity for change in Spain!

In Extracts 5a and 5b, mock naïvety was metadiscursively expressed by placing inverted commas around the term "'innocent'" (5a) and by expressing the dissonance between Évole's nonverbal (facial expressions) and verbal (e.g. not shouting) style (5b). Mock naïvety was also positively appraised in its replacement of—and hence a change from—high-affect prosody (needing to shout)—a possible reference to the verbally aggressive and overtly emotional style of some talk shows involving politicians and journalists in Spain (Brenes 2011; Garcés-Conejos Blitvich et al. 2010; Lorenzo-Dus 2007). The extracts illustrate some of the ways in which citizens verbalize a perceived sense of language change—where such change did not simply refer to modifications in the structural inventory of language (indeed, these were not explicitly commented upon) but to alterations in the way in which language should be used as part of social life, specifically when engaging with politicians in the media.

Conclusions

Salvados has been described as "a quirky but hard-hitting news show that has become an unlikely television success as crisis-plagued Spaniards try to figure out how their country got into the mess it is in."[22] At the time of writing, the reasons for that mess have not yet been fully unraveled, just as the story of the victims of the 2006 train accident is yet to be fully told. On September 3, 2014, I conducted an interview with the 3J Association vice president to discern the state of progress regarding the Association's efforts at ensuring a fair judicial investigation eight years after the accident. During the interview, she referred on various occasions to the invaluable role of the April 28 *Salvados* episode in rescuing the victims from social oblivion. She also referred to Évole's journalistic style as having been key to awakening citizens' conscience to the 3J Association's cause and, more generally, to the need for journalistic and social change in the country.

Her characterization of Évole coincided with many of the citizen comments examined in this chapter, which describe him as some kind of 'change activist'

within and outside his shows. In relation to Urban's (2001) theorizing
nange, Évole may be seen as one of a number of 'metacultural entrepre-
in the contemporary Spanish broadcasting scene whose communicative
contributing to stimulate, mediate, and evaluate change within the other-
pervasive Polarized Pluralist Model of political journalism.

what does that change entail, and to whom may it matter? The analysis
presented here shows that Évole's style relies on stances of moral evaluation, mock
naïvety, and ordinariness, all of which represent a departure from traditional forms
of political interviewing in the Spanish broadcast media. Within these, a different
way of discussing controversial issues in public is presented, in which verbal aggression (e.g. shouting) and unmitigated assertiveness (e.g. no hedging) are replaced
with stylistic dissonance and irony.

It is too early to evaluate the extent, let alone the durability, of the kind of
change being brokered by journalists like Évole. To start with, not everyone 'gets,'
let alone shares, Évole's ironic style—irony always carries a level of ambiguity and
indeterminacy in any case. Yet, the materials that I have examined, and the wider
uptake of Évole's style by other media (inter)nationally, suggests that his naïvety
is widely 'read' as mock. His style is not simply seen as indicative of potential
change within the genre of political broadcasting. It is also, and importantly, seen
to help galvanize and make discursively explicit a desire for language and social
change among the members of those discourse communities that actively engage
with him.

Appendix—Transcription conventions and Spanish-language extracts

Transcription conventions

CU / MS / LS *MCU / MLS*	Camera close-up / medium shot / long shot Medium close-up / Medium—long range shot
Laughs	Paralinguistic / nonverbal features of communication; also text not included owing to space constraints.
<u>Word</u>	Marked stress
?	Rising intonation
[	Onset of overlapping talk
=	Latching (no discernible gap) between the end of one turn and the beginning of the next turn
(.)	Short pause (a second or under)
(3.0)	Longer pause, in seconds

mm, er . . .	Filled pauses, hesitations . . .
an:::d	Prolongation ('stretching') of prior syllable
wor-	Syllable or word cut off abruptly
°quiet°	Syllable or word delivered quietly vis-à-vis surrounding speech

Extract 1 – Spanish

1   R   el tema de la baliza de señalización (.) esa era

2   <u>lógicamente</u> una de las palabras tabú principales

3   E   y no se os ocurrió en ningún momento pensar lo que

4   estamos haciendo es fraudulento?

5   R   (1.5) bueno (.) probablemente se nos pasó por la mente

6   que no era éticamente correcto y::: (.) er bueno nos

7   encontrábamos bajo una gran presión . . .

8   E   a ver si lo entien- (.) nadie se quejó y (.)

9   nadie dijo yo <u>no</u> hago eso?

10   R   nadie se atrevió (.) <u>absolutamente</u> nadie (.) <u>nadie</u>

11   E   y se puede dormir por la noche cuando se comparece

12   ante ante una comisión judicial y:: se da uno cuenta de

13   que el grupo que se representa no está diciendo la verdad?

14   R   (2.0) bueno creo que si no se tiene nada que ocultar se

15   puede dormir por la noche . . . en ese sentido yo tenía la

16   ventaja de

17   *. . . R explica que su área de responsabilidad no afectaba*
          directamente al accidente . . .

18   E   tuviste la impresión de estar mintiendo a la comisión?

19   R   no:: (.) la conversación se llevaba a::

20   °por decirlo de algún modo° hacia aquellas áreas que

21   convenía (.) en mi caso no =

22   E   = quieres decir que no mentías pero que no llegabas a

23   decir todo lo que sabías

24   R   correcto

25   *. . . R revela el robo del libro de registro del tren*

26   *siniestrado y todas sus copias . . .*

27   E   (2.0) es <u>terriblemente</u> cruel lo que me estás contando

28   R   sí (.) realmente terrible (.) pero es lo que sucedió

Extract 2 – Spanish

1	E	ooooh (.) ost-
2		está llamando Cotino
3	FP	te devuelve la llamada? =
4	E	= sí sí (.) es Cotino [to JC] Sr Cotino?
5	C	(.) sí soy yo (.) quién llama?[iv]
6	E	Sr Cotino? (.) sí (.) soy Jordi:: Évole (.) el director de
7		Salvados de la Sexta
8	C	no (.) no está
9	E	cómo que no está?
10	C	(2.0) no (.) no [está
11	E	[cómo? pero si me acaba de decir que
12		usted es el Sr Cotino
13	C	no (.) no [soy yo
14	E	[qué quiere decir que no?
15	C	soy su hermano
16	E	ah es usted <u>su</u> hermano (.) pues suena muy
17		parecido
18	C	claro (.) por eso somos hermanos
19	E	y::: su hermano no está en casa?
20	C	no (.) salió hace diez minutos
21		*... C explains that he answered*
22		*his brother's phone in case it was*
23		*his nephew calling ...*
24	E	no me estará engañando y será usted el Sr Cotino y no
25		quiere hablar conmigo (.) verdad?
26	C	no (.) no tengo motivo para mentirle (.) ni tengo el
27		gusto de conocerle =
28	E	= por supuesto =
29	C	= yo no me dedico a engañar a nadie (.)
30		adiós
31	E	(1.5) Sr Cotino?

[iv] From this point on, C's turns are transcribed as text on the screen.

Extract 3a.

@JordiEvole: Vas a conseguir con un programa de televisión más que todo el sistema judicial. Felicidades!!!

Extract 3b

@ JordiEvole: El poder de la televisión para cambiar—y mientras tanto otras personas haciendo un uso tan vil de ella. @JordiEvole, Felicidades.

Extract 4a

[Twitter]: esto es lo que necesitamos ahora: periodismo de calidad e independiente; que dejen de una vez de engañar a los ciudadanos!!

Extract 4b

[Twitter]: 58 minutos sin música o una sola imagen del accidente y sus víctimas—no nos dejemos engañar cuando nos dicen que no es posible hacer televisión de una forma diferente.

Extract 5a

Pocos periodistas saben cómo joder a esos cabrones hablándoles con un estilo tan 'inocente' como el de Évole. Los últimos 10 minutos no dejan lugar a dudas: http://www.youtube.com/watch?v=hQckavuirlQ.

Extract 5b

A diferencia de otros periodistas, Évole no necesita gritar para desafiar o ser escuchado. Una de sus miradas irónicas y los políticos se echan a temblar!! Qué refrescante para el periodismo español, y que oportunidad de cambio para España!

Notes

1. http://asociacionvictimasmetro.blogspot.co.uk/ (last accessed August 2016).

2. "sin vetos y con total garantía," http://asociacionvictimasmetro.blogspot.co.uk/ (last accessed August 2016). All translations into English in this chapter are by its author. Original texts (in Spanish) are presented either in footnotes or, in the case of Extracts 1–5, in the Appendix to this chapter.

3. These include the following: *Ondas Prize* (2008) for most innovative show; *Iris Prize* (Spanish Academy of the Sciences and Arts) for best reporter (2012, 2014) and best program (*Salvados*; 2014); *International Journalism Prize 'Manuel Vázquez Montalbán'* (political and cultural journalism category) in 2013 to Évole; and the *National Creativity Prize 'José María Recarte'* in 2014 to *Salvados*.

4. "renovar géneros periodísticos" and "establecer una agenda periodística propia y socialmente necesaria." http://www.elmundo.es/elmundo/2013/01/28/comunicacion/1359374937.html (last accessed July 2015).

5. Segments from Évole's speech at the *International Journalism Prize Manuel Vazquez Montalbán* award ceremony (2013): "en esta profesión, el silencio no conduce a nada" and "cuanto más se acerca el periodismo al poder politico, más se aleja de los ciudadanos."

6. Hallin and Mancini's (2004) work comparatively examined media systems in 18 Western democracies: Austria, Belgium, Canada, Denmark, Finland, France, Germany, Great Britain, Greece, Ireland, Italy, the Netherlands, Norway, Portugal, Spain, Sweden, Switzerland, and the United States. For recent developments of Hallin and Mancini's model, see, for example, Hardy (2008), as well as Hallin and Mancini's (2012) subsequent work on comparing media systems beyond the Western world.

7. The two other models are the North/Central Europe or Democratic Corporatist Model and the North Atlantic or Liberal Model.

8. The start of this period is tied to the world financial crisis of 2007–2008. It peaked in 2012, when the country was unable to bailout its financial sector and had to apply for a €100 billion rescue package to the European Union.

9. http://www.movimiento15m.org/ (last accessed August 2016).

10. This is, of course, his artistic name.

11. "Wyoming no se toca." See e.g. http://www.elconfidencialdigital.com/medios/ Respuesta-laSexta-Wyoming-toca_0_2143585621.html (last accessed July 2015).

12. http://www.vertele.com/noticias/ana-pastor-despedida-al-frente-de-los-desayunos-de-tve/ (last accessed July 2015).

13. Greatbatch (1998: 167) defines 'neutralistic interviewing' as "a manner or style of interviewing; it refers to patterns of IR [interviewer] conduct which can escape formal charges of bias—whether in the interview context itself or beyond."

14. *Asociación de Corresponsales de Prensa Extranjera* Prize, 2015.

15. "tergiversación desvergonzada"; "chusma." http://www.vertele.com/noticias/el-cofundador-de-upyd-llama-chusma-a-ana-pastor/ (last accessed July 2015).

16. See Transcription conventions on pp. 44–45. In the main text I show English translations of the source data. Spanish versions of all extracts are reproduced on pp. 45–47.

17. The four images included in Figure 2.1 can be viewed through Google images under the search term for 'Salvados episodio 28 de abril 2013.'

18. Interview segments, in English, available at: http://www.reuters.com/article/ 2013/04/11/entertainment-us-spain-crisis-tv-idUSBRE93A0CB20130411 (last accessed July 2015).

19. "con la misma media sonrisa con que lanza cargas de profundidad contra un cargo político envuelto en un caso de corrupción." http://www.revistavanityfair.es/actualidad/ articulos/jordi-evole-esto-es-un-juego-los-que-mandan-quieren-controlarte-y-tu-tines-que-mantener-tu-independencia/18220 (last accessed July 2015).

20. Each *Salvados* show is advertised by its channel a week before its broadcast.

21. *El follonero* was Évole's nickname in a previous television show, when his popularity began.

22. http://www.reuters.com/article/2013/04/11/entertainment-us-spain-crisis-tv-idUSBRE93A0CB20130411 (last accessed July 2015).

References

Androutsopoulos, Jannis. 2011. Language change and digital media: A review of conceptions and evidence. In Tore Kristiansen and Nikolas Coupland (eds.) *Standard Languages and Language Standards in a Changing Europe*. Oslo: Novus. 145–161.

Bentolila, Samuel, Pierre Cahuc, Juan J. Dolado and Thomas Le Barbanchon. 2012. Two-tier labour markets in The Great Recession: France versus Spain. *The Economic Journal* 122: 155–187.

Brenes Peña, Ester. 2011. *Descortesía verbal y tertulia televisiva.* Bern: Peter Lang.

Bucholtz, Mary. 2009. From stance to style: Gender, interaction and indexicality in Mexican immigrant youth slang. In Alexandra Jaffe (ed.) *Stance: Sociolinguistic Perspectives.* Oxford: Oxford University Press. 146–170.

Bustamante, Enrique. 2006. *Radio y televisión en España: Historia de una asignatura pendiente de la democracia.* Barcelona: Gedisa.

Coupland, Justine and Nikolas Coupland. 2009. Attributing stance in discourses of body shape and weight loss. In Alexandra Jaffe (ed.) *Stance: Sociolinguistic Perspectives.* Oxford: Oxford University Press. 227–250.

Coupland, Nikolas. 2001. Dialect stylisation in radio talk. *Language in Society* 30, 3: 345–375.

Coupland, Nikolas. 2007. *Style: Language Variation and Identity.* Cambridge: Cambridge University Press.

Coupland, Nikolas. 2014a. Language change, social change, sociolinguistic change: A meta-commentary. *Journal of Sociolinguistics* 18, 2: 277–286.

Coupland, Nikolas. 2014b. Sociolinguistic change, vernacularization and broadcast British media. In Jannis Androtsopoulos (ed.) *Mediatization and Sociolinguistic Change.* Berlin: De Gruyter. 67–98.

Du Bois, John W. 2007. The stance triangle. In Robert Englebretson (ed.) *Stancetaking in Discourse: Subjectivity, Evaluation, Interaction.* Amsterdam: John Benjamins. 139–182.

Fairclough, Norman. 2003. *Analysing Discourse: Textual Analysis for Social Research.* London: Routledge.

Forster, Ricardo. 2002. *Crítica y sospecha.* Buenos Aires: Paidós.

Garcés-Conejos Blitvich, Pilar, Nuria Lorenzo-Dus and Patricia Bou-Franch. 2010. A genre approach to impoliteness in a Spanish television talk show: Evidence from corpus-based analysis, questionnaires and focus groups. *Intercultural Pragmatics* 7: 689–723.

Glaser, Barney G. 1992. *Basics of Grounded Theory Analysis: Emergence vs. Forcing.* Mill Valley, California: Sociology Press.

Goffman, Erving. 1981. *Forms of Talk.* Philadelphia: University of Pennsylvania Press.

Greatbatch, David. 1998. Conversation analysis: Neutralism in British news interviews. In Allan Bell and Peter Garrett (eds.) *Approaches to Media Discourse.* Oxford: Blackwell. 163–185.

Hallin, Daniel and Paolo Mancini. 2004. *Comparing Media Systems: Three Models of Media and Politics.* Cambridge: Cambridge University Press.

Hallin, Daniel and Paolo Mancini. 2012. *Comparing Media Systems Beyond the Western World.* Cambridge: Cambridge University Press.

Hardy, Jonathan. 2008. *Western Media Systems.* London: Routledge.

Hepp, Andreas and Friedrich Krotz (eds.). 2014. *Mediatized Worlds: Culture and Society in a Media Age.* Basingstoke: Palgrave Macmillan.

Humanes Humanes, María Luisa, Manuel Martínez Nicolás and Enric Saperas Lapiedra. 2013. Political journalism in Spain: Practices, roles and attitudes. *Estudios sobre el Mensaje Periodístico* 19: 715–731.

Jaffe, Alexandra (ed). 2009. *Stance: Sociolinguistic Perspectives*. Oxford: Oxford University Press.

Livingstone, Sonia. 2009. On the mediation of everything. *Journal of Communication* 59, 1: 1–18.

Lorenzo-Dus, Nuria. 2007. (Im)politeness and the Spanish media: The case of audience participation debates. In María E. Placencia and Carmen García (eds.) *Research on Politeness in the Spanish-speaking World*. Mahwah, NJ: Erlbaum. 145–66.

Lorenzo-Dus, Nuria. 2009. *Television Discourse: Analysing Language in the Media*. Basingstoke: Palgrave Macmillan.

Luginbühl, Martin. 2014. Genre profiles and genre change. The case of TV news. In Jannis Androutsopoulos (ed.) *Mediatization and Sociolinguistic Change*. Berlin: De Gruyter. 305–330.

Musso, Pierre and Guy Pineau. 1985. *El audiovisual entre el estado y el Mercado. Los ejemplos italiano y francés*. *Telos* 27: 47–56.

Papatheodorou, Fotini and David Machin. 2003. The umbilical cord that was never cut: The postdictatorial intimacy between the political elite and the mass media in Greece and Spain. *European Journal of Communication* 18, 1: 31–54.

Roca-Cuberes, Carles. 2012. A comparison of broadcast political interviews in public and commercial television. *Proceedings of the 4th ECREA Communication Conference*. 189–212.

Swales, John. 1990. *Genre Analysis: English in Academic and Research Settings*. Cambridge: Cambridge University Press.

Tolson, Andrew. 2006. *Media Talk: Spoken Discourse on TV and Radio*. Edinburgh: Edinburgh University Press.

Traquina, Nelson. 1995. Portuguese television: The politics of savage deregulation. *Media, Culture & Society* 17: 223–238.

Urban, Greg. 2001. *Metaculture: How Culture Moves Through the World*. Minneapolis: University of Minnesota Press.

Web Forum Report, 2013–2014. http://www.weforum.org/.

3

Radio talk, pranks, and multilingualism: Styling Greek identities at a time of crisis
Tereza Spilioti

Introduction

In order to investigate the interplay between language change and social change, it is helpful to identify a context in which the catalyst of change is sufficiently obvious and accessible for observation. In addition, a sufficiently sophisticated conceptualization of the relationship between language and society is needed, particularly one that sees language change and social change as mutually constitutive processes. This chapter shows the potential to track these dynamics, by observing language-ideological shifts in the language forms and practices people laugh at, particularly through the ways in which humor is manifest in Greek media contexts in response to the Greek financial crisis.

Approaching language and social change as mutually constitutive processes has been advocated as a paradigm shift in sociolinguistics, from 'language change' to 'sociolinguistic change' (Androutsopoulos 2014b; Coupland 2009, 2014a, b). Acknowledging (and moving beyond) change limited to the language system, this new paradigm is open to change at the level of linguistic repertoires and practices, to language-ideological changes, and to a wider range of communicative, institutional, and media contexts (Androutsopoulos 2014b: 6; Coupland 2014b: 73). The relevance of media to sociolinguistic change, in particular, has been recently revisited: the media's multifaceted role cannot be subsumed under unidirectional accounts of 'media influence' or be relegated to the background as just an aspect of context (e.g. Androutsopoulos 2014a, b; Coupland 2014a; Stuart-Smith 2014). This chapter critically engages with aspects of that perspective on change, by examining how language use in the media can be revealing of processes of sociolinguistic change, but also by arguing that technologically mediated language use can be constitutive of sociolinguistic change in its own right.

51

Style, Mediation, and Change. Edited by Janus Mortensen, Nikolas Coupland, and Jacob Thøgersen
© Oxford University Press 2017. Published 2017 by Oxford University Press

The case investigated here is related to the so-called Greek debt crisis, which is taken as an example of the wider financial crisis in Europe and its consequential language-ideological and sociopolitical changes. In Greece, the crisis has resulted in acute socioeconomic changes that include major cuts in salaries and pensions, a significant rise in unemployment, and the implementation of austerity policies, accompanied by financial 'rescue packages' from international organizations such as the European Union (EU) and the International Monetary Fund. Notable sociopolitical changes can also be traced through the results of repeated parliamentary elections since 2009 and include, among others, distrust of political elites and the rise in popularity of smaller political parties, from far right to far left.

Focusing on a period of 'financial crisis' is particularly relevant to the study of sociolinguistic change in the media, since specific financial events (e.g. stock market crashes and sovereign defaults) operate as catalysts for change in both socioeconomic policies and popular discourses, often produced, circulated, and amplified in and through media. In the case of the Greek debt crisis (as well as wider 'crisis discourses' in Europe), public political debate in the media has centered on issues of national face and sovereignty (Boukala 2014; Wodak and Angouri 2014), arguably opening up space for ideological repositionings and collective renegotiations of perceptions and beliefs about the nation, national identity, and language.

"What is permissible to poke fun at publicly" (Woolard, with Bencomo and Soler-Carbonel 2013: 128) when it comes to language is very much conditioned by the language-ideological and sociopolitical discourses produced at a specific historical moment. For this reason media humor will tend to track sociolinguistic change by pointing to shifts in "what is considered to be funny about language" (Woolard with Bencomo and Soler-Carbonel 2013: 128). The present chapter engages with this issue by examining data that come from a radio show in which members of the public unknowingly become victims of humorous telephone pranks that get broadcast on national radio. As in Garfinkel's breaching experiments (Garfinkel 1967; cf. Heritage 1984), the prankster 'makes trouble' by breaching normative expectations, and humor arises from a subversion of the tacit background knowledge that otherwise enables interactants to recognize communicative events as belonging to particular types. Studying the devices used by pranksters "to produce and sustain bewilderment, consternation, and confusion" (Garfinkel 1967: 38) in conjunction with the victim's spontaneous responses helps us tease out the moving boundaries between what is considered marked and unmarked (sociolinguistic) practice at the specific sociohistorical moment.

In this particular context the use of English in the telephone pranks turns out to be significant, as knowledge of English is increasingly becoming an index of social identity, particularly in relation to education, age, and sophistication. Stylization of (Greek) English therefore represents a powerful device for subversion and humor and there is particular significance to the personas that get projected through seemingly erratic stylings. This leads to a discussion of the extent to which media performances in the current Greek context, similar to findings in other contexts (e.g. Woolard with Bencomo and Soler-Carbonel 2013), can be said to refract language-ideological change related to the sociocultural (re)alignment of languages, on the one hand, and sociopolitical alliances and discourses, on the other.

Language-ideological debates and sociopolitical processes

Language-ideological debates are historically embedded in simultaneous sociopolitical processes (Blommaert 1999: 3). As a result, language-ideological change can only be traced in relation to the historical unfolding of language debates and wider sociopolitical changes. In order to understand why certain language forms and practices are deemed laughable and, ultimately, in order to be able to link the media pranks under investigation with processes of sociolinguistic change, we need first to engage in a short, critical examination of language-ideological debates in Greece and situate the debates in the context of wider sociopolitical processes related to nation-building, globalization, and European integration.

In the late 19th/early 20th century language-ideological debates in Greece centered on the well-known Greek 'language question,' i.e. the "normative issue of which language the Greek people 'should' speak" (Frangoudaki 2002: 102). The prescription of a language standard was central in consolidating the sovereignty of the recently formed nation-state and in constructing a national identity which was often defined in relation to the "ancient past" (Frangoudaki 1992: 367). This language-ideological debate, fueled by the rise of two conflicting norms—archaic and purist or 'purified' *katharevousa*, on the one hand, and vernacular, 'of the people' *dimotiki*, on the other hand—often took the form of social and political conflict, where the public use of each norm was indexical of specific, often oppositional, political positions (Frangoudaki 2002).

It was not until 1976, when the Greek 'language question' was constitutionally resolved, that 'Standard Modern Greek' was recognized as the official language of the state and defined as the vernacular norm (with some archaic/learned forms), retaining the name *dimotiki* ('demotic Greek') (Moschonas 2009: 315). In the late 20th century Modern Greek standardization gave rise to a 'regime ideology,' according to which "the one and only language of the state, Modern Greek, should itself be pictured as a state, a territory or a regime, which comprises a pure and sacred interior that has to be kept intact by everything surrounding it" (Moschonas 2009: 294). This new ideology, which arguably still holds sway today, maintains some of the old ideals related to language purism and nationalism, coupled with a strong ideology of monolingualism, evident in the equation of one nation-state = one (pure) language (cf. Frangoudaki 1992; Moschonas 2009, 2014). Through this equation, issues related to language contact and maintenance, including the use of English in public and private domains, are given significant attention in language-ideological debates, especially in print media (Koutsogiannis and Mitsikopoulou 2003; Moschonas 2014). The every-day use of English loan words, the use of Latinized Greek script on the Internet, and the prospect of institutionalizing English as the second official language of the state are among the topics of heated debates in the media, whereby the use of 'non-Greek' (say, English, or any instance of 'mixed' Greek) is portrayed as an external threat to the internal cohesion of what is considered to be 'Greek' (Moschonas 2009: 307).

Assuming that language-ideological change is interrelated with sociopolitical changes, it is worth reflecting upon the socioeconomic events that marked the period of Modern Greek standardization in the 1980s and 1990s. According to Frangoudaki (1992: 374–377), the emergence of a dominant language ideology in Greece was related to the process of European integration.[1] More specifically, both purist and nationalist positions can be seen as responses to a perceived crisis of national identity in which 'being Greek' needed to be (re)defined and (re)positioned in view of the new socioeconomic alliances being forged in Europe. The robustness of the association between language-ideological change and sociopolitical change is supported by the resurgence of language purism and monolingual ideals that was evident in other European countries at the time. For example, Stevenson and Mar-Molinero (2006) and Spitzmüller (2007) report similar public and media debates on the concepts of language and nation in response to the social process of 'Europeanization' in other countries such as Spain and Germany in late 1990s.

The beginning of the new millennium marked a range of sociopolitical changes within the EU, including the implementation of the new European monetary union (the creation of the Eurozone). In the context of Greece, changes in education policies, often hinging on the new sociopolitical conditions of increased mobility, and cross-border cooperation, have impacted upon people's expectations about one's fluency in English. The increasing mobility of students and the workforce within (and beyond) the EU, together with the new legislation for provision of English as a compulsory 'foreign language' to all pupils at the age of eight, has contributed to making English-language competence a relatively routine expectation, with the further effect that the nonfluent use of English is indexically marked.

Overlaid on the strong monolingualism ideal before the millennium, we therefore witness the emergence of an ideal of English/national language bilingualism.[2] Koutsogiannis and Adampa's (2012) study of digital literacy practices among Greek teenagers in 2006 shows that attitudes toward multiliteracies (including multilingualism/bilingualism and computer literacies) vary in terms of social class and socioeconomic background. Parents and teenage students from middle and upper socioeconomic backgrounds seem to orient positively toward the ideal of English/Greek bilingualism (Koutsogiannis and Adampa 2012: 228, 231). Unlike the strong monolingualism voiced in press publications of the late 20th century, both Greek and English are accepted as media of instruction in privileged private schools and seen by parents who send their children to these schools as resources for participating in both local oriented and globally oriented (online) communities. In other words, English-language proficiency is in this context seen as just as important as Greek, as part of a language repertoire that may help secure a successful future in an increasingly expanding world.

If this account of language-ideological change is accurate, we should anticipate seeing media performances in the Greek context consistent with the two competing 'ideals'—that is, the continuing regime ideology of monolingualism alongside the emerging ideal of English/national language bilingualism. The media pranks that we will turn to in the next section were broadcast and circulated during the initial stages of the still developing Greek debt crisis—that is, from 2009, when the prospect of a Greek economic default was made public, to 2011, when the crisis deepened and a second EU bailout package was announced.[3] As I will argue in the following, the pranks are in various ways related to language issues and therefore have the potential to tease out and call into question normative expectations and stereotypes alluding to established ideals. In doing so, they reveal reconfigurations in the nexus of language, national and political ideologies in Greece at a time when the position of the nation-state in Europe and perceptions of national identity have resurfaced in public and political debate.

Data: Media pranks on *Greekophrenia*

Research on language ideologies in the media has often focused on texts that explicitly deal with language issues (e.g. Moschonas and Spitzmüller 2010; Thurlow 2006). Although such research sheds light on the role that media have as brokers of certain language ideologies, primarily voiced by language experts and professionals, it does not necessarily capture how language and sociopolitical ideologies are invoked, played out, and experienced in interaction. One way of exploring such processes is to look at media genres that do not have explicit language-ideological aims, particularly in the context of interactive 'talking media,' such as TV talk shows or radio phone-ins.

The data used in this chapter provide a window onto such media interactions. They concern a series of telephone pranks that appeared on the satirical radio show *Ελληνοφρένεια* ('Greekophrenia'; a pun on 'schizophrenia'), broadcast daily on one of the national broadcasting stations in Greece (SKAI TV/radio; REAL FM since 2011). The show has a strong political edge and aims to criticize politicians, government actions, public institutions, and so on. As noted on *Greekophrenia*'s Twitter account, the show is "a daily satire with the people who 'shape' Modern Greek history as the protagonists" (my translation).[4]

The specific data set is composed of sequences that occur in the final section of the show, entitled 'The People' (*O Λαός*): it features telephone calls from listeners of the show, as well as telephone pranks targeting politicians, government officials, and members of the public. The person who takes the calls—and the mastermind of the pranks—is one of the two male radio hosts, known as *Αποστόλης Μπαρμπαγιάννης* (*Apostolis Barbayiannis*). During the first half hour, listeners of the show are encouraged to call the station to speak to *Apostolis* and share their views or comments on current news. Extracts of such telephone conversations are edited and get broadcast during the final section of 'The People,' which lasts for about 15 minutes.

Amidst the telephone calls transferred to the radio host, there are people who happen to call the TV/radio station's call center for other reasons and end up being put through to *Apostolis*. As a result, a subset of the calls broadcast on 'The People' segment of the show includes telephone conversations where *Apostolis* takes the role of the prankster, playfully deceiving and confusing callers who, for example, really wish to speak to the station's journalists. The data analyzed in this chapter are a subset of these pranks in which the radio host puts on a distinctive speech style, identified by listeners and fans of the show as '*Apostolis*'s English.' The recognizability of this styling is evident in the fact that the specific pranks are searchable on social media (e.g. YouTube) through the specific label (in Greek, e.g. 'Ελληνοφρένεια—Τα Αγγλικά του Αποστόλη' 'Greekophrenia—*Apostolis*'s English'). As will be illustrated in the following sections, '*Apostolis*'s English' exhibits extensive mixing of features of Greek and English, accompanied by marked changes in pitch and pace of delivery. Language mixing also takes the form of morphosyntactic interference (evident in nonsensical calques in English), phonological shibboleths of 'non-native' accent in Greek, and other instances of code-switching.

Overall, the analysis draws on 12 prank calls aired on the radio show during the initial stages of the Greek debt crisis. The pranks are often isolated, edited out from their original context (i.e. the radio show), and subsequently circulated by listeners across social media or uploaded separately on the show's website. The wide circulation of the pranks across media suggests that they can be viewed as separate media events that have gained their own significance and recognizability among fans of the show. This form of cultural expression—and, particularly, its satirical and often explicitly political content—is akin to the type of edits/remixes of media footage that have proliferated in social media during the period of financial crisis in Greece. The edited (or remixed) media footage circulated online have satirical or ironic effects and arguably function as a public critique of dominant ideologies (cf. Georgakopoulou 2014). As Papanikolaou (2011: 4) argues, "even though not always related to the crisis directly," such forms of cultural expression "can assume, in the current climate, a radical political position." In the case of prank calls, traces of such sociopolitical positions are embedded in metadiscourse that is produced while conventional knowledge and understanding of the situation at hand is called into question and challenged by the prankster's behavior.

Victims or *dupes*: Telephone prank openings

According to Bauman (1986: 36; see also Goffman 1974; Trester 2013), practical jokes, hoaxes, and pranks are instances of "expressive routines of victimization" that can be defined as "enactments of playful deceit in which one party or team (to be called *trickster*) intentionally manipulates features of a situation in such a way as to induce another person or persons (to be called *victim* or *dupe*) to have a false or misleading sense of what is going on, and so to behave in a way that brings about discomfiture (confusion, embarrassment, etc.) in the victim." In other words, a practical joke operates within a "fabricated frame" (Goffman 1974) wherein one participant constructs a given situation as play, while the other party understands it as real (Seilhamer 2011: 678). In the case of the media pranks under investigation, the fabricated frame is first activated backstage when people who happen to ring the TV and radio station's call center are unknowingly put through to speak to the show's host, *Apostolis*. This fabricated frame, though, can collapse if it is not effectively sustained and reinforced by both verbal and nonverbal means in the telephone call opening and throughout the interaction. This section focuses on the opening sequences of the telephone pranks in my sample. In doing so, we can gain a better understanding of the victim's profile in the specific subset of *Greekophrenia* pranks, especially as revealed in the identification sequence of telephone call openings (cf. Schegloff 1986). The section also highlights the language resources mobilized by the caller (victim) and the host (prankster) during the initial stages of the prank and discusses their significance for the staging of the prank as well as their potential for language-ideological work, as will be documented further in the analysis.

Overall, four general categories of victims feature in my data. The first group includes callers who ring the station's call center from abroad in order to contact journalists or media celebrities. Extract 1 illustrates the opening of a prank with this type of caller, where a representative from Polish radio (labeled 'C,' for Caller) wishes to speak to a journalist/news analyst who works at the station (SKAI). In terms of language resources used in this extract, we notice that English elements appear in the speech of the radio host ('H,' i.e. *Apostolis*) (line 3) in response to the use of English by the caller in her first turn (line 2).

Extract 1[5]

1   H: ναι
          hello

2   C: hello it's [name] from the Polish radio (.) can I=

3   H: =Polish radio yeah tell me=

4   C: =can I talk to Mr (.) <u>Babis</u> Papadimitriou?

The second category of victims is constituted by viewers/listeners and professionals who appear to call from within Greece but seem more fluent in English than Greek. Often, it turns out during the interaction that these callers are in fact non-Greek nationals.[6] They call to seek more information about, and possibly comment on, a particular show. In addition to their use of English, it is also typical to find mixing of English and Greek in these calls, particularly in the caller's initial turns. This is illustrated in Extract 2: the caller is a freelance journalist who wishes to contact a SKAI journalist in order to write a story about the environment and animal welfare. The caller uses Greek in her first turn (line 2) but mixing of language resources is noted in the form of phonological interference in the pronunciation of the Greek journalist's name (line 4) and use of both codes in line 6, followed by similar shifts in the speech of the radio host.

Extract 2

1   H: λέγετε
           hello

2   C: ναι γεια σας
           yes hello

3   H: γεια σας
           hello

4   C: μήπως είναι εκεί ο κύριος Yorgo Yorgo Karamitsoglou
           is Mr Yorgo Yorgo Karamitsoglou there

5   H: Karamitsoglou?

6   C: ναι yeah
           yes yeah

7   H: where are you calling from? από πού τηλεφωνείτε:?
           where are you calling from? where are you calling fro:m?

In the third category we find viewers/listeners who are fluent in both Greek and English and who appear to be based in Greece. The reasons for their calls are similar to those discussed previously; for example, the caller in Extract 3 rings the station's call center in order to find out when the new series of Oprah Winfrey's show will be broadcast. As evident in the opening section below (especially line 5), the switch to a different, more performed, style by the host (marked by significant changes in pace and volume, as well as repetition) appears to come in response to English elements inserted in the caller's speech. In line 4, for example, 'show' is pronounced as [ʃɔʊ] instead of [sou] (the latter representing how the loan 'σόου' (meaning 'show') would sound in Standard Modern Greek).

Extract 3

1 H: ναι
      hello

2 C: ναι μια ερώτηση
      hello just a question

3 H: βεβαίως
      of course

4 C: για το:: show της Oprah σε ποιον μπορώ να ρ-
      fo::r the Oprah's show who could I a-

5 H: > το sh- show της Oprah< wh- WH WHAT?
      > the Oprah's sh- show< wh- WH WHAT?

Finally, the role of the victim in certain prank calls is also found to be projected onto persons who act as mediators between callers and the prankster, and who are fluent in both Greek and English. Extract 4 illustrates the opening turns of a prank segment where the initial caller (C1) asks a third party (Caller 2, C2) to intervene and talk to the prankster on his behalf. This segment appears later in the prank and the new speaker/caller also becomes the victim of the prank.

Extract 4

After 17 turns of interaction between the host/prankster and the caller (C1) who is trying to report something on the current broadcasting program, the caller hands the phone to a third party (Caller 2, C2) who is a fluent speaker of both Greek and English.

18 C1:   I know Psyri yes what about it?

19   >wai- wait a minute I'll put you through to someone<

20 H: wh- wha:?

21 C2:   ναι:?
       hello:?

22 H: ΕΛΑ (.) ΕΛΛΑΔΑ εδώ
       HEY (.) this is GREECE

23 C2:   τι πάει να πει Ελλάδα εδώ=
       what do you mean this is Greece=

Extracts 1–4 illustrate that the set of *Greekophrenia* pranks studied in this chapter primarily target speakers who either opt to use English or draw on both Greek and

English in their conversation with the call taker. In other words, the victims are speakers who deviate from the monolingualism ideal that has long been a prevalent language ideology in Greece. It appears that it is precisely their deviation from normative ideals about language use that makes them targets for victimization in the telephone pranks. The national broadcasting, though, of extended sequences of bilingual interaction and the wider popular hype about speakers' command of English were largely unattested in the Greek mediascape of the late 20th century. Insofar as changes in media performances, and particularly in what is permissible to laugh at publicly, are indicative of wider processes of sociolinguistic change (cf. Chapter 1, Introduction), it is worth probing more into the language-ideological aspects of such interactions. As will become evident in the analysis of longer prank sequences below (Extracts 5–7), the victimization of callers, together with the prankster's performance, paint a more complicated picture where such deviations from a monolingualism ideal are associated with new values and ideals related to sociopolitical changes.

The following section provides a more detailed analysis of the speech style(s) performed by the radio host and the types of personas projected to the prankster and the victims through styling and metadiscursive commentary. The analysis focuses on three separate prank calls with bilingual speakers (with varying degrees of fluency in each language) as prank victims. The two first sections of the analysis concern pranks targeting speakers who fall primarily under the second category of victims: that is, speakers who are more fluent in English than Greek (probably non-Greek nationals who live in Greece). The third section focuses on a prank extract featuring a fluent bilingual who is included in the final category of victims mentioned above: that is, a speaker who becomes the target of the prank in her attempt to mediate and facilitate interaction between the prankster and the initial caller.

Radio pranks in action

The social and ideological meanings of performed stylings in the media may be difficult to interpret, both for the analyst and for the people involved, in this case the prank victim and the audience. Especially when entering the realm of stylized talk—that is, "the knowing deployment of culturally familiar styles and identities that are marked as deviating from those predictably associated with the current speaking context" (Coupland 2001: 345)—the simultaneous embedding of multiple and, at times, dissonant voices enhances ambiguity and makes the task of identifying and pinning down any projected personas a particularly elusive task (cf. Coupland 2001, 2007: 149–154; Jaffe 2000; Woolard et al. 2013). But, at the same time, such ambiguity arguably renders this type of stylistic performance particularly appropriate for studying sociolinguistic change, as such performances are indexically rich and highly reflexive.

In an attempt to address this methodological issue, my analysis of *Apostolis's* seemingly erratic stylings in the following media pranks draws on three key inter- pretive resources. In each subsection, I first attend to the inferable indexical mean- ings of the style(s) the prankster performs. Then, assuming that the prankster's talk is always played against the speech of the victim, I focus on how *Apostolis's* stylings draw on and strategically manipulate speech features characteristic of the callers. Finally, I draw on metadiscourse which is often generated by the breach of normative expectations in telephone pranks and which, to some extent, refers to the indexical stereotypes at play in the interaction.

APOSTOLIS'S ENGLISH #1

The first extract selected for analysis (Extract 5) offers an instantiation of the style the radio host often performs in the telephone pranks known as "*Apostolis's* English."[7] The reason the (male) caller rang the station is not clear from the broad- cast segment, as the prank is very short and the topic seems to be focusing primarily on issues of language fluency.

Extract 5

1	H:	παρακαλώ
		hello
2	C:	hello μιλάτε αγγλικά?
		hello do you speak English?
3	H:	yes of course=
4	C:	=you do? thank you so much are you SKAI television?
5	H:	eh::: no I am a <u>human</u> nature (.) I am a human
6	C:	huh huh huh no I know you are <u>not</u> SKAI television
7		but I mean is the company SKAI television?
8	H:	the comp- you speak with very good eh::
9		προφορά you know preference? I don't know the word and
		accent you know preference? I don't know the word and
10		I don't understand you because I'm a- I'm a villager=
11	C:	=huh huh huh huh=
12	H:	=ναι villager <u>Greek</u>
		=yes villager <u>Greek</u>
13	C:	I see (.) ok
14	H:	βλαχοέλληνας and I can't speak English very best
		peasant-<u>Greek</u> and I can't speak English very best

15   C: oh you speak it very well

16   H: eh wait a second=

17   C: =ok=

18   H: =to give you <u>someone</u> (wh)o speaks φαρσί

     =to give you <u>someone</u> (wh)o speaks fluently

Following the caller's prompt to switch to English (line 2), *Apostolis* shifts to the performed style identified as 'his English.' In terms of delivery, his talk includes a number of features that are not typical of the usual fast-paced and fluent speech delivery found in other types of pranks and other instances of him interacting with the public. In the example above, marked repetitions (lines 5, 10–12), hesitations (lines 5, 8), and false starts (line 8) contribute to the projection of a rather 'labored' style that contrasts with his normal pace of delivery[8] and, thus, can be interpreted as highly staged and performed.

The performed style draws on exaggerated mixing of Greek and English elements that is achieved, through (1) insertion of Greek elements within clauses where English appears to serve as a base language (lines 8–9, 12, 14, 18); (2) repetition of the same content in both languages, together with the creation of awkward calques in English (e.g. *villager Greek* for *βλαχοέλληνας* 'peasant-Greek'); (3) other phenomena of language interference that result in marked and nonstandard lexical choices (e.g. the use of *preference* for *accent*, echoing the immediately preceding Greek word *προφορά* [profora] 'accent,' line 9), grammatical inaccuracies (e.g. use of 'best' as adverb, line 14), and marked pronunciation evident in fronting of vowels and neutralization of phonemic contrasts between alveolar and palato-alveolar consonants (e.g. *villager* pronounced as [vilatzer], line 10). Together with the exaggerated mixing of language resources and grammatical inconsistencies, the radio host's talk also displays pragmatic inconsistencies. Lines 4–5 illustrate a case where the host responds to the caller's identification request (*are you SKAI television?*), by referring to his human state and not his role as representative of the broadcasting organization, a role that is pragmatically relevant to the frame of customer-service interaction the caller thinks they operate on.

Based on the stylistic choices outlined so far, *Apostolis* seems to be styling 'Greek-accented English'; that is, a style of English that follows phonetic patterns associated with the Greek system (i.e. preference for front and open vowels and lack of palato-alveolar consonants, at least in Standard Modern Greek) and displays morphosyntactic constructions that include Greek elements or are word-for-word translations. Such marked and nonstandard elements in the radio host's speech are also isolated and quoted in listeners' comments to the pranks that are circulated online. The online comments that show appreciation of the host's performance (and 'his English' in particular) indicate that the audience recognizes '*Apostolis*'s English' as performative (and, ultimately, laughable) in the specific context.

The style of 'Greek-accented English,' as described previously, connotes social contexts of language contact and, more specifically, second-language learning or tourist encounters. Similarly, the prank constructs a context where the prankster appears like the local (Greek) call operator and the victim is an English speaker. As the prank unfolds, 'Greek-accented English' is contrasted with the fluent English spoken by the caller. This contrast is also metadiscursively framed by means of explicit evaluations by the radio host: in fact, many of the features associated with the performed style are manifest during the metatalk about the interactants' fluency in English. Furthermore, the different speech styles (i.e. 'fluent standard English' vs. 'Greek-accented English') appear to project different personas, underlining a contrast between the fluent, courteous, and lighthearted English and the nonfluent, incompetent, and uncomprehending Greek. The stressed delivery of 'Greek', both in English (line 12) and Greek (line 14), and its use within the compound label of 'villager/peasant-Greek' further supports an association between 'Greek-accented English' and Greekness, as well as parochialism. It can be argued that, while styling 'Greek-accented English,' the radio host deauthenticates and stigmatizes the projected persona of 'non-fluent peasant-Greek,' through distancing himself from the animated voice and the associated sociocultural values. In doing so, the stereotype of 'Greek as parochial' is foregrounded, thrown out for scrutiny and ridicule for the fans of the show.

OPRAH FROM AKRATA

The second extract selected for analysis (Extract 6) is taken from a prank that was aired in 2009 and subsequently uploaded on the show's website with the title *Oprah from Akrata*. Akrata is a small town, located about 150 km to the west of Athens. The caller (a female viewer of SKAI TV) appears to be calling from this small town (line 8), to receive some information about an episode of the Oprah Winfrey show that was previously broadcast by the TV station.

Extract 6

1	C:	ε ΣΚΑΙ τηλεόραση?
		eh SKAI TV?
2	H:	βεβαίως πείτε μου
		of course tell me
3	C:	ναι γεια σας μπορείτε να με συνδέσετε σας παρακαλώ με
		yes hello could you please put me through to
4		κά:ποιον που μπορεί να μου δώσει
		so:meone who could give me

5   πληροφορίες για την εκπομπή σας στις ε (.)
           information about your show at eh (.)

6   πέντε (.) ώρα το πρωί της (inaudible) της Oprah?
           five (.) o'clock in the morning of (inaudible) of Oprah?

7   H: της Oprah?
           of Oprah?

8   C: ναι
           yes

9   H: eh (.) wait a minute (.) eh (.) where are you from?

10   C: ehm actually I'm calling from Akrata but (.) ehm=

11   H: =from Akrata?

12   C: yeah I'm in=

13   H: oh yeah this is the προφορά from Ακράτα (.)
           oh yeah this is the accent from Akrata (.)

14   in Ακράτα δηλαδή έτσι μιλάνε
           so in Akrata that's how they speak

15   C: oh

16   H: oh?

17   C: wh- where have I called?

18   H: SKAI channel

19   C: SKAI channel yea- I needed=

20   H: =I I can help you=

21   C: =I=

22   H: =I can help you (.) you <u>want</u> Oprah show?

23   C: yeah I <u>sa:w</u> a show on (.) five o'clock Thursday morning

24   H: p<u>ardon</u>?

25   C: five o'clock πέντε η ώρα το πρωί <u>Thursday</u>?=
           five o'clock five o'clock in the morning <u>Thursday</u>?=

26   H: =five o'clock yes (.) yes στις πέντε=
           =five o'clock yes (.) yes at five

27   C: =but I NEED the <u>title</u> of the show be- [(inaudible)]

28   H: [the <u>title</u> of the <u>show</u>]

29   C: the <u>book</u> that she had it's e:hm=

30 H: =o:::h=

31 C: =so

32 H: are you socialist?

33 C: pardon?

34 H: are you socialist?

35 C: am I <u>what</u>?

36 H: socialist

37 C: socialist?

38 H: <u>yes</u> (.) you vote e:h for George?[9]

39 C: I don't <u>vote</u> in Greece huh huh

40 H: ah-o:::h <u>what</u> a pity <u>what</u> a pity > κρίμα κρίμα <

        ah-o:::h <u>what</u> a pity <u>what</u> a pity > (what a) shame (what a) shame <

41   κρίμα because I hear your προφορά is excellent (.)

        (what a) shame because I hear your accent is excellent (.)

42   and you have to be:::: in επικρατείας του ΠΑΣΟΚ

        and you have to be::::: in the ballot paper of PASOK[10]

43 C: oh you know this is getting out of hand now (.)

44   is this <u>really</u> SKAI channel? Hhh

45 H: anyway τα ψιλοχάνω κιόλας γιατί είμαι και λίγο <u>βλάχος</u> Έλληνας

        anyway I don't get everything of course because I'm sort of a <u>peasant</u> Greek

46   δεν τα πιανω όλα τα Αγγλικά περιμένετε να σας συνδέσω ε

        I don't get all the English wait to put you through eh

47   to Oprah's Winfrey show yeah wait

Unlike the situation in Extract 5, the caller in Extract 6 initially appears as a fluent speaker of Greek, producing a syntactically rather complex request in the opening section of the conversation (lines 1–6). The request, though, ends with what is perceived as a more 'standard' English pronunciation of the name 'Oprah' [oʊpɹæ:]. Together with the occurrence of a diphthong (rather than a close-mid back vowel) at the beginning, the use of the alveolar approximant [ɹ]—instead of an alveolar tap or a short trill of the sort that one expects to find in 'r' clusters with plosives in Standard Modern Greek (Arvaniti 1999: 169)—is picked up by the radio host and echoed in his speech (line 7). From this point onward, the host/ prankster shifts to the performed style, already identified as '*Apostolis*'s English' and manifest, here, in (1) the insertion of Greek elements within clauses where English serves as a base language (lines 13–14 and 40–42); (2) repetitions (lines

13–14, 26, 40); and (3) pauses and hesitations (line 9), as well as marked changes in pace (lines 40–41).

In terms of accent, *Apostolis* regularly displays elements of 'Greek-accented English,' evident in, among others, more fronted vowels and unaspirated plosives (e.g. in [piti] for "pity," line 40). At the same time, though, he is crossing to a more 'standard' English accent, evident in his use of a diphthong for the initial sound of Oprah's name (e.g. [oupɹɐ] line 7).[11] Similar inconsistencies also appear at the level of grammar: unmarked grammatical constructions (line 38: "yes (.) you vote e:h for George") are produced together with marked and non-standard clauses (line 22: "you want Oprah show").

In addition to inconsistencies related to 'Greek-accented English,' Extract 6 illustrates some inconsistencies that are noted in the radio host's delivery of Greek words, especially elements that have been previously uttered by the caller. Phonological shibboleths of 'L2 accent' in Greek can be found in how the town ('Akrata') is uttered by *Apostolis* in line 11 [ɐkɹɐtɐ],[12] following the caller's [ɐkɹəʔæ], as well as the production of a much more centralized vowel in the interjection 'oh' [əʊ:] (line 16), instead of the mid back [ɔː] typical of Standard Modern Greek. These examples reveal strategic manipulation of phonological properties that appear in the caller's speech, enhancing and underlining inconsistency in the radio host's verbal performance. The effect of such inconsistencies, sustained through crossings into the style of the caller, is increased confusion and discomfiture on the part of the victim. This confusion triggers the need to reassess the setting and the interactional frame (customer-service interaction) that the victim understands as 'real' in the given situation (line 17: "wh- where have I called?").

By appropriating the voice of the caller (albeit in a fleeting and somehow incomplete manner), the host arguably projects a particular persona onto the caller/victim that the listening audience is invited to recognize. The double-voicing (Bakhtin 1986) potential of stylized speech enables the performer to move between personas, using different styles in order not only to evoke cultural stereotypes in his own performance (e.g. the nonfluent peasant-Greek of Extract 5) but also to construct particular representations of the callers. Indeed, what contributes to the popular appeal of the media pranks is arguably that while they play a trick on individual callers, they also tend to victimize the caller as a particular persona.

Extract 6 illustrates how the caller is victimized as a persona that has specific political and ideological positions. This is achieved not only through the aforementioned fleeting stylizations of the caller's speech but also—and primarily—through metadiscursive evaluations of her speech style. Metalinguistic comments (lines 13–14 and 40–42) offered by the host/prankster bring to the fore the voice of the caller and her 'accent' in particular. The first metalinguistic comment (lines 13–14) follows a request that invites the caller to identify herself in terms of place of origin or nationality ("where are you from?," line 9). Stereotypical associations between location and speech/accent come into play when the metacomment foregrounds perceived incongruities between the caller's accent and her location. Such incongruities capitalize on sociolinguistic stereotypes according to which residents of small rural towns cannot display a 'standard' English accent. Such beliefs are invoked in the metalinguistic statement ("this is the accent from Akrata") that the radio host ironically repeats in line 13. For humorous purposes, such metalinguistic comments, together with the host's stylizations of the caller's speech, are aimed at foregrounding such incongruities, and through irony, they effectively deauthenticate and undermine the persona of the caller.

Metatalk again becomes relevant after a request that invites the caller to identify herself in terms of her political beliefs. The question, which is repeated through multiple turns, carries certain presuppositions that align the caller with the Greek social democratic party ("are you socialist?," lines 32, 34). The then leader of the social democratic party (Georgios 'George' Papandreou) is a Greek politician who was born and educated in the United States (see note 9). His competence in English and Greek has been debated in the media, with his fluency in English receiving praise in popular discourse. The metalinguistic comment ("your accent is excellent," line 41) brings to the fore associations between fluent (Greek and English) bilingualism and certain sociopolitical positions. Rather than projecting the 'foreigner' (e.g. 'English') persona to this caller (who also doesn't vote in Greece, as she proclaims in the broadcast), the telephone prank metadiscursively links the fluent Greek-English bilingual persona of the caller with the governing political party and the political elites at the time.

Unlike Extract 5 where styles of English (Greek-accented English and fluent English) are used as resources in order to contrast the local/Greek with the non-Greek/English, Extract 6 illustrates a prank where different contrasts are projected. The radio/host prankster continues to self-reflexively position himself as 'peasant-Greek' (line 45–46), achieved again through styling 'Greek-accented English.' His overall style, though, is much more inconsistent here, partly due to his stylization of phonological features associated with 'standard' English in the caller's speech. Drawing on the strategic manipulation of varying styles of English and the metadiscursive comments at the end of the broadcast, this prank seems to establish a contrast between speakers of 'Greek-accented English' and fluent bilingual speakers, with the latter acquiring certain political and ideological associations. In this prank, fluent Greek-English bilingualism is indexing a particular political elite, with references to the political party and leader who announced that Greece was on the brink of default and negotiated the first bailout package from the European Union.

HAVE YOU HIRED YOUR OWN ENGLISHMAN TO DO YOUR ERRANDS?

The final extract selected for analysis is constituted by the final segment of a long prank. Unlike the previous cases, the caller in this extract has not initiated the call. As illustrated in Extract 4, the fourth category of prank victims concerns third parties who act as mediators between the prankster and initial callers. Similar to the prank opening of Extract 4, the third party here also seems to be somebody in close physical proximity to the initial caller at the time of the call. In line 50, the third party (female caller, C2 below) takes the floor, after the initial caller (a male English speaker) finds it impossible to communicate meaningfully with the prankster and hands the phone to her. In the extract that follows, we see that the (new) victim turns out to be a bilingual speaker who is fluent in both languages and speaks with a Standard Modern Greek accent.

Extract 7

1–49   [. . .]

50   C2:   ε ναι παρακαλώ μ' ακούτε?
              eh yes hello can you hear me?

51   H: yes

52   C2:   ναι είναι εκεί το κανάλι ΣΚΑΙ?
              yes is this SKAI channel?

53   H: what do you mean?

54   C2:   ναι μιλάω ελληνικά μπορείς να μου μιλήσεις ελληνικά
              yes I speak Greek can you speak Greek to me

55   και να μου πεις αν είναι εκεί το κανάλι ΣΚΑΙ?
              and tell me if this is SKAI channel?

56   H: ε και τι βάζεις τον ξένο να συνεννοηθούμε τότε μίλα από την αρχή
              eh and why are you asking the foreigner to speak then speak first

57   τον ξένο βάζεις να πάρει τηλέφωνο?
              are you asking the foreigner to make the phone call?

58   C2:   άνθρωπέ μου δικό του ήταν τ-
              man it was h-

59   H: έχεις αγοράσει Άγγλο δικό σου να σου κάνει τις δουλειές
              have you hired your own Englishman to do your errands

60   σε περίοδο κρίσης έχεις άνθρωπο να σου παίρνει τα τηλέφωνα?
              during the crisis do you have somebody to take your calls?

Extract 7 starts with the female person who is asked to intervene (by the initial caller) and who switches to Greek as soon as she takes the floor. In response to this strategic switch by the new caller/mediator, the prankster continues to perform his style of 'English.' It is only when language ("Greek") becomes topicalized in line 54 that *Apostolis* switches to Greek and returns to his usual fast pace of delivery with minimal hesitations or pauses.

As is evident in lines 56–57, the radio host continues the frame of the prank by subverting the roles the two callers play on the phone. Rather than treating C2 as a mediator who has been asked to intervene by the main caller, *Apostolis* treats her as the main caller who has "hired" (line 59) the initial (fluent English) speaker to make the phone call for her. In this extract, the discursive work of projecting a particular persona to the victim of the prank is not achieved through stylization but through explicit metadiscursive framing of what the victim does. Similar to what we saw in Extract 6, the fluent bilingual caller (C2) is indexed as 'elite' by attributing to them signs of wealth. In lines 59–60 in particular, the social context of the financial crisis is explicitly invoked by the prankster/host to underline the contrast between the caller's construed affluence and widespread financial strains at times of crisis. In this prank, *Apostolis*, with his 'Greek-accented English,' is contrasted to both victims: the initial caller ('standard' English speaker) who is labeled the "foreigner"/ "Englishman" (lines 56 and 59) and the fluent bilingual speaker who is portrayed as (Greek) 'affluent elite.'

Discussion

Considering that humorous performances in the media are "rather distorted refractions of actual community speech practices" (Woolard et al. 2013: 128), it can be argued that the popular telephone pranks discussed in this chapter offer a metapragmatic commentary on language practices in Greece and the socio-cultural values associated with such practices at the beginning of the so-called Greek debt crisis. More specifically, the pranks shed light on ongoing shifts in the sociocultural alignment between Greek and English whose relative 'status' has become the focus of language-ideological debates in the media in recent decades. At the same time, the analysis reveals the sociopolitical associations that different 'languages' and mediated language practices can gain at times of crisis; in this particular case as part of a highly conflictual and polarized political debate (cf. Angouri and Wodak 2014) concerning issues of national sovereignty and identity in relation to wider political and economic alliances, specifically the EU.

In my analysis, I have approached the pranks on *Greekophrenia* as a distinct public participation media genre where laypersons are unknowingly induced, as prank victims, into a fabricated situation that is doubly deceiving: they believe that the call taker (who is really a high-profile radio host, identifiable by the audience as the prankster) is an operator at the radio/TV station's call center, and they are unaware that the interaction (or segments of the interaction) will be broadcast. On the other hand, the audience and the radio host are aware of both the fabricated frame of customer-service interaction and the jocular frame of broadcast prank. In other words, the key participants (prankster, victim, and audience) constitute a triangle of deceit where entertainment is partly achieved by the victim's failure to interpret the situation as a joke. The struggle for re-establishing interactional order, in spite of—and in response to—the overt violations of social and language norms orchestrated by the prankster, offers a window onto discourse that allows us to study underlying metapragmatic and metalinguistic values. In the pranks, we witness the online dialogic (re)negotiation of social norms about language use and indexical associations, played out through stylized and metadiscursively rich talk which eventually gets circulated as public discourse in a range of media ('old' and 'new').

Stylization, as a reflexive and metaphorical process, constitutes a key element of the mediated performances that the prank calls facilitate. Styling personas, such as the nonfluent peasant Greek (incongruent with the fabricated frame of customer-service interaction), contributes to the violation of accepted social norms and confuses the prank victims. Such stylizations consolidate sociocultural profiles (or "exemplary" speakers in Agha's 2003 terms) and increase people's awareness of ideological values associated with particular ways of speaking and acting. As Coupland (2014b: 76) points out, "social actors become aware of culture and of cultural change, but also of cultural continuity, precisely when a level of cultural reflexivity at a sufficient scale or representation is achieved." The analysis of the language resources used in the stylizations and the personas styled in such performances sheds light on language-ideological change as captured in the stereotyped semiotic and ideological values associated with these personas and their talk.

In the case of Greece, the blending of styles and languages has been a popular resource for media parodies of character types in films, advertising, and so on for decades. As for the use of English elements in particular, previous studies documented the styling of character types, such as the "newly-rich" of the 1960s Athenian society (Georgakopoulou 2000: 122) and the aspirational "peasant" (who wants to come across as urban/cosmopolitan, cf. Archakis et al. 2014: 52–53), by inserting individual English words while conversing in Greek. Although *Apostolis*'s performance echoes this tradition of stylistic humor, it is distinct—or even anomalous—in relying not only on 'Greek-accented English' (see Extract 5) but also on a more sophisticated engagement with varying styles of English (e.g. stylization of 'standard' English elements, as they appear in some callers' speech; cf. Extract 6). In short, we see more variation in the way English is used—and more variation in what English is used *for*—in these pranks than is attested in the contemporary Greek sociolinguistic literature.

What seems like an 'anomaly' of my data set (compared to what has been discussed so far in the Greek literature) can be interpreted in relation to both media genre and potential change in the sociocultural alignment of Greek and English. To start with the latter, a more secure position for English in the public domain, achieved among other things through the earlier introduction of English as a compulsory subject at school and the increasing mobility of student/workforce in Europe, arguably encourages media stylizations of English and bilingual talk, as it presupposes sufficient familiarity with the relevant stylistic resources and allows its "public profanation in more hybridizing performances" (Woolard et al. 2013: 129). Second, the sorts of data that have been studied in this chapter—spontaneous, humorous interactions that cannot be planned in advance—also hold the potential of revealing less crystalized forms of stylistic humor and more ambivalent language-ideological positions than pre-scripted performances (cf. Archakis et al. 2014). This may explain why different styles of English have not generally, in the Greek context, been documented as key resources for stylistic humor in studies focusing on scripted genres such as comedy sketches, sitcoms, and advertisements.

Having suggested that the stylings examined in this chapter point to a change in the sociocultural alignment between Greek and English, it remains to explore how they may refract language-ideological change, especially in relation to the two aforementioned 'ideals' of 'monolingualism' and 'English/national language bilingualism.' Despite the increased acceptance of English in the public domain, the playful and strategic manipulation of both English and Greek elements in the radio host's performance draws on a continuing 'regime ideology' of monolingualism. The related ideologies of language purism and language differentiation are invoked in performances where hybrid language practices (manifest in the performed style of 'Greek-accented English' or stylizations of phonological shibboleths of L2 accent in Greek) become the target of stylistic humor. At the same time, attention to the personas projected through the prankster's stylings and his metadiscursive commentaries suggests that the emerging ideal of English/national language bilingualism has been gaining impetus since the turn of the 21st century. In my analyses of Extracts 6 and 7, which featured fluent Greek-English bilingual callers, I noted that the prankster projects onto the victim the persona of a particular type of Greek elite, associated with affluence and political power. This indicates that Greek-English bilingualism carries a certain prestige. However, as the pranks unfold it transpires that the 'fluent bilingual' elite is doubly fooled and ironized: first, through the radio host's fleeting stylizations of the caller's accent and, second, due to the fact that they are fooled by the 'fool,' i.e. the incompetent, nonfluent and 'peasant-Greek' radio host.

The metadiscursive association of language use with sociopolitical positions reflects a wider debate about politics and language stereotypes that came to prominence in Greece during the initial stages of the unfolding crisis. Thus, 'Tsipras's English' (*Τα Αγγλικά του Τσίπρα*), referring to the speech style of the left-wing party leader and current Prime Minister (cf. '*Apostolis*'s English') is another keyword that will yield a series of YouTube videos where online users comment and laugh at nonfluent elements in his speech. The recasting of political debate in terms of folk ideologies about language and the new indexical values attached to fluency in English are aptly illustrated in the following extract which was published in an opinion piece about politics shortly after the period examined in this chapter:

> It is even more important what their [the politicians'] English reveal about themselves. About Papandreou for example? His English reveals that he is probably a world citizen and not a nationalist; that his thinking is influenced more by foreign *think tanks* than Greek unions; that he reads the FT, The Economist and The Guardian more than the Greek press. [. . .] What about Tsipras's poor English? It reveals, first and foremost, somebody who, probably, was not a very good student or, at least, somebody who never went abroad to live; somebody who is not elite and who will even snub the high society; [. . .][13] (my translation)

In the initial stages of the developing crisis, from which the radio pranks investigated here are sourced, the tension between the local/parochial and the global/cosmopolitan is strongly associated with language stereotypes about nonfluent vs. fluent bilingual speakers. Fluency in English, in particular, is used as a resource in order to recast intranational political differences that have resurged during the crisis, rather than distinctions between local/Greece and global/Europe we find in earlier language-ideological debates (i.e. before 2000).

Media performances of the type studied in this chapter contribute not only to reinforcing indexical relations between linguistic forms and social meanings (e.g. 'poor English' indexing peasant-ness, Greek-ness, etc.) but also to increasing visibility and social awareness of new socioculturally meaningful contrasts that center around knowledge of English (as a lingua franca), rather than the official standard language, Greek. Such contrasts between, for example, fluent and less/nonfluent speakers and their indexical values offer additional resources for reflecting upon and debating the position of the Greek nation-state within Europe and the world. The wide circulation of media footage with satirical content (e.g. pranks) through social media can accelerate the diffusion of such representations and their language-ideological impact.

Acknowledgements

An earlier version of this chapter was presented at the Copenhagen Round Table on 'Sociolinguistics and the Talking Media: Style, Mediation, and Change' (University of Copenhagen, June 12–13, 2014). I am grateful to all participants for their valuable feedback and, particularly, to Janus Mortensen, Nikolas Coupland, and Jacob Thøgersen who generously engaged with my work and offered critical suggestions and comments. I would also like to thank Alison Wray and Gerard O'Grady for providing useful comments on different parts of the manuscript, as well as Argyro Kantara for her invaluable help with data collection and transcription. All remaining shortcomings and errors are mine.

Transcription conventions

C	caller
H	host
hhh	audible breathing
huh huh	laughter
(.)	very brief pause
[word]	overlapping speech
wo-	cut-off of prior sound
word?	rising inflection
word=	latching
<u>word</u>	stressed word or sound
word	louder compared to surrounding speech
wo:rd	stretching of prior sound
>word<	fast pace
word	quiet speech
word	English translation of utterances/ expressions in Greek
(word)	transcription comments

Notes

1. In contrast to the pre-1976 era when different beliefs about language norms tended to index conflicting political ideologies, both Frangoudaki (1992) and Moschonas (2009) have pointed out that the *regime ideology* (to use Moschonas's term) of the late 20th century cut across political differences and boundaries.

2. Research on print/digital media discourse in European countries, like Greece or Germany, also attests to a pattern of bilingual (English/national language) discourse where English appears as a "complementary code used in addition to ('on top' of) the predominant national language" (Androutsopoulos 2012: 209).

3. *BBC News.* Greece Profile—Timeline. Available at: http://www.bbc.co.uk/news/world-europe-17373216 (last accessed August 7, 2016).

4. Ellinofreneia. 2015. *ELLINOFRENEIA (@Ellinofreneia) on Twitter*. Available at: https://twitter.com/ellinofreneia (last accessed August 7, 2016).

5. English translation of turns including Greek elements is provided under the original in *italics*. See transcription key for additional conventions.

6. When asked by the host where they are from, callers in the data set report England, South Africa, Australia, and Germany as countries of origin.

7. At the time of writing, the audio file is still available on the show's website, archived together with other popular pranks, and clearly tagged by the site producers as Αγγλικά Αποστόλη #1 ('Apostolis's English #1').

8. Cf. the relative lack of the aforementioned features when 'moving out' of this style in Extract 7.

9. Georgios (also known as George) Papandreou, Greek politician, leader of the social democratic party (PASOK) and Prime Minister (2009–2011).

10. PASOK stands for Panhellenic Socialist Movement (Greek social democratic political party).

11. In other pranks, *Apostolis* engages in a more 'Greek-accented' pronunciation of Oprah as [oprɐ].

12. This is in stark contrast with how the same word is uttered with a broad Standard Modern Greek accent twice in line 11 as [ɐkrɐtɐ].

13. Nikolopoulos, G. Tsipras's English [Τα αγγλικά του Τσίπρα]. *protagon.gr*. Available at: http://www.protagon.gr/?i=protagon.el.article&id=15321 (May 18, 2012) (last accessed August 7, 2016).

References

Agha, Asif. 2003. The social life of cultural value. *Language & Communication* 23, 3–4: 231–273.

Androutsopoulos, Jannis. 2012. English 'on top': Discourse functions of English resources in the German mediascape. *Sociolinguistic Studies* 6, 2: 209–238.

Androutsopoulos, Jannis. 2014a. Beyond 'media influence.' *Journal of Sociolinguistics* 18, 2: 242–249.

Androutsopoulos, Jannis. 2014b. Mediatization and sociolinguistic change: Key concepts, research traditions, open issues. In Jannis Androutsopoulos (ed.) *Mediatization and Sociolinguistic Change.* Berlin: De Gruyter. 3–48.

Angouri, Jo and Ruth Wodak. 2014. 'They became big in the shadow of the crisis': The Greek success story and the rise of the far right. *Discourse & Society* 25, 4: 540–565.

Archakis, Argiris, Sofia Lampropoulou, Villy Tsakona and Vasia Tsami. 2014. Linguistic varieties in style: Humorous representations in Greek mass culture texts. *Discourse, Context & Media* 3: 46–55.

Arvaniti, Amalia. 1999. Standard Modern Greek. *Journal of the International Phonetic Association* 29, 2: 167–172.

Bakhtin, Mikhail M. 1986. *Speech Genres and Other Late Essays* (ed. Michael Holquist; trans. Caryl Emerson and Michael Holquist). Austin: University of Texas Press.

Bauman, Richard. 1986. *Story, Performance, and Event: Contextual Stories of Oral Narrative.* Cambridge: Cambridge University Press.

Blommaert, Jan. 1999. The debate is open. In Jan Blommaert (ed.) *Language Ideological Debates.* Berlin: De Gruyter. 1–38.

Boukala, Salomi. 2014. Waiting for democracy: Political crisis and the discursive (re)invention of the 'national enemy' in times of 'Grecovery.' *Discourse & Society* 25, 4: 483–499.

Coupland, Nikolas. 2001. Dialect stylization in radio talk. *Language in Society* 30: 345–375.

Coupland, Nikolas. 2007. *Style: Language Variation and Identity.* Cambridge: Cambridge University Press.

Coupland, Nikolas. 2009. Dialects, standards and social change. In Marie Maegaard, Frans Gregersen, Pia Quist and J. Norman Jørgensen (eds.) *Language Attitudes, Standardization and Language Change.* Oslo: Novus. 27–49.

Coupland, Nikolas. 2014a. Language change, social change, sociolinguistic change: A meta-commentary. *Journal of Sociolinguistics* 18, 2: 277–286.

Coupland, Nikolas. 2014b. Sociolinguistic change, vernacularization and broadcast British media. In Jannis Androutsopoulos (ed.) *Mediatization and Sociolinguistic Change.* Berlin: De Gruyter. 67–96.

Frangoudaki, Anna. 1992. Diglossia and the present language situation in Greece: A sociological approach to the interpretation of diglossia and some hypotheses on today's linguistic reality. *Language in Society* 21, 3: 365–381.

Frangoudaki, Anna. 2002. Comment: Greek societal bilingualism of more than a century. *International Journal of the Sociology of Language* 157: 101–107.

Garfinkel, Harold. 1967. *Studies in Ethnomethodology.* Cambridge: Polity.

Georgakopoulou, Alexandra. 2000. On the sociolinguistics of popular films: Funny characters, funny voices. *Journal of Modern Greek Studies* 18, 1: 119–133.

Georgakopoulou, Alexandra. 2014. Small stories transposition and social media: A microperspective on the 'Greek crisis.' *Discourse & Society* 25, 4: 519–539.

Goffman, Erving. 1974. *Frame Analysis: An Essay on the Organization of Experience.* Cambridge: Cambridge University Press.

Jaffe, Alexandra. 2000. Comic performance and the articulation of hybrid identity. *IPRA Papers in Pragmatics* 10, 1: 39–59.

Koutsogiannis, Dimitrios and Bessie Mitsikopoulou. 2003. Greeklish and Greekness: Trends and discourses of "glocalness". *Journal of Computer-Mediated Communication* 9, 1.

Koutsogiannis, Dimitrios and Vassiliki Adampa. 2012. Girls, identities and agency in adolescents' digital literacy practices. *Journal of Writing Research* 3, 3: 217–247.

Moschonas, Spiros. 2009. 'Language Issues' after the 'Language Question': On the modern standards of Standard Modern Greek. In Alexandra Georgakopoulou and Michael Silk (eds.) *Standard Languages and Language Standards: Greek, Past and Present.* London: Ashgate. 293–320.

Moschonas, Spiros. 2014. The media on media-induced language change. In Jannis Androutsopoulos (ed.) *Mediatization and Sociolinguistic Change.* Berlin: De Gruyter. 395–426.

Moschonas, Spiros and Jürgen Spitzmüller. 2010. Prescriptivism in and about the media: A comparative analysis of corrective practices in Greece and Germany. In Sally Johnson and Tommaso Milani (eds.) *Language Ideologies and Media Discourse: Texts, Practices, Politics.* London: Continuum. 17–40.

Papanikolaou, Dimitris. 2011. Archive Trouble. *Fieldsights–Hot Spots, Cultural Anthropology Online,* http://www.culanth.org/fieldsights/247-archive-trouble, October 26, 2011.

Schegloff, Emmanuel. 1986. The routine as achievement. *Human Studies* 9: 111–151.

Seilhamer, Mark Fifer. 2011. On doing 'being a crank caller': A look into the crank call community of practice. *Journal of Pragmatics* 43: 677–690.

Spitzmüller, Jürgen. 2007. Staking the claims of identity: Purism, linguistics and the media in post-1990 Germany. *Journal of Sociolinguistics* 11, 2: 261–285.

Stevenson, Patrick and Clare Mar-Molinero. 2006. Language, the national and the transnational in contemporary Europe. In Clare Mar-Molinero and Patrick Stevenson (eds.) *Language Ideologies, Policies and Practices: Language and the Future of Europe.* Basingstoke: Palgrave Macmillan. 1–10.

Stuart-Smith, Jane. 2014. No longer an elephant in the room. *Journal of Sociolinguistics* 18, 2: 250–261.

Thurlow, Crispin. 2006. From statistical panic to moral panic: The metadiscursive construction and popular exaggeration of new media language in the print media. *Journal of Computer-Mediated Communication* 11, 3: 667–701.

Trester, Anna Marie. 2013. Telling and retelling prankster stories: Evaluating cleverness to perform identity. *Discourse Studies* 15, 1: 91–109.

Wodak, Ruth and Jo Angouri. 2014. From *Grexit* to *Grecovery*: Euro/crisis discourses. *Discourse & Society* 25, 4: 417–423.

Woolard, Kathryn, with Aida Ribot Bencomo and Josep Soler-Carbonell. 2013. What's so funny now? The strength of weak pronouns in Catalonia. *Journal of Linguistic Anthropology* 23, 3: 127–141.

4

Styling syncretic bilingualism on Welsh-language TV: *Madamrygbi*

Nikolas Coupland

Introduction

Minority language movements tend to invest heavily in minority language media.[1] Broadcasting in the endangered language and the availability of relevant technologies for web-based interaction are typically seen as forms of institutional support for small languages. Classical approaches to modeling the ethnolinguistic vitality of languages (e.g. Landry and Allard 1994a, b) make this relationship explicit, and it is not surprising that planners and activists have lobbied intensively for media resources to exist and to be protected. The Welsh-language fourth television channel in Wales, S4C (*Sianel Pedwar Cymru*, 'Channel Four Wales') is no exception, having been launched in 1982 in the wake of a campaign of protest and civil disobedience which included a hunger strike by Gwynfor Evans, the sole member of Parliament representing *Plaid Cymru*, the Welsh Nationalist Party (at that time). Institutional support for Welsh media continues to be a priority. For example, the current Welsh Assembly Government, with devolved authority from the Westminster Parliament in London, has recently announced a new funding initiative titled the "Welsh Language Technology and Digital Media Grant."[2] Media matter to minorities.

The radical social and technological changes that have affected contemporary media services and markets, however, have unsettled the assumption that national governments and broadcasters can impact directly and positively on the vitality of a minority language, simply by creating platforms for greater mass-mediated usage. Different national agencies have, in any case, followed different principles dictating *how* a minority language should be mediated. For example, Ireland's TG4 television channel—which in some ways is closely equivalent to S4C in Wales—has worked under a less restrictive policy on how Irish and Irish-English bilingualism

Style, Mediation, and Change. Edited by Janus Mortensen, Nikolas Coupland, and Jacob Thøgersen
© Oxford University Press 2017. Published 2017 by Oxford University Press

should be represented in its programming (Kelly-Holmes 2012). TG4 gives higher priority to viewer ratings, over language-ideological considerations in the service of revitalizing the minority language, than S4C does—TG4 is not as concerned to follow an Irish-only policy as S4C is to follow a Welsh-only policy (as discussed in the next section).

A wider consideration, however, is that different forms of globalization are progressively challenging the naturalness, or taken-for-granted-ness, of 'one nation, one language,' and this is the ideology that originally motivated most campaigns for national broadcasting in minority contexts.[3] In Wales, new conditions for media production and consumption have arisen not only in material terms—a diversification of media platforms and modes of engagement—but also in terms of the intensified, multiply mediated reflexivity of linguistic and cultural representation. The very concept of 'national broadcasting in a national language' already sounds dated in social environments (like Wales) which are demonstrably plural. The mechanisms of national language broadcasting persist, including the S4C television channel in Wales, but the language-ideological basis of their existence and the practical footings on which they represent their linguistic and cultural constituencies are changing.[4]

Against this general background, in this chapter I present a case study of one mediated persona that appears quite regularly on S4C. The case study illustrates changing broadcasting norms in Wales, but it also gives insights into how those changes, and wider sociolinguistic change, can be promoted by mediated performance. The persona is *Madamrygbi*, a young female 'comedy rugby interviewer' character created and performed, mainly in Welsh, by actor Eirlys Bellin. Rugby—*rygbi* in Welsh, pronounced identically—is generally considered to be the 'national game' of Wales. I am interested in how the *Madamrygbi* persona works *against the grain* of (what we can probably call) traditional norms of national Welsh-language broadcasting in Wales, also *against the grain* of how rugby is conventionally positioned and represented in Welsh media. Rugby coverage is, in fact, one of S4C's few high-value program categories in terms of audience reach, against a backdrop of much-criticized 'value for money' assessments of the channel. As I explain in more detail later, authenticity is strongly implicated in the traditions and conventions of both national broadcasting and in public discourse around rugby in Wales. In essence, the case for a Welsh-language television channel has rested on the assumption that Welsh is 'the language of Wales,' just as rugby is 'Wales's national game,' and deep emotional and moral currents have flowed in both dimensions. *Madamrygbi*, on the other hand, opens up these quasi-religious authenticities of Welsh language and sporting culture to new types of scrutiny. She does this in ways that resonate with the globalization-induced social changes that I referred to previously.

In order to appreciate how *Madamrygbi* exposes and challenges these myths and tensions, we need to look closely at how Eirlys Bellin creatively styles the *Madamrygbi* persona and at how her persona is mediated into the public consciousness of the viewers she reaches. There are, very clearly, both static and dynamic aspects to these processes. *Madamrygbi* as a character has become strikingly unique and recognizable to many S4C viewers, but also to some networks of social media users in Wales, in threads of interest and engagement that *Madamrygbi's* appearances on Welsh television have promoted. She is a consolidated character with 'a distinctive style'—which inevitably proves to be a composite, multimodal confection of visual, bodily, and linguistic features, stances, and relational designs. A growing community of media consumers in Wales knows how the *Madamrygbi* persona 'works' and what it indexically stands for. Yet Eirlys Bellin continually refreshes and adds to the character, in a series of new 'rugby interviewing' contexts and episodes (one of which I will examine in detail in this chapter), but also through her in-character engagement in social media. Each episode, in either an 'old' or 'new' media context, is a fresh opportunity to restyle the persona, to reanimate it, and to attach new nuances to it.

Madamrygbi is therefore both an established characterological figure, even a celebrity figure in Welsh media and rugby circles, yet a persona always in the making. As I explain later, *Madamrygbi* is slowly developing her own (fictional) biographical narrative, across several mediated episodes in which she comes into contact with Welsh rugby stars who, non-fictionally (or perhaps we should say less fictionally) are celebrities in their own right. The *Madamrygbi* case merits attention because she brings new metalinguistic and metacultural perspectives into focus: she shows us new possible ways of construing language, media, and sport in Wales. She playfully disrupts old certainties and authenticities, while exploring the possibility that newer forms of authenticity can be found in performance.

Before coming to the case study itself, in the next two sections I fill in some further detail about language and bilingualism in Wales and Welsh media, and then explain the ways in which I hope to bring the concepts of style, media, reflexivity, authenticity and change into dialogue with each other to support the case study analysis.

Competing perspectives on bilingual Wales

Two interconnected emphases have dominated the traditional account of bilingual Wales, as they have in similar sociolinguistic contexts: first, the assumption that minority and majority language codes occupying the same social space should be treated as wholly separate entities; second, the assumption that demography and enumeration are of primary importance in evaluating a language code's strength or vitality, principally by surveying how many people use it. These emphases have traditionally existed in academic sociolinguistics, but also in the language policy and planning field (in which some sociolinguists have been active) and, to some extent, in wider public discourses. For example, as data from the 2011 UK census started to be reported in Welsh media in 2012, reports centered on the fact that the data showed a small decline in the (self-reported) number of speakers of Welsh in Wales above three years of age to 562,016, from a total population in Wales of approximately three million, relative to data from the previous census in 2001. These accounts then tended to deal with the changing sociological and geographical patterns underlying the headline numbers, noting, for example, that Welsh was "more resilient" in the north-west than the south-west "heartland" area. (The quote-marked terms were frequent in the reports.) Another point covered was that the balance of urban relative to rural speakers had changed by 2011, as a result of compulsory learning of Welsh in schools to age 16, given that the urban south-east of Wales has the highest population densities in Wales.

Social trend statistics inevitably capture political and public imaginations and they are a necessary basis for some sorts of policy decisions, but these emphases keep particular language-ideological values to the fore. They consolidate the view that the dominant sociolinguistic agenda in Wales *properly is* 'bilingual Wales.' In consequence, public discourse in Wales rarely addresses issues of *multi*lingualism (e.g. in relation to transnational mobility). In relation to bilingualism itself, repeated accounts of the demographic relativities between speakers of Welsh and English in Wales have generated a dominant model of what I have previously called 'parallel-text bilingualism' (Coupland 2012), premised on the need to promote Welsh and English as equivalent and equal linguistic 'options' or 'choices'—a particular interpretation of 'parallel monolingualisms' (cf. Duchêne and Heller 2007, 2012; Heller 2008)[5]. Legislation to protect the use of Welsh "on the basis of equality" (with English), such as the 1993 Welsh Language Act and the 2011 Welsh Language Measure, is couched in exactly these terms. As a result, the planned future of Welsh is constructed on the basis of Welsh needing to 'catch up with' and 'exist alongside' English, rather than functioning in rich and variable patterns of bilingual Welsh-English interplay at the level of practice.

Under these ideological conditions it has been possible to construe Welsh as an authentic national language, and speakers of Welsh (even though they are almost all bilingual—almost everyone speaks English) as authentic speakers. Authenticity often confers and is conferred by authority (Coupland 2014a), and the relatively new office of *Comisiynydd Y Gymraeg*/the Welsh Language Commissioner (from 2012) was instituted in order to monitor public-sector organizations' compliance with laws requiring use of both languages, and to penalize noncompliance. Once again, all of this squeezes out any recognition of the clear fact that the linguistic relationship between Welsh and English in Wales has been, as we might expect, a highly syncretic one, and that on a day-to-day basis bilingual practice is itself syncretic, the resources of the two codes 'growing together' and being used together (Coupland 2012; Gal and Irvine 1995; Urciuoli 1995).

It is not surprising, therefore, that the Welsh-language television channel in Wales, S4C, came to operate under a set of *Canllawiau Iaith*, 'language guidelines,'[6] which include the following prescriptions and proscriptions (given here in English translations from the original Welsh):

Extract 1: Quotations from *Canllawiau Iaith* 'Language Guidelines' S4C (2008)

> The basic objective is to provide a high quality S4C television service through the Welsh language . . .

> Not all spoken language practices qualify for coverage . . . For example, rapid colloquial speech can be very attractive to viewers who use the dialect of the area, but very difficult to understand by viewers who are not familiar with the dialect . . .

> need for accuracy . . . correct noun gender . . . give assistance to the general public but don't coerce . . .

> the service function of helping to expand the use of contemporary Welsh vocabulary, where it can be done without compromising understanding and enjoyment of the program . . .

> cherish and promote rich Welsh vocabulary . . . but without risking lack of understanding . . .

> need to supervise and control the use of English words in program to ensure they are consistent with the standard appropriate to the program . . .

S4C is therefore explicitly committed to delivering its program schedule "through the Welsh language" (as opposed to, in some sense, bilingually), but also through some version of standard Welsh, with the potential "use of English words" being "controlled." These priorities are generally respected by S4C program makers, notwithstanding that some sports programs have recently begun to offer viewers a choice of either Welsh or English match commentary, but with Welsh-only anchors, trailers, post-match discussion, and so on in the same programs.[7] S4C's resistance to representations of syncretic bilingualism is such that a recent, successful detective drama series, modeled on 'Danish noir' television drama, has been filmed in two separate versions, Welsh and English.[8] This is indicative of the normative anti-syncretic context in which (and indeed, against which) *Madamrygbi* styles her own sometimes syncretic and often transgressive mode of bilingual practice.

Media, reflexivity, and change

In drawing a distinction between language change and sociolinguistic change (Coupland 2009, 2014b; and see Chapter 1 in this volume) colleagues and I have attempted to identify a theoretical space where a wide agenda of changes at the interface between language and society can receive due attention. The language change paradigm, which is clearly the most coherent perspective on change in sociolinguistics, deals with formal changes in linguistic structure—changes in particular forms, as in 'sound change,' in repertoires or registers, or in the social distribution of forms (e.g. Labov 2001). No attention is paid to whether and how such formal changes are *or are not* sociolinguistically significant (in the sense that language/society relations are or are not demonstrably reconfigured). Sociolinguistic change, on the other hand, focuses on sociolinguistically significant change, *whether or not* formal language change is at issue. Clear-cut instances of sociolinguistic change will therefore include shifts in language-ideological values, reconfigurations of normative frameworks for language use and changing footings for interpersonal and social engagement through language and discourse. Whereas language change research has seen little relevance in media processes and data, mediation in general and mediatization (if we accept one of its key definitions, as the progressive and massive upsurge in technologically mediated language use, cf. the discussion in Chapter 1) have substantial roles to play in sociolinguistic change. A methodological and interpretive shift is also entailed in this distinction. Studying mediated performance, for example, may even be able to reveal sociolinguistic change *in progress*—change being enacted in the pragmatic construction of particular mediated sequences—as opposed to change being made visible by comparing 'before and after' snapshots in the manner of language change research.

If we briefly go back to the traditional account of the ethnolinguistic vitality of the Welsh language, we can say that this has been framed in ways more reminiscent of language change than of sociolinguistic change. It is difficult to assess the significance of small changes in reported statistics for the use of Welsh ('before and after,' in the manner of data from successive censuses). On the other hand, relative stability in the demographics of Welsh language use in Wales (which is what we have seen between 1971 and 2011, where the declared percentages of the population using Welsh ranged between 20.8 and 19.0) have been accompanied by highly significant, if in some ways empirically elusive, sociolinguistic changes.

The crux of these changes is, in summary, globalization, which is creating new forms of complexity and fluidity in center-periphery relations (Pietikäinen et al. 2016). So, a 'peripheral' space (Wales), and particularly 'peripheral' spaces *within* Wales (its traditional Welsh-speaking 'heartlands' in the north-west and the south-west), are nowadays able to market themselves on the basis of, for example, tourism or high-quality artisanal products. The Welsh language is being repositioned, in some contexts of commercial marketing, as an icon of 'smallness,' 'oldness,' and 'interesting cultural difference,' and this discursive shift is in many ways incompatible with nationalistic appeals to language rights and entitlement. It is becoming more difficult to represent Wales in sociolingustic terms as being 'an endangered minority language.' Duchêne and Heller's (2012) glossing of such changes—which are quintessentially sociolinguistic changes—as the discourse of 'pride' being assimilated into discourses of 'profit' is highly apposite in the Welsh case (Coupland and Kelly-Holmes in press).

Mediatization invites analysis most basically because, more and more, identities and interpersonal relationships and interactions are technologically mediated. But mediatization's importance in terms of sociolinguistic change is to be found in the new affordances and new demands of the technology—new networking arrangements impacting, for example, on how 'localness' and national identity are indexed—and in the new conditions for sociolinguistic and cultural engagement that reflexivity creates. Heightened cultural reflexivity inevitably accompanies mediatization. So-called old media, television and radio, in their own shifts into multichannel broadcasting and multiplatform consumption, on-demand as much as consumed-when-broadcast, increasingly represent cultural and linguistic diversity more densely, relative to which audiences reassess their own identities and social conditions.

Beck, Giddens and Lash (1994—more than 20 years ago) were first to argue that the late-modern social order is generally more reflexive, in a process they called "reflexive modernization." However, perhaps the most important sociolinguistic resonance in their social theory has to do with detraditionalization—how traditional sociolinguistic structures tend to lose their determining power in late modernity. Elaborating on this view, Archer (e.g. 2012) stresses "the reflexive imperative," where reflexivity becomes a burden and an obstacle to life progression and decision making. Archer says that we can no longer rely on "similars and familiars," the networks of people like ourselves, our families and peers, who traditionally served as anchoring points.

This combination of increased reflexivity and detraditionalizing tendencies in globalized late modernity is highly relevant to style, media, and change (this book's programmatic concerns) and to the *Madamrygbi* analysis that I present in the next two sections. The challenge is to show how particular mediated designs and performances contribute new sorts of reflexive, metacultural awareness, and then to show how such innovative characterizations achieve particular detraditionalizing effects. What is it about a given performance that works to shake up our traditional understandings of ourselves, our social belongings, and our cultures? The *Madamrygbi* case gives us some very particular insights into those processes, in relation (as I hinted at the beginning of the chapter) to the traditionally 'sacred spaces' of Welsh language, Welsh media, and Welsh rugby, with splashes of discursive resistance to established norms of gender and sexuality, in passing, too.

The *Madamrygbi* persona

As Eirlys Bellin[9] explains in an extensive interview that she agreed to give about her work, she had previously developed versions of the character, originally simply named *Rhian*, in comedy stand-up venues, in English, including at the Edinburgh Fringe Festival. She also performed *Rhian*, in character, unknown to the organizers, as a candidate for a role on a well-known reality TV show. This history already shows how Bellin has been eager to blur the boundary between the *Rhian* fictional character (who evolved into *Rhian Madamrygbi Davies, Madamrygbi* for short) and the plausibly nonfictional person she can be taken for when adopting this guise. In the interview Bellin says that she had often seen unsophisticated young female Welsh rugby fans, sometimes "hammered" (drunk), on trains, and used them as models for the *Madamrygbi* persona. She says she had often thought that "Rhian could work in that world." As we shall see, this indeterminacy, the permeable boundary between reality and fiction, is fundamental not only to the *Madamrygbi* persona but also to what it/she is able to achieve, relationally and metaculturally.

As the 'comedy rugby interviewer' version of the persona, *Madamrygbi* came to prominence in 2010, in Welsh, on a weekly Saturday night S4C television show titled *Jonathan*.[10] The still shots in Figure 4.1 have been used in online promotions of the show.

The 'Jonathan' in question is Jonathan Davies (photographed on the right of Figure 4.1), a former Welsh international rugby player who is nowadays also a prominent pundit (expert commentator) on televised rugby, in Wales and beyond. He is the principal host of his own *Jonathan* show, whose guests include other prominent rugby players and rugby-linked personalities. The show is performed live in front of a beer-drinking studio audience, mainly comprising members of particular Welsh rugby clubs who are invited to attend in rotation. The three silhouetted figures (to the left in Figure 4.1) are Jonathan Davies (in the center of the group) plus the show's two other regular hosts, Nigel Owens (left), currently a leading international rugby referee, and Sarra Elgan (right), a female S4C presenter. The light-hearted and often sardonic key of the show is implied in Jonathan's facial expression in the figure, also in the apparently dissonant semiotics of Nigel, a rugby referee, blowing his whistle and Sarra's model-like pose, visually paralleling Nigel's whistle with her hairdryer.

The *Jonathan* show itself is therefore constructed counter-normatively, in several respects. The show is rugby-themed, but it mediates rugby issues into frames based on gossip and banter (teasing and mock-aggressive relational talk). It is based on personalized and insider perspectives on rugby rather than on rugby's traditional public ideologies and representations. While Jonathan and Nigel enjoy

FIGURE 4.1 Promotional images for the S4C *Jonathan* show

authoritative standing in the serious world of rugby in other media contexts, the *Jonathan* show orients to rugby as an intimate recreational interest in which they have insider knowledge. It is important to emphasize that Welsh rugby continues to be iconized metaculturally, as a key element of the "heart and soul" of Wales (cf. Richards, Stead and Williams 1998[11]). Banter is not alien to the ethos of rugby, but what is distinctive about the *Jonathan* show is how it promotes banter onto the frontstage of mediated rugby in Wales. The show also challenges established gender and sexuality norms for rugby (Elias and Dunning 1986), partly through Sarra Elgan's and Eirlys Bellin's roles in the show, but also partly through the fact the Nigel Owens is gay, a theme that is often a focus for mock-censorious banter in the show. The *Jonathan* show's counter-normativity is therefore politically progressive, as well as amusing.

The *Madamrygbi* persona offers the show a particularly distinctive way of performing the show's counter-normativity, and a way of creatively elaborating on this in a wide range of non-studio locations. *Madamrygbi* is a 'roving reporter' character who, we are asked to believe, is able to insinuate herself into circumstances where she can opportunistically conduct filmed interviews with rugby celebrities. I will focus (in the next section) on *Madamrygbi*'s filmed interview with Jamie Roberts, who has been a leading Welsh international player for several years. I chose this interview because Jamie Robert's had himself become, at the time of filming, a character in *Madamrygbi*'s fictional biographical narrative. In several previous episodes she had confessed to being in love with Jamie—for example asking another Welsh rugby star, Shane Williams, in another filmed encounter, to set her up with a "hot date" with Jamie.[12]

Madamrygbi styles herself as a naïve, sexy female rugby fan who is passionate about Welsh rugby and about Welsh rugby players, particularly Jamie. Her name, *Madamrygbi*, is in fact a syncretically bilingual form. It borrows the English word 'mad' (in the sense of 'crazy' or 'passionate') and links it with the Welsh preposition *am*, 'about'—'crazy about rugby,' in punning relation to 'Madam rugby,' which would be the default English interpretation. In character, *Madamrygbi* is in awe of Welsh rugby players' celebrity and physical attractiveness, unable to credit her 'good fortune' in getting close to them and interacting with them, however gauche and rude she then occasionally ends up being while interviewing them. How *Madamrygbi* came to have her 'interviewer' role is never explained fully within the fictional account, but it is clearly a plot device that allows her to stage one-on-one interviews in front of the camera.

Madamrygbi's visual style is easier to show than to describe, see Figure 4.2. In this image she is wearing a red Welsh rugby shirt (*Cymry* is Welsh for 'Wales') bearing the red dragon national symbol. She is wearing the sort of plastic cowboy hat that, with the characteristic incongruity of sporting paraphernalia, is sold to fans on international match days. Only slightly less incongruent are large yellow and green inflatable plastic daffodils (the daffodil is another national symbol of Wales)

FIGURE 4.2   Eirlys Bellin as *Madamrygbi*

and a head-covering soft-fabric daffodil that goes some way to bodily transforming a rugby fan into a human daffodil. *Madamrygbi* sometimes wears the daffodil
head dress, for example when she appears in character in the crowd at international matches, and she is not alone in doing this. As I suggested earlier in relation
to banter, the semiotic displays of rugby fandom in the real worlds of real rugby
supporters can already be playful and highly stylized in these ways. So although
Madamrygbi's use of these resources may be accelerated and more intense relative
to most actual fans' self-styling, it is not unique to her. What *is* unique to her is how
she is able to embed the persona of a naïve, overheated (or in *Madamrygbi*'s English
neologism, 'ecstatical') rugby fan into new contexts and relationships.

   Madamrygbi's red-painted fingernails are quite important resources in her
bodily and gestural style. The gesture she is performing in Figure 4.2 is a stylized expression of embarrassed incredulity, which involves mock-fanning of her
face with her fingers. Bellin reminds me, in the interview, that *Madamrygbi* commonly refers to this particular gesture (self-referentially, in character, in English,
often interposed into a Welsh utterance) as either "non-silent scream" or "silent
scream." "Silent scream" is used when *Madamrygbi* feels she is not in a situation
where screaming is allowed, and when she purportedly has to suppress what would
otherwise be an involuntary response cry. *Madamrygbi* often audibly accompanies the bodily gesture with the relevant metapragmatic utterance, usually the
verbalized expression "silent scream" itself (not dissimilarly to when someone
might say "groan" instead of, or in addition to, actually groaning). As we will see,
Madamrygbi's performances are shot-through with set-piece facial, gestural, and
linguistic expressions of this sort, and their recurrence across new contexts makes
them familiar and quotable elements of *Madamrygbi*'s style.

   It is interesting to keep in mind Bellin's own descriptions of the *Madamrygbi*
character (again from interview data). She suggests that *Madamrygbi*'s use of Welsh
helps to locate her as a "nonacademic" speaker (whereas Bellin herself is in fact an

academic linguist by training and a first-language Welsh-speaker by upbringing, even though that upbringing was outside Wales). She emphasizes social class as a key component of the portrayal—*Madamrygbi*, she says, is "definitely not middle-class"—and feels that *Madamrygbi* often emerges as "the underdog who doesn't know she is the underdog." To this extent Bellin herself locates *Madamrygbi* as a sympathetic character, albeit one whose naïvety is often revealed to be faux-naïvety, as she changes footing in interviews with players in order to wrong-foot them (cf. the mock naïvety of Évole, the journalist whose style is analysed by Lorenzo-Dus in Chapter 2).

Madamrygbi interviews Jamie Roberts

Eirlys Bellin, as *Madamrygbi*, filmed a series of short interviews, including the one transcribed in Extract 2, with leading Welsh rugby players for the *Jonathan* show while the players rested between matches at the 2011 Rugby World Cup in New Zealand. I was interested to learn how the episodes were set up. Bellin explains that media interviews with players needed to be agreed in advance by the Wales Media Manager travelling with the team, and that filming had to be scheduled on predesignated "media days." Also, players to be interviewed received a measure of advance warning of the questions *Madamrygbi* would ask, and they generally had some appreciation of *Madamrygbi*'s interviewing style. Bellin also explained, however, that a good level of trust existed between her and the players, who might expect to be wrong-footed by her mix of straight, 'rugby interviewer-type' questions and what she calls "something ridiculous." At the same time, she says that "it's *not all* pre-planned."

Jamie Roberts was aware of the evolving fictional plot (that *Madamrygbi* loves him and intends to marry him), and Bellin also explains that the media company under whose aegis the films were made had taken advice about how to avoid potential legal problems if the Jamie connection and narrative might be perceived as being "too real." On the other hand, she agrees that her interviewing really does confuse and embarrass Jamie. Extract 2 is a transcript of the whole interview, which is available on YouTube.[13] Each numbered line of the transcript represents the original interview exchange, with an English translation below it in italics. Underlining in the original data transcript lines is a rough-and-ready way to highlight words or partial utterances that could be taken to be 'in English,' even though the matrix language of the overall exchange is generally 'Welsh.' Some forms in the numbered lines are italicized, intended to imply that attributing them to 'Welsh' versus 'English' is impossible, sometimes because competing criteria would lead to different attributions, or that this sort of attribution is irrelevant (which may actually be the case overall). Welsh orthographic alternatives are, nevertheless, sometimes available for ambiguous forms, and I have chosen to use those in the transcript.

Extract 2: *Madamrygbi* (MR) interviewing Jamie Roberts (JR) at the Rugby World Cup.

MR: 1   fi yma (.) gyda'r <u>actual</u> (.) *Jamie Roberts*
            I'm here (.) with the actual (.) Jamie Roberts

         2   *Jaimie* (.) sut ti'n teimlo am fod yn y <u>semi-final</u>?
            Jaimie (.) how are you feeling about being in the semi-final?

JR: 3   <u>just amazing really</u> bod ni'n warae mewn (.) <u>semi-final</u> cwpan y byd
            just amazing really that we're playin in (.) the world cup semi-final

         4   a (.) yn sicr [laughs] bod Cymru *er* yn nol gatre (.) yn mynd <u>crazy</u>
            and (.) for sure [laughs] Wales er back home is going crazy

         5   ar y funed *so* gobeithio bod ni gallu neud y *busnes* dydd Sadwrn
            at the moment so hoping that we can do the business Saturday

MR: 6   sut mae dy drwyn?
            how's your nose?

JR: 7   trwyn yn *okay* mae heb torri (.) nes i cael er <u>bang</u> arno fe (.)
            nose is okay it's not broken (.) I got er a bang on it (.)

         8   <u>black eye</u> fel ma nhw'n dweud ond ma fe'n <u>fine</u>
            black eye as they say but it's fine

MR: 9   *okay* fi *jyst* ishe ti gal gwbod (.) like hyd yn oed gyda trwyn fel
            okay I just want you to know (.) like even with a nose like

        10   Mike Tyndall bydde ti <u>like</u> y <u>fittest man</u> ar yr <u>actual planet</u>
            Mike Tyndall you're like the fittest man on the actual planet

JR: 11   diolch yn fowr (.) <u>nice one</u> (.) sai <u>quite</u> na (.) yn erbyn
            thanks a lot (.) nice one (.) I'm not quite there (.) against

        12   *Mike Tyndall* to (.) dal da fi gwallt *so*
            Mike Tyndall yet (.) I've still got hair so

MR: 13   alle ti ddisgrifio <u>ideal</u> *rygbi* <u>fan</u> ti?
            can you describe your ideal rugby fan?

JR: 14   rhywun sydd yn <u>passionate</u> iawn
            someone who's really passionate

MR: 15   *tic*
            tick

JR: 16   er rhywun sydd yn *u:m* (.) <u>drunk</u> yn y <u>terraces</u>
            er someone who's u:m (.) drunk in the terraces

MR: 17   *tic*
            tick

JR: 18 [laughs] er (.) rhywun sydd yn er (.) gweiddu (.) trwy gydol
               [laughs] er (.) someone who er (.) shouts (.) all the way through

        19 y gêm
               the match

MR: 20 *tic*
               tick

JR: 21 a rhywun sydd yn er (.) cynrychioli Cymru
               and someone who er (.) represents [supports?] Wales

MR: 22 [gasps] (.) fi yn <u>like</u> (.) <u>hundred percent ideal fan</u> *rygbi* Jamie (.) *agh:*
               [gasps] (.) I am like (.) a hundred percent Jamie's ideal rugby fan (.) agh:

MR: 23 cwestiwn ola Jamie (.) <u>ovs</u> (.) fi ishe trafod priodas ni (.)
               last question Jamie (.) ovs I want to discuss our wedding (.)

        24 bydde ti'n falch o weud bo fi di *sorto* pob dim (.) okay (.)
               you'll be pleased to know that I've sorted everything (.) okay (.)

        25 ma *Adam Jones* (.) yn mynd i fod yn <u>bridesmaid</u> (.)
               Adam Jones (.) is gonna be bridesmaid (.)

        26 fi di ffeindio ffrog a phopeth (.) ma *Warren G* yn mynd i fod
               I've found a dress and everything (.) Warren G is gonna be

        27 yn weinidog (.)
               the minister (.)

        28 yr unig *problem* yw bo ti *jyst* ddim yn ffonio fi (.) *so* <u>like</u>
               the only problem is that you just don't call me (.) so like

        29 beth yw'r <u>deal?</u>
               what's the deal?

JR: 30 *um* (.) colli rhif ti fi'n meddwl
               um (.) lost your number I think

MR: 31 allai *sorto* hynnu mas nawr
               I can sort that out right now

JR: 32 ((*sorry*)) [laughs] ((*sorry*)) [laughs]
               ((sorry)) [laughs] ((sorry)) [laughs]

MR: 33 cai gael sws?
               can I have a kiss?

JR: 34 [stylized kiss] *mwah*
               mwah

The main analytic agenda here is to understand how styling and mediatization (in the sense of televisual mis-en-scène techniques) function in the data, but it seems useful to break this agenda down into three themes—genre, identity, and linguistic/discursive resources. We can ask:

- What media genre is enacted here and how is it managed?
- What identities are performed and how do they interface, relationally?
- What key resources are deployed, including code resources ('Welsh' and 'English')?

In terms of *genre*, we have seen that *Madamrygbi* presents herself as some form of 'rugby interviewer,' and that Jamie has agreed to participate in a 'media interview.' Sports interview discourse is rather formulaic; indeed, Bellin reports that the Welsh rugby stars complain about having to "do interviews" where "the same old issues" come up. *Madamrygbi*'s opening question (line 2) conforms closely to the predicted norm, asking Jamie for a personal assessment of how he is "feeling about being in the semi-final" of the World Cup. Jamie's response falls well within the bounds of a predictable answer—"amazing," [people] "back home … going crazy," "hoping we can do the business" (i.e. win the next match). The second question (line 6) is also norm-conforming, if we know (as *Madamrygbi* and most viewers certainly did) that Jamie had a "bang" on his nose in the previous match, which he confirms and plays down in his answer.

Nonverbal aspects of the performances and camera work in the opening of the interview, however, hint that the 'media interview' frame is not so securely in place. *Madamrygbi*'s line 1 utterance, as its surface pragmatics suggest, is said to camera. She has a beaming smile and points a finger toward Jamie, shifting in her seat. *Madamrygbi* is signaling her awed surprise at conducting this interview, perhaps particularly with Jamie, and her nervousness, and of course these traits fall outside the normative range of a sports interviewer's orientation. Not only Jamie's initial responses but his own bodily demeanor, on the other hand, index a 'straight' and conventional stance. He is responding as the genre predicts he would, except perhaps for his small laugh in line 4.

Madamrygbi's turn over lines 9–10 clearly and radically breaks the genre frame (if we agree that it was generally holding at first). She makes a personalized declaration ("I … want you to know") of her physical attraction to Jamie, that he is "the fittest man on the … planet." Genre norms allow sports interviewers to praise their interviewees but not to express lustful attraction to them. The declaration leaves Jamie with a discursive space where he has to respond to *Madamrygbi*'s accelerated personal compliment in front of the camera. He shows self-control and thanks her, moving on to a mild joke about how, despite his nose injury, he is "not quite there against Mike Tyndall" (an English player with a bent nose), partly because, unlike Tyndall, he still has hair.

The remainder of the episode, which Bellin confirms has been edited post-filming, is organized around two main topics. The first is a sequence where Jamie has to describe his ideal fan (lines 13–22), which *Madamrygbi* sets up to allow her to make another personal declaration, said ('ecstatically') to camera, that she herself meets all his criteria—she serially ticks them off, implying that her list and Jamie's are identical. The second topic is *Madamrygbi's* planned wedding with Jamie, incorporating her accusation (in a shifted key, now mock-aggressive) that Jamie never phones her, for which he apologizes (lines 23–32). The episode closes with *Madamrygbi's* opportunistic request for a kiss, which Jamie laughingly provides, with a visually and linguistically stylized "mwah." So the 'sports interview' genre frame is never reconstructed, even though *Madamrygbi* unconvincingly indicates (at line 23) that she is putting her "last question" at that point. The 'ideal fan' sequence conforms more to a chat-show genre, and the 'wedding' sequence is more like soap opera.

The frame switches and dissonances contribute to the overall impression created that the 'interview,' if that is what it is, is fundamentally inauthentic. *Madamrygbi*, if she is 'an interviewer,' is also inauthentic, both because (in the fictional world) she adopts inconsistent and incoherent stances but also because (viewed against background assumptions of how sports interviewers normatively conduct themselves) she both underperforms (she is incompetent) and overperforms (she transgresses). Beyond that, however, *Madamrygbi's* performance provides ample evidence to TV audiences that she wants us to recognize and judge her inauthenticities. In short, her performance is a complex stylization; she leaves the 'brush strokes' of her artistic performance 'visible,' and she challenges audiences to deal interpretively with this indexical problem. This performed inauthenticity loosens up conventional social meanings. Jamie himself is caught in the uncertain territory between the authentic and the inauthentic. He knows that *Madamrygbi* is a 'comedy' rugby interviewer. And yet, Jamie really *is* a star rugby player, he *is* being asked (one or two) relevant questions about the World Cup (and responding normatively to them), and the episode *is* being broadcast to a Welsh rugby-watching audience.

The *identities and relationships* that conventionally fill out the rugby interview genre are, as we have already seen, playfully supplanted and erratically switched during the episode. *Madamrygbi* styles herself—initially, while 'interview' is still plausibly the genre frame in place—as an interviewer of sorts, but as an incompetent one. (For example, she prominently holds up a cue card, as if she needs to read her questions aloud.) When, as noted earlier, she shifts in her seat, she performs nervousness but also coquettishness, anticipating her "fittest man" declaration, and this is one of the means by which the interview frame is destabilized. Her declaration itself is performed as if it is utterly guileless, styled to betray the unsophisticated and naïve understanding of relationships that *Madamrygbi* brings to her quest for Jamie. Her metric for love is how "fit" (that is, sexually attractive) Jamie is, and she tells him to his face that he is "like the fittest man on the ... planet."

Eirlys Bellin has said (at interview) that she wants to construct *Madamrygbi* sympathetically, and that she is aware that there is a category of young female Welsh rugby fans, for whom the cultural stereotype 'ladette' might be appropriate, among whom the *Madamrygbi* character could 'work.' We are entitled, anyway, to see a dimension of sociocultural critique at work behind the playfulness and planned awkwardness of the *Madamrygbi*/Jamie relational narrative. Might Welsh rugby, for some types of follower, be nothing to do with 'the national game' and its nationalistic 'heart and soul' resonances? Might it rather be, for some, a parade of fit young men? It is particularly interesting that Jamie himself is willing to comply, to an extent, with his 'interviewer's' sexualized approach to him, however inauthentic he knows it to be. He produces good-natured, coherent responses to *Madamrygbi*'s exuberant declarations, including his "thanks" (line 11) for the "fit" compliment. It is Jamie who volunteers (line 16) that an ideal fan would be someone who is "drunk in the terraces." He even plays along with aspects of the "you just don't call me" complaint (lines 28–32). *Madamrygbi* ends the complaint with the mock-aggressive expression "what's the deal?". In speech act terms this interrogative is a demand for an account, but at the same time the utterance shifts their putative relationship onto some sort of commercial basis. Jamie lamely suggests (line 30) that he may have lost her telephone number, and apologizes, although by that point he is dissolving in embarrassed laughter. He may be apologizing, in his real persona, for eventually failing to sustain his fictional role as the object of *Madamrygbi*'s desires, more than he is apologizing to *Madamrygbi*, in his own fictionalized and inauthentic persona, for losing the phone number.

So far, I have made rather few comments about the specific linguistic and discursive resources through which the genre play and identity play is achieved, and I have referred to the data in their translated English version only, even though the textual detail is stylistically crucial to the meanings and effects achieved. *Madamrygbi* has a repertoire of set expressions, linguistic and nonverbal, that function as shortcuts to her persona, because they index her stances and her world view. Some of them are English-sourced expressions, like the word *actual*, which is a very productive resource. There are two examples in Extract 2. The first is in line 1, where she introduces Jamie (to camera) as "yr actual Jamie Roberts." *Madamrygbi*'s sycophancy is often expressed in extreme-case formulations (Pomerantz 1986); in fact she sees the celebrity world in extreme, absolute terms, as if it could not be more attractive, and this is also, therefore, a way of indexing her naïvety. So in line 1, she is introducing us to the rugby star she sees as, we might say, 'the one and only' Jamie Roberts, and the expression "yr actual Jamie Roberts" might have a much more personal relevance (or might have been chosen in order to imply that relevance) for her than it would typically have, for example, as an introductory remark in a TV chat show.

It matters that the phrase "yr actual" is a syncretic blend—a resource that, in conventional etymological terms, blends Welsh and English forms; *yr* is the Welsh definite article, whose /r/ is phonologically conditioned by the following vowel. *Madamrygbi* uses "yr actual" again in her (line 10) declaration, "bydde ti like y fittest man ar yr actual planet," whose complement noun phrase has exclusively English lexis linked by Welsh-only grammatical particles. In fact it is a catch-phrase that she uses regularly across the many interviews she has filmed. There are other resources that work to similar effect, including the (English) abbreviation "ovs" ('obviously') in line 23 (and she often uses it when a point she is making is not at all obvious to others, but implied to be obvious within her own world view). But I suggest there is little relevance in tracing the language origins of individual words and particles to their source languages in this way (as my rough-and-ready coding in the extract does). The better stylistic generalization is that, particu-larly at moments of high emotional involvement, when *Madamrygbi*'s expressive character identity (Bednarek 2011) needs to be most distinctively indexed, she draws from a repertoire of syncretic expressions that neutralize the code distinc-tion between the two languages. We see this again in line 22, when *Madamrygbi* has positively 'ticked off' all of Jamie's attributes for being an ideal rugby fan—they are criteria that she meets in full. She gaspingly says (again to camera) "fi yn like (.) hundred percent ideal fan rygbi Jamie (.) agh:." The 'gasp' (which is my weak coding of a complex semiotic performance of high affect—euphoric facial expression, breathy voice, frantic hand gesturing) is the onset to an (almost) 'silent scream,' which, as mentioned earlier, is one of *Madamrygbi*'s stock meta-expressive resources. My (again inadequate) transcription "agh:" is the extended culmination of the (almost) silent scream, red nail polish being rampantly dis-played by the face-fanning fingers.

We can say that the extract as a whole shows a good deal of code syncretism, even though Jamie's parallel use of English lexis (as noted earlier, I have under-lined these fairly clearly 'English' forms in the transcript) is more like conventional intrasentential code-switching than blending for expressive purposes. This is con-sistent with Jamie being a 'new speaker' of Welsh, who probably doesn't have the relevant Welsh lexis at his disposal. (In fact, his use of "cynrychioli" ['represents'] at line 21 may be an inapprioriate lexical choice.) However, the main point to bear in mind here is that episodes like these are quite flagrantly flouting S4C's Welsh-only principles (cf. the section on *Competing perspectives on bilingual Wales*), and this generalization holds for *Madamrygbi*'s linguistic style in general. This is some-thing that Eirlys Bellin is fully aware of, and she clearly sees some critical value in *Madamrygbi*'s performances in this regard, as Extract 3 shows.

Extract 3: Eirlys Bellin commenting on Madamrygbi's style of Welsh.
> . . . she [*Madamrygbi*] makes it OK to not speak perfectly . . . for young people that's really important (.) so often in school you're told (.) [you] have to mutate [follow grammatical mutation rules] correctly (.) you have to do this and that (.) don't speak English don't speak English

Conclusion: Desacralizing Welsh language and culture?

The cultural impact of *Madamrygbi*'s persona is, of course, not restricted to the one episode I have dealt with, not even to the whole run of celebrity interviews she has filmed over recent years, nor even to the long-running *Jonathan* show itself. We saw earlier how Eirlys Bellin has 'worked up' the *Madamrygbi* character over time, and its prominence on the S4C television channel has allowed it to circulate in several other media. On Twitter, for example, Bellin continues to dialogue with her followers, in posts like the one in Extract 4.

Extract 4: A *Madamrygbi* tweet, February 6, 2015.
    Amser dechrau'r parti #chwegwlad !Pob lwc bois! C'mon Cymru!
    Time 2 start this #6nations party!Good luck boys! Go Wales!
    NON SILENT SCREAM

The first line translates as 'Time to begin the party #six nations! Good luck boys! Come on Wales!,' although the tweet embeds its own translation, and 'non-silent scream' is always voiced in English. (The 'six nations' is the annual international rugby competition involving Wales, Scotland, Ireland, England, France, and Italy.) Bellin has also made appearances, in character, in schools in Wales, aiming to promote bilingualism among learners. As noted earlier, she herself commonly attends rugby matches in character—which is an interesting form of mass-mediated circulation, whether or not they are televised—and there are online images of young female rugby fans attending matches in the visual character of *Madamrygbi*.[14] Bellin says in the interview, "I love taking a fictional character into a real setting . . . I find that very exciting."

Madamrygbi's fictional domains include book publishing: she had published a mock-autobiographical account of her marriage to Jamie in the book *Madamrygbi: Y Briodas* (Bellin 2012). The Welsh-language press has sometimes published critical reactions to her linguistic style, including the comments of one correspondent to the Welsh newspaper *Y Cymro* ('The Welshman'), who had read the 'Wedding' book and charged Bellin with using *iaith erchyll cwbl hurt* ('horrifying, totally absurd language'), and *ffwlbri cableddus* ('blasphemous mockery'). In this particular commentator's view, it seems that Bellin is indeed intruding into the 'sacred' Welsh cultural space which, for some, the Welsh language can still be taken to represent. I am not aware of any parallel objections from Welsh rugby supporters, although it is evident that *Madamrygbi*'s performances do intrude on that 'sacred space' to some extent, too. On the other hand, as the sport has professionalized, players and supporters have already recognized that different forms of commodified reinterpretation are now part of its public face (cf. supporters carrying or wearing plastic and fabric daffodils, mentioned earlier), which we could easily see as forms of secularization.

It seems most significant that Bellin and *Madamrygbi* are *able* to perform syncretic bilingualism on publicly funded Welsh television, at a time when the 'Welsh-only' prescription is apparently still in force. In this context, we have to see Bellin/*Madamrygbi*'s performances as a critical challenge to hegemonic, Welsh-only broadcasting norms—a challenge launched through humor, which is well-appreciated by audiences of the *Jonathan* show, even if it still stirs a degree of public controversy. In fact, the controversy itself could be said to be an important part of the process of sociolinguistic change. As Urban (2001) has argued, in his theorizing of cultural change and of 'how culture moves through the world', change can only be said to have happened when it is *evaluated* to have changed, and when meta-level accounts of culture and change are in circulation. The same perspective in relation to language and society would be that sociolinguistic change has to incorporate, and has to be theorized as incorporating, metalinguistic and metadiscursive processes.

This idea opens up possible lines of critical insight into the roles of authenticity and inauthenticity in sociocultural change also. It would be unconvincing to suggest that Madamrygbi's demonstrable inauthenticities—her stylized and fractured representations of the rugby interviewer, her 'phoney' relational narrative with Jamie Roberts, or her 'improper' Welsh—are reasons why she cannot play a part in meaningful social and sociolinguistic change. It is more convincing, I believe, to argue the converse. I suggested at the outset that 'tradition' in Wales, at least in respect of language and rugby, has been founded on presumed authenticities—language and rugby as two poles of authentic cultural Welshness. Why that should have been the case is entirely understandable, in the frames of reference that were mainly in sight in the pre-globalization era. Minoritized Welsh language and culture needed to cling on to historical anchoring points and essentialisms, and to wrap them up in authenticating discourses. However, more reflexive times are making it less feasible to continue to construct tradition this way.

Mediatization increasingly opens up wider horizons on linguistic and cultural diversity, and it relativizes our perceptions of cultural categories and boundaries. We could try the generalization that, whereas the traditional role of media was to contain, consolidate, center, and standardize cultural 'content,' this role has flipped to being one of multiplying, comparing, and critiquing it. Whereas stylizing representations of culture, under traditional ideological regimes in earlier cultural conditions, was troublesome and could even be considered disloyal, 'straight' representations have nowadays come to seem dull, dated, and indeed romanticizing. There is clearly still a place for romanticizing discourses and accounts, in the name of heritage mediation, but this cannot be the dominant representational frame. If this is right, then *in*authenticity assumes new metacultural value, if only the value of working outside traditional frames. In this light, in relation to Wales, *Madamrygbi* seems to be a highly contemporary figure.

Notes

1. I am grateful to my two co-editors of this book for their incisive comments on an earlier version of this chapter, as well as to Sari Pietikäinen, Helen Kelly-Holmes, and Alexandra Jaffe for their many helpful many discussions of this case study in connection with a different book project. Remaining deficiencies are of course my own.

2. See http://gov.wales/topics/welshlanguage/promoting/grants/technology-and-digital-media/?lang=en. This and other online sources listed in this chapter were last accessed on August 6, 2016.

3. 'One nation one language' could of course only apply, at the level of practical implementation, in very selective domains in Wales, such as on S4C, as an ideologically constituted Welsh-only space. Majority-language (English) usage, and broadcasting, dominate overall.

4. Pietikäinen et al. (2016) examine the impacts of globalization on Sámi, Corsican, Irish, and Welsh languages and language-related practices.

5. See the policy documents *Iaith Pawb* 'Everyone's language' (Report 2008-9) and *Iaith Fyw, Iaith Byw* 'A Living Language, a Language for Life' (2011), both available at the National Assembly for Wales website (Wales.gov.uk/docs/).

6. *Canllawiau Iaith* 'Language Guidelines' S4C (2008) are available at www.s4c.co.uk/production/downloads/guidelines/Canllawiau.

7. Occasional drama series also contain small elements of code-switched dialogue.

8. In Welsh, for broadcast on S4C, the series is titled *Y Gwyll*; in English, for broadcast on BBC, it is titled *Hinterland*.

9. For further background see http://www.eirlysbellin.com/; Twitter @madamrygbi. I am particularly grateful to Eirlys Bellin for supporting this project and for providing her own personal insights into how she has created and developed the *Madamrygbi* persona. I am also grateful to Angharad Hodgson for her assistance in profiling *Madamrygbi* on the basis of other data, including Eirlys Bellin's live performances in a range of venues.

10. See http://s4c.co.uk/adloniant/e_jonathan.shtml.

11. The expression *Heart and Soul* features in the title of this book, which (like its sequels) is a serious academic analysis of the cultural prominence of rugby in Wales. The book's cover features a close-up image of Jonathan Davies in his playing days.

12. My analysis of that particular episode appears in Chapter 5 of Pietikäinen et al. (2016). These and other episodes are available via *Madamrygbi*'s YouTube channel (www.youtube.com/user/madamrygbi).

13. At https://www.youtube.com/watch?v=P-wGDFq19NU.

14. Madamrygbi's Twitter account is a good source of examples of this sort, including images of young fans performing the 'silent scream,' as Bellin herself does on the cover of her fictional autobiography—see the next paragraph in the main text.

References

Archer, Margaret. 2012. *The Reflexive Imperative in Late Modernity*. Cambridge: Cambridge University Press.

Beck, Ulrich, Anthony Giddens and Scott Lash. 1994. *Reflexive Modernisation: Politics, Tradition and Aesthetics in the Modern Social Order*. Cambridge: Polity Press.

Bednarek, Monika. 2011. Expressivity and televisual characterization. *Language & Literature* 21, 3: 3–21.

Bellin, Eirlys. 2012. *Madamrygbi: Y briodas* [*Madamrygbi: The Wedding*]. Talybont: Y Lolfa.

Coupland, Nikolas. 2009. Dialects, standards and social change. In Marie Maegaard, Frans Gregersen, Pia Quist and J. Normann Jørgensen (eds.) *Language Attitudes, Standardization and Language Change*. Oslo: Novus. 27–50.

Coupland, Nikolas. 2012. Bilingualism on display: The framing of Welsh and English in Welsh public spaces. *Language in Society* 41: 1–27.

Coupland, Nikolas. 2014a. Language, society and authenticity: Themes and perspectives. In Véronique Lacoste, Jakob Leimgruber and Thiemo Breyer (eds.) *Indexing Authenticity: Sociolinguistic Perspectives*. Berlin: De Gruyter. 14–39.

Coupland, Nikolas. 2014b. Sociolinguistic change, vernacularization and broadcast British media. In Jannis Androutsopoulos (ed.) *Mediatization and Sociolinguistic Change*. Berlin: De Gruyter. 67–96.

Coupland, Nikolas and Helen Kelly-Holmes. In press. Making and marketing in the bilingual periphery: Materialization as metacultural transformation. In Jillian Cavanaugh and Shalini Shankar (eds.) *Language and Materiality*. Cambridge: Cambridge University Press.

Duchêne, Alexandre and Monica Heller (eds.). 2007. *Discourses of Endangerment: Ideology and Interest in Defence of Languages*. London: Continuum.

Duchêne, Alexandre and Monica Heller. 2012. *Language in Late Capitalism: Pride and Profit*. London: Routledge.

Elias, Norbert and Eric Dunning. 1986. *Quest for Excitement: Sport and Leisure in the Civilizing Process*. Oxford: Basil Blackwell.

Gal, Susan and Judith Irvine. 1995. The boundaries of languages and disciplines: How ideologies construct difference. *Social Research* 62: 967–1001.

Heller, Monica. 2008. Language and the nation-state: Challenges to sociolinguistic theory and practice. *Journal of Sociolinguistics* 12: 504–524.

Kelly-Holmes, Helen. 2012. Multilingualism and the media. In Marilyn Martin-Jones, Adrian Blackledge and Angela Creese (eds.) *Routledge Handbook of Multilingualism*. London and New York: Routledge. 333–346.

Labov, William. 2001. *Principles of Linguistic Change: Social Factors*. Malden, MA and Oxford: Blackwell Publishers.

Landry, Rodrigue and Réal Allard. 1994a. Diglossia, ethnolinguistic vitality, and language behaviour. *International Journal of the Sociology of Language* 108: 15–42.

Landry, Rodrigue and Réal Allard. 1994b. Ethnolinguistic vitality: A viable construct. *International Journal of the Sociology of Language* 108: 117–144.

Pietikäinen, Sari, Helen Kelly-Holmes, Alexandra Jaffe and Nikolas Coupland. 2016. *Sociolinguistics from the Periphery: Small Languages in New Circumstances*. Cambridge: Cambridge University Press.

Pomerantz, Anita. 1986. Extreme case formulations: A way of legitimizing claims. *Human Studies* 9: 219–229.

Richards, Huw, Peter Stead and Gareth Williams (eds.). 1998. *Heart and Soul: The Character of Welsh Rugby*. Cardiff: University of Wales Press.

Urban, Greg. 2001. *Metaculture: How Culture Moves Through the World*. Minneapolis: University of Minnesota Press.

Urciuoli, Bonnie. 1995. Language and borders. *Annual Review of Anthropology* 24: 525–546.

PART II

The Business of Style

THE STYLE OF BUSINESS

5

Brand styling, enregisterment, and change: The case of *C'est Cidre*

Helen Kelly-Holmes

Companies and brands often exploit the indexical values of specific linguistic resources as part of the styling of a brand or product. The objective is to link the product or brand to the place associated with the particular language used and, simultaneously, to exploit associated meanings in relation to that particular place. Concepts such as 'impersonal bilingualism' (Haarmann 1989), 'language display' (Eastman & Stein 1993; Hornikx, van Meurs & Hof 2013), and 'linguistic fetish' (Kelly-Holmes 2005, 2014) have been used to describe this phenomenon and to draw attention to two key aspects of such advertising strategies: (1) the linguistic styling involved is generally not a reflection of everyday bi- and multilingualism in the particular sociolinguistic context[1] and (2) the symbolic functioning of the linguistic styling takes precedence over any referential communicative function. Thus, we typically find a slogan or chunk used for 'decorative' effect with important information being conveyed in the dominant domestic language.[2]

Marketing and advertising texts are important sites for signaling and also contributing to sociolinguistic change (see Cook 2001). For example, advertising language can maintain, challenge, or create new linguistic norms as well as document usage and practices. Linguistic fetish and styling in advertisements both rely on and contribute to enregisterment, the process by which "sets of linguistic choices can come to be understood as varieties" (Johnstone 2011: 660) and become means of indexing membership of particular class, regional, age, and similar categories (Agha 2003, 2007; Silverstein 2003). Enregisterment is a necessary condition for commodification (Johnstone 2009), and for the use of such styles in advertising there needs to be some existing enregisterment of that style. However, the use of the style in advertising also contributes to further enregisterment. We can see that media texts, including advertising, are a key site for enregisterment of this type of linguistic styling and a place where we can find evidence of change. As

Style, Mediation, and Change. Edited by Janus Mortensen, Nikolas Coupland, and Jacob Thøgersen *manipulate the ads*

#

Androutsopoulos (2014) points out, mediatized circulation is an important aspect of the enregisterment process because it allows for very large scale responses to one particular text (cf. Agha 2003: 269).

In this chapter, I would like to explore one particular example of brand styling which both relies on and contributes to the enregisterment of 'fake French' and the French linguistic fetish in advertising. The case studied is an advertisement for European lager brand, *Stella Artois*'s latest product, a cider, and the ad's posting and discussion on YouTube. I would like to propose that the brand is in fact making use of a metaparodic frame, in Coupland's (2012) terms, simultaneously asserting and parodying its stylized or 'fake' French speaking, and that the consumer needs to co-construct this metaparody. Much contemporary marketing discourse is premised on the co-creation of value between a producer and an active rather than a passive consumer. Consumers are expected to co-create value in a whole range of ways, value being understood here as not "only the functional and economic value of goods and services, but also the consumer's interpretation of consumption objects, including products, brands, and services" (Pongsakornrungsilp and Schroeder 2011: 305). They may do this, for example, by using products for identity work, forming networks around products, giving feedback on products and suggestions for new products, and carrying on 'did-you-see?' conversations about ads (see Brodie et al. 2013; Sicilia and Palazón 2008). Some of this co-creation also involves sharing ads, discussing ads, and modifying them. Both the *Stella Artois* advertisement itself and responses to its posting on YouTube show how linguistic styling in advertising as well as audience responses to it and consumer co-constructions contribute to sociolinguistic change through enregisterment and, more importantly, highlights how enregisterment "unfolds by means of speech chains that link mediatized representations to mediated responses" (Androutsopoulos 2014: 34; see also Bednarek, Chapter 6, this volume).

Styling *Stella Artois*

Stella Artois, as stated above, is a well-known brand of lager across Europe. Although the brand's origins are in the Belgian city of Leuven, it is owned by one of the largest international brewery companies, *AB InBeV Corporation*, whose portfolio includes beer brands such as *Budweiser* (American) and *Beck's* (German). Despite complicated ownership structures in the contemporary market, country of origin remains a key marketing tool, with transnational or global ownership by conglomerates and holding companies often hidden from view or, at least, not accentuated in advertising that seeks to associate brands with particular places (cf. Kelly-Holmes 2005, for a discussion of country of origin from a marketing perspective, and cf. Jaffe and Nebenzahl 1999; Usunier 2006). While brewing continues in the historic site of origin, Leuven in Flanders, Belgium, the beer is also brewed in the United Kingdom, other parts of Europe, Australia, and Brazil.

The advertisement in question was designed by a UK-based advertising agency, *Mother*, to coincide with the launch of the new *Stella Artois*-branded product, a cider targeted directly at the UK market. The advertisement is recognizable as high-end in terms of a number of factors such as production values, design detail, and length. The brand name for the new cider, '*cidre*,' makes use of the French word for cider, although English is the de facto language of the target audience in the United Kingdom. The Flemish/Dutch word, which would be *cider*, a homograph but not a homophone of the English word, is also not used. The ad features the fictional president, *Le Président* (Figure 5.1a), marching hurriedly to the television studio with his attentive entourage to make an urgent statement, "*une annonce importante*" (Figure 5.1b), in relation to the difference between cider and *cidre*, apparently in response to rumors that *Stella Artois* is launching a new cider rather than a new *cidre* (see Extract 1 for a full transcript).

The language used is of course just one part of the styling of the brand. Other aspects include the music, set, costumes, and visual styling, as well as movement and gesture. The president and all the participants are dressed in 1960s costumes, and the studio is a retro set. There is no music in the first, business-like part of the ad (lines 1–5 of Extract 1). Then, in the middle of line 5, to signal a mellowing of mood, jazz musicians start to play (visible in the background, see Figure 5.1c), which seems incongruous for an important announcement. A number of key sounds also make up part of the soundtrack, for example marching boots in the introduction and the sound of the glass being filled up as the drink is poured (line 10). The set and staging use a number of different devices: the 1960s character is reminiscent of the early days of television with fairly minute attention to detail in creating congruence between the set and the costumes; this congruence and the faux seriousness of the broadcast are threatened by the rather amateur prop of an apple tree (Figure 5.1c)

FIGURE 5.1 Screenshots from the *C'est Cidre* advertisement. Reproduced from www.vimeo.com/ 26392571 under 'fair use' standards.

and a pull-down board (Figure 5.1d) which poke fun at this attempt, and the attention to detail in terms of costume and setting add to the humor of the ad. In terms of movement and gesture, the president is seen as a man of action in the first half of the ad, marching decisively to the studio for the announcement, sitting down, and beginning. There is then less movement, reflected by more laid-back music, and the frantic atmosphere gives way to a slower pace as he describes the features of the product. The frantic pace returns somewhat at the end with the clumsy use of the pull-down (teaching) board to demonstrate the product.

The aim of the ad ostensibly is to emphasize the French name of the product to invoke its origin as a product from "the continent" (line 8), which is understood as "from mainland Europe" for the UK audience, and differentiating it from cider, which is made in the United Kingdom. Extract 1 is a transcript of the advertisement with French words marked in italics (further conventions are explained at the end of the chapter under *Transcription conventions*). *Le Président* (LP in Extract 1) uses a stylized and hyperbolic French accent throughout together with a fluent, poetic style.

Extract 1: Transcript of the *C'est Cidre* advertisement[3]

The president is walking to the television studio, surrounded by handlers. We hear the marching click of their shoes. One female handler brushes off his jacket as he enters the studio. All are dressed in 1960s clothing.

1　A:　*une annonce importante de Stella Artois* (. . .)
　　　　{an important announcement from Stella Artois}
　　　　((shot of president shuffling papers on desk; camera moves to the president, seems to be caught unawares))

2　LP:　good evening *mesdames et messieurs* (.)
　　　　　　　　{ladies and gentlemen}
　　　　((looking directly at the camera, maintains eye contact with the audience throughout))

3　　　　it has come to my attention that >there is word on the
4　　　　street that< (.) >*Stella Artois*< is about to launch a *mocking themselves*
5　　　　c̲ider (. .) no >↓nononono< (. .)
　　　　((four screens display the same shot of the president))

6　　　　>*Stella Artois*< is launching a *cid̲re* (.) not c̲ider (.)
　　　　　　　　((jazz band starts to play))

7　　　　*cid̲re* for gentlemen and woman who can appreciate a
8　　　　sophisticated drink (.) made with apples on the continent
9　　　　which then cross the sea and take the compliment of being
10　　　poured over ice (.) please (. . .) into something I like
　　　　((raises glass expectantly, filled from a unseen source))

11   to call a chalice (.) so next time you hear such a

12   fallacy *mon ami* recall this conversation between you and
                {my friend}

13   me or if there are too many words, just remember the

14   refreshing (. .) <u>re</u>, and not <u>er</u> (. .) *c'est cid<u>re</u>* (. .) not
                                {it's *cidre*}
        ((moves out from behind the news desk; pours over ice, takes a
        drink; screen drops down))

15   <u>ci</u>der (.) from >*Stella Artois*< (.) >*bonsoir*<
                                {good evening}

Stylization can be understood as the deliberate imitating or voicing of another in a hyperbolized manner (see Coupland 2007). In the *C'est Cidre* ad, as already noted, the stylization is of fake French or the French linguistic fetish. It is interesting that the impression that I got when listening to the ad was contradicted when I carried out the transcription, since, as we can see, there are very few token words in French, roughly 15 out of a total of 126. The announcer (A in the transcript) speaks completely in French (line 1), but the president speaks in English with only a small number of words and phrases in French highlighted in italics (lines 2, 6, 7, 12, 14, 15). As Cook (2001: 74) points out, advertising "carries a heavy proportion of its meaning paralinguistically," and we can see here how the stylization of the French speaker is largely achieved by the use of the hyperbolized accent. The small number of French words would be easily understandable to the viewer in the United Kingdom from either secondary schooling in French—the predominant first foreign language taught in that country at secondary school level—and, I would argue, also from the use and enregisterment of French-accented English and fake French. The latter is enregistered through mediatized, stylized performances, involving a mixture of a hyperbolized French-accented English with token French words, which is well established and enregistered as a stable variety for media audiences in the United Kingdom and other countries (cf. García Vizcaíno 2011; Hornikx, van Meurs and Starren 2007; Kelly-Holmes 2000, 2005).

In the *C'est Cidre* ad there is an 'overshoot' (Bell and Gibson 2011) or hyperbolization in terms of the accent, which affects almost every word. It is important to point out that while this is a hyperbolization in relation to French-accented English, it is perfectly in line with mediatized, stylized fake French speaking. The main linguistic feature is the president's emphasis on the uvular /r/, which is a classic index of French speaking for Anglophones, and which distinguishes *cidre* from cider in lines 6 and 14. The print advertising in the campaign also reproduced this by printing the name as 'cid<u>re</u>', with underlining for emphasis. In this, the ad's ". . . metapragmatic work that focuses on the form of words as much as on their meaning objectifies these linguistic forms in ways that iconize or rhematize them and allow them to gather value, articulate social relations, and potentially circulate more widely than originally intended" (Shankar and Cavanaugh 2012: 361).

Conversely, we can say that, for this degree of hyperbolization in the accent, we would expect many errors in proficiency and accuracy (syntactical, lexical, and grammatical), and in general fluency of expression. However, the president talks fluently (there are no repairs), is able to alter his pace and pitch for stylistic effect (lines 4, 5, 6, 15), displays insider knowledge of British discursive culture in terms of his use of "the continent" (line 8) and the idiom "word on the street" (lines 3–4), and uses language for rhythmic and prosodic effect (cf. Cook 2001 in relation to this feature of advertising). The president is generally accurate in his lexis, grammar, and syntax, although some of his phrasings and lexical choices are somewhat idiosyncratic (lines 9–10, lines 12–13), but not out of keeping with his styling as a French speaker of English for acculturated media audiences in the United Kingdom. Thus, when he uses French, it is not because he is lacking an English word but as part of his personal style ("mesdames et messieurs" in line 2; "mon ami" in line 12; "bonsoir" in line 14). As Androutsopoulos (2007) points out in relation to the movie *Spanglish*, the combination of hyperbolized accent and fluency is much more common in stylized media performances and portrayals of bilinguals than any attempt to represent authentic code-switching and mixing practices.

The purpose of these linguistic and paralinguistic choices (the tokenistic but strategic use of French coupled with the hyperbolized French accent, pacing, pitch, etc.) appears to be to index or reference particular social meanings for the audience, in this case a notional French speaker. The French linguistic fetish also references higher-order indexicalities (Silverstein 2003; cf. Johnstone 2009, 2011)—not just a notional French speaker of English, then, but also French people in general and the positive and negative associations of French culture and French products. Beyond this, it also indexes, I would argue, a notional European foreignness and non-Britishness in the case of the specific target audience for the ad. This is explicitly referenced by the president in line 7 of the text, where he mentions the production of *cidre* on the continent. The French speaking is as much about emphasizing the 'non-Britishness' of the brand as marking its 'Frenchness.'

Brand styling as a resource for audience creativity and enregisterment

The *C'est Cidre* advertisement was posted to the video-sharing website YouTube, which enables uploading, viewing, sharing, and discussion of videos, in July 2011. YouTube is free to view and supported by paid advertising, but in order to upload or comment on content, (free) membership is required. There is some regulation and moderation of content by YouTube in relation to inappropriate postings. The site is localized geographically, and to a certain extent linguistically; for example, the site offers 61 language versions and 74 country options as top-level domains. Posting an advertisement to YouTube as a regular content item involves a remediation (Bolter and Grusin 2000; see also Bednarek, Chapter 6, this volume) of it—it is mediated again, but in a different way. The contemporary context of digital and social media enables multiple remediations and it is often not possible to point to the first mediation of a particular text. Remediation brings the potential for different audiences, repeated viewings of texts which were traditionally designed to be one-offs or viewed only occasionally, and the potential lengthening of the lifespan of the ad. The genre of the ad thus changes as a result of this remediation from monologic to peer-to-peer. The YouTube posting enables many-to-many and one-to-one communications to occur, in contrast to the one-to-many communication of television advertising.

The YouTube posting had 46,479 views after it was uploaded in July 2011 by *anabarlin*[4], a UK-based user, according to their profile, and this is their only upload. Postings to YouTube must be captioned, and the captioning is an important aspect of the re-entextualization (Bauman and Briggs 1990) of the ad:

Extract 2

Le President comes on TV to make an important announcement. *Stella Artois* is not launching a cider. Stella Artois is launching a ciDRE.

Videos are also categorized; in this case, the categorization is, surprisingly, 'News and Politics.' Up to the point when the video was taken down (May 2014), it had received 85 comments, 124 likes, and 13 dislikes. There were 64 contributors, and almost all (56) contributed only once. Using Herring's (2004) criteria for evaluating online communities, the levels of interaction, and so on, are low, and we can see this as a fleeting type of community.

We can see the ad and its posting and discussion on YouTube as an example of the phenomenon Androutsopolous identifies in terms of the way in which mass media "make metapragmatic typifications of registers available to large audiences for recontextualizations and response" (2014: 32). Taking their cues from the 'metapragmatic typifications' found in the ad, contributors use a variety of resources provided or hinted at by the ad and by their fellow posters to respond to and debate the ad, the main topic being the fake French styling. For example, they engage in play or crossing (Rampton 1995; see also Hill 1999 regarding junk Spanish), as in the two examples that follow (Extracts 3 and 4), where the posters pick up on the hyperbolization of accent in the ad and the perceived fakeness and recreate the phonetic features employed:

Extract 3

zis adveeertt gitttss oonn myyy teeeettz—ooo hh ooo hh oooo hh ooooohhhh—ahh ahh ahhh ahh—i ve found theee remmmote—gooooooodbyyyhheee !!!! stuuuuppeeeedd !!!!!

Extract 4

Why, I'ad no idea zat une chalice of ze soi-disant 'cidre' would time-travelle you back to ze sizteez

The top comment on the site, in terms of number of likes received, was "What a wankre;" the poster changes the well-known pejorative British slang term *wanker* to *wankre*, which involves deliberately playing with the ad's emphasis on the uvular /r/. We can see the play here as a as an example of how "mediatized representations of language in society prompt subsequent mediatized representations and mediated responses in which audiences creatively recontextualize media fragments by exemplary speakers into their own performances" (Androutsopoulos 2014: 36). This type of play with the uvular /r/ is also practiced by other posters, as in the next example which also subverts another pejorative British slang term *tosser*:

Extract 5

So would that make him a wankre, tossre maybe? (Wolfy101)

In Extract 6, we see another type of language play. The contributor originally posted in English, complaining about *Stella*'s inconsistency in terms of using French:

Extract 6

What bugs me about these Stella Artois adverts is that this cidre (sorry... cidre) carps on abouts its "Europeaness" by maintaining that it is to be pronounced in the French style, yet the earlier Stella Artois 4 adverts were called *Stella Artois* 'Four' by the voice-over. Sure it should have been called *Stella Artois* Quatre? (TheMicksterdee)

They then come back and post in French, claiming to have run their original comment through Google Translate for fun and urging fellow contributors to back-translate it in order to understand it:

Extract 7

Une publicité du double standard. Pourquoi Stella Artis souligner que ses cidre est le Français quand il appelle un certain lager Stella Artois Four. Run it through Google Translate. That's how I got it in French! LOL (TheMicksterdee)

One of the main themes running through the discussion is the use of fake French for styling a brand that is in fact considered Flemish. Some of the posts seek to uncover *Stella Artois*'s advertising strategy of using the French linguistic fetish in preference to using Flemish, the brand's 'real 'or 'true' language of origin, which is not sufficiently enregistered in the same way for UK audiences:

Extract 8

the only reason why Stella Artois does NOT put cider on their bottles is because it is cider in Flemish and it would never sell

Extract 9

In Flemish it is CIDER!!! Who are these idiots? Stella Artois is Flemish. It is from Leuven NOT Louvain

Extract 10

> Stella is from Flanders where people speak Dutch not French. Ceci n'est pas un representation correcte.

Extract 11

> its not bloody cidre its cider. Stella Artois is not bloody french its flemish. Stella Artois stop with your identity crisis

Rather than experiencing an identity crisis, it seems more likely that *Stella Artois*'s strategy of styling itself through fake French could be understood as an example of 'metaparodic framing' (Coupland 2012). Metaparody is "a multiply voiced reference that incorporates parodying one's own role as a parodist" (2012: 18), and it can be seen as a particularly reflexive form of self-parody. The brand's language play, display, and deliberate disregarding of language-territory equivalences can be seen as an invitation to consumers to play and display, and disregard the language-territory equivalences made in 'straight' country-of-origin messages. In the process they co-construct the metaparody and by extension value for the brand. And, we can see recognition of this metaparodic framing by some of the posters. For example, in response to Extract 11, where the identity crisis of the brand is proposed, one poster writes:

Extract 12

> This attempt to be French does make for some remarkably interesting commercials. Realizing the irony makes them, in a way, better too.

This is acknowledged by other posters also:

Extract 13

> I don't know what's worse - the fact that they can market a beverage based on an alternative pronunciation, or the fact that it's working. I really want a cidre now.

Extract 14

> L'avertissment C'est cool, n'est pas?

In its *C'est Cidre* campaign, *Stella Artois* is styling itself using fake French, and also parodying this styling. It is using the French linguistic fetish as a legitimate resource for marketing a Belgian (Flemish) product, while simultaneously making a joke about this usage. The brand's performance of French not only indexes the notional French speaker and relevant associations but also works as a code for authenticating foreignness/distinction for the UK audience. It is both exploiting and further reinforcing higher-order indexicalities and at the same time making a joke about this exploitation. And, while the brand is challenging and parodying the primacy of territoriality by constructing indexical credibility for itself as a French 'speaker,' it is also simultaneously exploiting this and reinforcing territoriality and established categorizations of region and language.

Discussion

Stylized performances reference "sociocultural groups whose varieties are enregistered with local or international cachet" (Bell and Gibson 2011: 562), and the use of the French linguistic fetish by *Stella Artois* can be seen as an example of this. Audience, as Bell and Gibson remind us, is crucial in terms of such performances, since the linguistic forms used must be able "to index those forms' performed histories, resonances shared between performer and audience" (2011: 270). However, this explanation does not cover the creativity and parody involved either in the original advertisement or in the audience responses to it. This is not a clear case of a register or variety which is linked to a local dialect or variety. Instead, the French linguistic fetish based on fake French is already a stylized resource, based on the target audience's and the brand's perception of what a French speaker stereotypically sounds like and how French speakers are represented in media and marketing discourses. Thus, the contributions to the YouTube discussion can be seen as stylized performances in Coupland's (2007) terms, which are not straightforward selections from a repertoire but which involve strategic and context-specific play with indexicalities. Given the contemporary levels of mediatization, "the proliferation of media communication in all areas of social life" (Androutsopoulos 2014: 10), media are key sites for establishing, maintaining, and challenging indexicalities of this kind rather than simply representing them. It can be argued that the French linguistic fetish and its indexicalization are relatively stable both for the UK audience and to a certain extent globally, and that it has been "inscribed" (Bauman and Briggs 1990) in the sociolinguistic culture through the use of mediatized fake French in a whole range of television programs and films and French linguistic fetish in advertising (Kelly-Holmes 2000, 2005).

We can thus see how a process of enregisterment is at work here. It enables performances of fake French and reinforces the indexicalization of these linguistic choices thereby creating conditions for brands and companies to both exploit and parody in the future. Not surprisingly, stylized performances are often designed to draw the audience's attention to existing indexicalities, and can also contribute to their maintenance as well as the creation of new ones, media being a set of key sites where indexicalities are learned, outside the immediate physical and geographic environment. They rely for their success on the audience making the necessary connections and having the necessary cultural knowledge to do so, as outlined earlier. Discussions about the advertisement on YouTube show evidence of the changing enregisterment of stylized French-speaking. However, there is also more at work here than simply the creation of norms, and we can see evidence of something beyond the use of enregistered styles too. First, we can see how styles can be enregistered in different keys—so there is enregistered 'French-accented English,' which has to do with how foreign accents of English index foreignness in both positive and negative ways for a British public, but then there is also enregistered 'fake French' and metaparodic French-accented English, which is utilized as a linguistic styling device both by the advertiser and by the contributors to the YouTube site. So we can see how both the advertisement itself, with its metaparodic and knowing stance, and the responses to it, are not just using an existing, enregistered style for a predictable purpose but are also complicating and even destabilizing this enregisterment (mocking it even in the case of the advertisement) and adapting it for use, depending on who the joke is actually on or about. In the process, of course, all these texts are adding layers to the enregistered meanings of the linguistic resources of 'French-accented English' and 'fake/parodic French-accented English.'

The *C'est Cidre* ad, its mediation and remediation, viewing and repeated viewing, sharing, liking and disliking, and discussion on YouTube, are also part of an ongoing, changing dialogue about French-European relations and otherness in the target culture, the United Kingdom in this case, as well as being part (synchronically and diachronically) of the intertextuality of advertising, TV, and other performances of French speaking—fake and straight—for this particular audience. Indexicalities, such as those at work here, are particular to sociolinguistic cultures, although as a result of growing globalization of media and branding, some are designed to have resonance among an international and often global audience (cf. Kelly-Holmes 2010 regarding McDonald's use of linguistic indexicalities in a global advertising campaign).

Finally, as we can see from the example of *C'est Cidre*, linguistic styling, and also parodic linguistic styling, carry both opportunities and risks for a brand, particularly when we look at the role of consumers in co-constructing value for the product and meaning for the ad and the brand. While I have argued that the stylized performance and the use of fake French in the ad are framed metaparodically, it is important to note, as the range of contributions on YouTube evidences, that not everyone would appear to 'get the joke.' There is considerable work required on the part of the consumer in co-creating value for the brand and the advertisement. Stylized performances such as the *C'est Cidre* ad seek an acculturated audience (Coupland 2007), who know the genre, understand the intertextual links and indexicalities, and get the joke—this is all a lot of work for the target audience, and, as is clear from the discussion on YouTube, this is far from a straightforward process. Johnstone points out that it is important to consider other hearers/viewers, not just the acculturated audience, and she argues that "focusing on the multiple interpretative schemata brought to bear by actual audience members" enables us to get a glimpse into "how performance can be implicated in cultural and linguistic change" (2011: 659). The *Stella Artois* ad, its remediation to YouTube, and its discussion there offer us one such glimpse.

Transcription conventions

<u>emphasis</u>
((non-verbal))
(.) (. .) (. . .)—pauses of increasing length
< > increase in pace; >< decrease in pace
French words
{qwerty} translation of French words

Adapted from: http://homepages.lboro.ac.uk/~ssca1/sitemenu.htm
© c.antaki@Lboro.ac.uk.

Notes

1. It should be noted that these concepts have been used to explore bi- and multilingual advertising to bilinguals (e.g. Santello 2015), and advertising in complex multilingual situations involving minority languages (e.g. Coupland 2012; Coupland and Kelly-Holmes in press), English as a second language (e.g. Bhatia 2001, 2007), and accent (e.g. O'Sullivan 2013).

2. See e.g. Alm (2003) on English in advertising in Ecuador; García Vizcaíno (2011) in relation to the use of English, French, and Italian in Spanish airline Vueling's advertising; Gerritsen et al. (2000) on English in Dutch commercials; Griffin (1997) on English in advertising in Poland; Hornikx, Van Meurs & Starren (2007) for a study of French, German and Spanish in Dutch advertising; Kasanga (2010) on the use of English in advertising in DR Congo; Piller (2001) regarding multilingualism in German advertising; Santello (2015) on the use of Italian in Australian advertising.

3. The transcript is based on a video that was posted on YouTube. This particular posting is no longer available, but the video is at present available on a number of other sites, including http://vimeo.com/26392571 (last accessed August 22, 2016).

4. As the forum is in the public domain and a password is not needed to view the discussion, I have used the original posters' names as given on the site. This particular posting of the advertisement and discussion are no longer available on YouTube.

References

Agha, Asif. 2003. The social life of a cultural value. *Language & Communication* 23: 231–273.

Agha, Asif. 2007. *Language and Social Relations*. Cambridge: Cambridge University Press.

Alm, Cecilia Ovesdottor. 2003. English in the Ecuadorian commercial context. *World Englishes* 22, 2: 143–158.

Androutsopoulos, Jannis. 2007. Bilingualism in the mass media and on the internet. In Monica Heller (ed.) *Bilingualism: A Social Approach*. Houndmills: Palgrave Macmillan. 207–230.

Androutsopoulos, Jannis. 2014. Mediatization and sociolinguistic change: Key concepts, research traditions, open issues. In Jannis Androutsopoulos (ed.) *Mediatization and Sociolinguistic Change*. Berlin: De Gruyter. 3–48.

Bauman, Richard and Charles L. Briggs. 1990. Poetics and performance as critical perspectives on language and social life. *Annual Review of Anthropology* 19: 59–88.

Bell, Allan and Andy Gibson 2011. Staging language: An introduction to the sociolinguistics of performance. *Journal of Sociolinguistics* 15, 5: 555–572.

Bhatia, T. K. 2001. Language mixing in global advertising. In Edwin Thumboo (ed.) *The Three Circles of English*. Singapore: UniPress. 195–215.

Bhatia, Tej K. 2007. *Advertising and Marketing in Rural India*. New Delhi: Palgrave MacMillan India.

Bolter, Jay. D. and Richard Grusin. 2000. *Remediation: Understanding New Media*. Cambridge, MA: MIT Press.

Brodie, Roderick J., Ana Ilic, Biljana Juric and Linda Hollebeek. 2013. Consumer engagement in a virtual brand community: An exploratory analysis. *Journal of Business Research* 66, 1: 105–114.

Cook, Guy. 2001. *The Discourse of Advertising* (2nd ed.). London: Routledge.

Coupland, Nikolas. 2007. *Style: Language Variation and Identity.* Cambridge: Cambridge University Press.

Coupland, Nikolas. 2012. Bilingualism on display: The framing of Welsh and English in Welsh public space. *Language in Society* 41: 1–27.

Coupland, Nikolas and Helen Kelly-Holmes. In press. Making and marketing in the bilingual periphery: Materialization as meta-cultural transformation. In Jillian Cavanaugh and Shalini Shankar (eds.) *Language and Materiality.* Cambridge: Cambridge University Press.

Eastman, Carol M., and Roberta F. Stein. 1993. Language display: Authenticating claims to social identity. *Journal of Multilingual and Multicultural Development* 14, 3: 187–202.

García Vizcaíno, María José. 2011. Code-breaking/code-making: A new language approach in advertising. *Journal of Pragmatics* 43, 8: 2095–2109.

Gerritsen, Marinel, Hubert Korzilius, Frank van Meurs and Inge Gijsbers. 2000. English in Dutch commercials: Not understood and not appreciated. *Journal of Advertising Research* 40, 4: 17–31.

Griffin, Jeff. 1997. Global English invades Poland: An analysis of the use of English in Polish magazine advertisements. *English Today* 13, 2: 34–41.

Haarmann, Harald. 1989. *Symbolic Values of Foreign Language Use: From the Japanese Case to a General Sociolinguistic Perspective.* Berlin: De Gruyter.

Herring, Susan. 2004. Computer-mediated discourse analysis: An approach to researching online behavior. In Sasha Barab, Rob Kling and James H. Gray (eds.) *Designing for Virtual Communities in the Service of Learning.* Cambridge: Cambridge University Press. 338–376.

Hill, Jane H. 1999. Styling locally, styling globally: What does it mean? *Journal of Sociolinguistics* 3: 542–556.

Hornikx, Jos, Frank van Meurs and Marianne Starren. 2007. An empirical study of readers' associations with multilingual advertising: The case of French, German and Spanish in Dutch advertising. *Journal of Multilingual and Multicultural Development* 28, 3: 204–219.

Hornikx, Jos, Frank van Meurs and Robert-Jan Hof. 2013. The effectiveness of foreign-language display in advertising for congruent versus incongruent products. *Journal of International Consumer Marketing* 25: 152–165.

Jaffe, Eugene D. and Israel D. Nebenzahl. 2001. *National Image and Competitive Advantage: The Theory and Practice of Country-of-Origin Effect.* Frederiksberg: Copenhagen Business School Press.

Johnstone, Barbara. 2009. Pittsburghese shirts: Commodification and the enregisterment of an American dialect. *American Speech* 84, 2: 157–175

Johnstone, Barbara. 2011. Dialect enregisterment in performance. *Journal of Sociolinguistics* 15, 5: 657–679.

Kasanga, Luanga A. 2010. Streetwise English and French advertising in multilingual DR Congo: symbolism, modernity, and cosmopolitan identity. *International Journal of the Sociology of Language* 206: 181–205.

Kelly-Holmes, Helen. 2000. Bier, parfum, kaas: Language fetish in European advertising. *European Journal of Cultural Studies* 3, 1: 67–82.

Kelly-Holmes, Helen. 2005. *Advertising as Multilingual Communication.* Houndmills: Palgrave-MacMillan.

Kelly-Holmes, Helen. 2010. Global marketing and language. In Nikolas Coupland (ed.) *The Handbook of Language and Globalization*. Oxford: Wiley-Blackwell. 475–492.

Kelly-Holmes, Helen. 2014. Linguistic fetish: The sociolinguistics of visual multilingualism. In David Machin (ed.) *Visual Communication*. Berlin: De Gruyter. 135–151.

O'Sullivan, Joan. 2013. Advanced Dublin English in Irish radio advertising. *World Englishes* 32: 358–376.

Piller, Ingrid. 2001. Identity constructions in multilingual advertising. *Language in Society* 30: 153–86.

Pongsakornrungsilp, Siwarit and Jonathan E. Schroeder. 2011. Understanding value co-creation in a co-consuming brand community. *Marketing Theory* 11: 303–324

Rampton, Ben. 1995. *Crossing: Language and Identity among Adolescents*. London: Longman.

Santello, Marco. 2015. Advertising to Italian English bilinguals in Australia: Attitudes and response to language selection. *Applied Linguistics* 36, 1: 95–120.

Shankar, Shalini and Jillian R. Cavanaugh. 2012. Language and materiality in global capitalism. *Annual Review of Anthropology* 41: 355–369.

Sicilia, Maria and Mariola Palazón. 2008. Brand communities on the internet: A case study of Coca-Cola's Spanish virtual community. *Corporate Communications: An International Journal* 13, 3: 255–270.

Silverstein, Michael. 2003. Indexical order and the dialectics of sociolinguistic life. *Language & Communication* 23: 193–229.

Usunier, Jean-Claude. 2006. Relevance in business research: The case of country-of-origin research in marketing. *European Management Review* 3, 1: 60–73.

6

(Re)circulating popular television: Audience engagement and corporate practices
Monika Bednarek

Introduction

Growing up in a small town in Germany in the 1980s and 1990s I was fascinated by American television series such as *MacGyver, Star Trek: Next Generation, Miami Vice, Quantum Leap,* and *The X-files*. I would watch these programs dubbed into German, unless they were broadcast in a 'dual audio' format on Swiss television (which some German locations could receive) or during a brief period when TV series were broadcast 'unscrambled' via a British satellite channel. I could buy merchandise (especially posters and books), although I sometimes had to travel to a special store in a bigger city. I did not talk about these TV series with any other fans unless they were part of my circle of friends. This changed with the arrival of the Internet, when it suddenly became possible to chat to others in forums or via email, and to engage with fan fiction. But this was the start of the Internet, and by the time I was more familiar with it and more resources came to exist, I had outgrown my fandom. There has been much socio-cultural change since then, including the rise of international media companies and transnational fan cultures with significant impact on identity and community building. As Hermes puts it:

> Popular cultural texts help us to know who we are, and include us in communities of like-minded viewers and readers. While, formerly, the nation might have been thought to have primarily organized our sense of belonging, our rights, and our duties ... , it is now facing serious competition from international media conglomerates as well as from fan cultures ... that invite us into new types of collectivities that stretch far beyond national borders and produce small self-enclosed enclaves within the nation. (2005: 1)

115

Style, Mediation, and Change. Edited by Janus Mortensen, Nikolas Coupland, and Jacob Thøgersen © Oxford University Press 2017. Published 2017 by Oxford University Press

This chapter focuses on processes whereby both international media conglomerates and transnational fans circulate or recirculate fictional television and thereby create different styles of fandom, whether for commercial gain or for the negotiation of identity and community membership. More specifically, the chapter discusses four key processes of (re)circulation, illustrating them with examples drawn mainly from the US TV series *The Big Bang Theory* (*BBT*).

In this chapter I use Androutsopoulos's conceptualization of sociolinguistic change (2014, following Coupland 2009) as a relatively broad concept which encompasses the study of changing relations between language and society, at all levels, with a focus on language practices, and not limited to spoken language: exploring sociolinguistic change means "examin[ing] language practices and linguistic flows across media and institutional contexts" (Androutsopoulos 2014: 6) and "integrates processes of socio-cultural change such as globalization, commodification and, indeed, mediatization" (Androutsopoulos 2014: 7).

While there has been some recent interest in the sociolinguistic analysis of television series (e.g. Richardson 2010; Stuart-Smith 2011; Tagliamonte and Roberts 2005), for a long time TV series were neglected in sociolinguistic research. Not only is the language used in TV series an example of mass-mediated, scripted language which may be regarded as "artificial" (Androutsopoulos 2014: 3), it is also an example of 'artificial' language that is not highly valued—in contrast to other forms of fiction, say, literary narrative. As a prime example of pop culture, it has long been deemed unworthy of study, although this has changed more recently in relation to 'quality' television. Pennycook argues that "if popular culture is indeed so popular, and, moreover, closely bound up with English and globalization, we would be foolish to ignore it or to reduce it to dismissive comments about 'pop culture'" (Pennycook 2007: 81). While Pennycook (2007) explores hip-hop, my own research has focused on TV series. I have outlined their significance in detail elsewhere (Bednarek 2010: 7–11, 2012: 199–202), so I will only briefly summarize this argument here.

US television series are popular cultural products, consumed by millions of viewers world-wide, many of whom speak English as a second or foreign language or use a different national variety. Audiences engage with the characters and narratives as well as the language of these fictional worlds, including in online and offline conversations with others. More specifically, audiences spend a lot of time watching television series in general and often follow a particular TV series over many years—this creates significant depth of engagement. There is both psychological engagement through processes such as parasocial interaction, (wishful) identification, or affinity/liking (Cohen 1999; Giles 2002) as well as linguistic engagement through texts such as threads, blogs, review columns, and fan fiction about television series (Richardson 2010: 89–92). To name but a few possibilities, audiences can engage with the linguistic content of televisual narratives (e.g. taking up certain catchphrases or commenting on the use of swearing), their narrative elements (e.g. personalizing and speculating about events and interpreting characters), or the values and ideologies represented (e.g. reacting to the representation of LGBTIQ characters). Such engagement happens both within and across cultures, and within and across languages. For example, Australian audiences engage both with Australian and with British or American TV series, and with TV series in their own and in other languages (for instance, Scandinavian drama series with English subtitles). To give another example, German audiences regularly engage with US TV series, as illustrated in Extract 1, from a German radio interview with an accountant and a chemist discussing *BBT* in relation to its 'nerdy' characters.

Extract 1: Discussing *BBT*

> Tobias Mueller: Also, das ist 'ne Serie über Nerds und Nerds, das sind—um das kurz Mal zu beschreiben—das sind Leute, die, sag' ich jetzt einfach mal zum Beispiel Star Trek-Fans, die diese Themen für sich privat ein bisschen übertreiben.
>
> ['Well, that is a series about nerds, and nerds, that's, to describe it briefly, that's people, who, for example I would say Star-Trek fans, who exaggerate these topics in their private lives a bit.']
>
> Peter Schweizer: Dann gibt es Leonard, den anderen der beiden Physiker, er ist klein, nicht unbedingt muskulös und hat eine Brille, darüber hinaus Asthma und eine Reihe weiterer Allergien—auch das ein verbreitetes Nerd-Klischee; ich bin übrigens selbst auch Allergiker.
>
> ['Then there is Leonard, the other of the two physicists, he is small, not very muscular and wears glasses, on top of that he has asthma and a number of other allergies—that's another well-known nerd cliché; by the way, I myself am an allergy sufferer, too.'][1]

In this extract the two interviewees discuss an important aspect of characterization in the show—nerdiness (Bednarek 2012). The loan word *Nerd* indicates that this is a concept that was not originally lexicalized in German. (The closely related English word *geek* is also used as loan word in German, e.g. *das Kochbuch für Geeks*—'the cookbook for geeks'). Other aspects of the televisual narrative that are discussed elsewhere in this interview include humor or particular plot elements. Also noteworthy in this example is that the speakers compare their own 'real-life' identities to those of fictional characters, accomplished here through a first person statement about the speaker's own health issues. This is a good example of how television fulfills needs for social interaction, relationship, and identity building by helping viewers to bond with characters, to talk to others about television series, and to compare their own identity with those of televisual characters (Selby and Cowdery 1995: 186). In sum, the significance of television series extends beyond mere consumption and reaches across cultures; also, television series constitute significant contemporary products of popular culture that are worthy of study in sociolinguistics and beyond. It is also worth noting that TV series have attracted a high level of academic attention outside linguistics, for instance in cultural and media studies.

One area of sociolinguistic research that *has* looked at fictional television includes work on its potential influence on language change, such as Stuart-Smith's (2011) work on soap opera. This chapter does not concern itself with this area of sociolinguistic change but rather looks at *mediatization* processes (see Androutsopoulos 2014 for an overview). As I understand them here, mediatization processes are processes whereby mass and new media influence social practices and social life, which includes *processes of (re)circulation*—processes whereby mass media content and mass media language are circulated and recirculated among transnational communities. The chapter will first explore these processes with respect to fan T-shirts for *BBT*, before examining them in the context of social media. While my main focus in this chapter is on mediatization processes and sociocultural change, I will also draw on the notion of style. Style is here understood in a relatively broad sense, as "a way of doing something" (Coupland 2007: 1), including ways of speaking, ways of performing identity, and ways of using and combining semiotic modes—that is, including multimodal styles (e.g. verbal-visual). In this sense, I will argue that (re)circulation processes can be associated with different styles of fandom, and that there are both similarities and differences between T-shirt texts and social media texts, for instance in terms of their potential for style and styling.

The Big Bang Theory, fan T-shirts, and sociocultural change

Since this chapter illustrates (re)circulation processes with examples drawn mainly from *BBT,* and starts by looking at fan T-shirts, it is worth providing some background on both. As described in Bednarek (2012), *BBT* is a contemporary US sitcom about two young physicists, Sheldon and Leonard, their scientist friends Howard Wolowitz and Raj Koothrappali, and their new neighbour Penny, a pretty blonde who wants to be an actress but works as a waitress. In later seasons, two other female characters, Bernadette and Amy, join the cast. A main source of humor in the sitcom is the contrast between these very different characters, making use of stereotypes about nerds and 'dumb blondes,' but also showing the nerds to viewers as a community. The sitcom has been highly successful in terms of both industry awards and audience figures and is watched in many countries outside the United States, including China, Germany, Albania, Brazil, Lithuania, Costa Rica, and France—to name but a few.

As noted previously, the focus of this chapter is first on (re)circulation processes in one popular product of merchandise: the TV fan T-shirt.[2] Such T-shirts are associated with a particular TV series (in this case, *BBT*) and typically reference the series in various ways. Adopting Pennycook's (2007: 53) notion of transtextuality, they contain "intertextual echoes" and at the same time constitute instances of "posttextual" engagement. T-shirts have recently started to attract the attention of sociolinguists, such as Johnstone (2009), who explores the commodification of Pittsburgh speech on T-shirts, and Coupland (2012), who explores T-shirts in relation to how they frame the Welsh language and bilingualism. However, neither of these sociolinguistic studies focus on television fandom, and they do not concern language that is *already* embedded in a commercial product (the TV series), which is heavily marketed internationally. I have seen people wearing *BBT* T-shirts on the streets of Sydney and in the subways of Munich; I have seen an image of a girl wearing one in *The Guardian Weekend* (21 September, 2013: 54) and have seen them exhibited in shop windows in London and Stockholm (Figures 6.1 and 6.2); they are also available online for purchase and shipping worldwide.

Thus, these T-shirts exemplify the rise of both transnational television and its marketing, two areas of significant sociocultural change. First, since the late 1970s (Sinclair, Jacka, and Cunningham 1996: 1) or mid-1980s (Barker 1997) the audiovisual landscape has begun to shift significantly, moving toward a transnational television landscape. For instance, there is extensive importing and localization of US TV programs, genres, and genre conventions outside the United States (Sinclair, Jacka and Cunningham 1996). While this process is multidirectional (with the United States also importing or adapting non-US TV programs and genres), it initially favored the West and in particular the United States (Barker 1997: 5; Berry 2001). Internationally, American programs sell more than others (*NOTA International TV Trends* 2011/2012), and they attract high audience numbers in several countries outside the United States (*Scripted Series Report* 2010/2011). The first decade of the 21st century was characterized by the international rise of American TV series (*Scripted Series Report* 2010/2011). Thus, US TV series are

FIGURE 6.1 Notting Hill, London

FIGURE 6.2 Gamla Stan, Stockholm

regularly watched by many audience members outside the United States and gain fans there. Legal and illegal technology has also made it much easier for audiences to access these TV series in their original, rather than dubbed versions. It is hence not surprising to see fans of a US television series outside the United States, as in the case of the *BBT* T-shirt wearers.

Second, these T-shirts illustrate shifts in the *marketing* of TV series by multi-national corporations, although such marketing has a long history. For example, merchandising for the 1950s TV series *I love Lucy* exceeded $50 million and included clothes, dolls, jewelry, albums, books, music, and even furniture and bedroom suites (Landay 1999). Nevertheless, Berry argues that the impact of marketing "on film and television has been felt primarily since the 1960s" (Berry 2001: 264). *Star Wars* (dating from the late 1970s) is widely cited as "the point at which entertainment licensing began to grow exponentially" (Raugust 1996: 12), with television-related merchandise licensing 'exploding' in the 1980s and 'maturing' in the 1990s, with TV series such as *Beverly Hills 90210* generating "hundreds of millions of dollars in total retail sales of licensed products" (Raugust 1996: 12), with about half of the retail sales coming from overseas markets, in particular Europe (Raugust 1996: 84–86). Indeed, a trend emerged in the mid-1990s toward an increasingly international, multi-territorial licensing business (Raugust 1996: 113–115). The Internet has also made it easy for fans to buy merchandise, whether it was produced for the United States or for the international market. Hence it is now relatively easy for international fans of a US television series to acquire associated merchandise. Thus, we can expect to see consumer products like the *BBT* T-shirts outside the United States.

As far as *BBT* in particular is concerned, executives are clearly aware of its commercial potential, as indicated in this quote about marketing products:

> "The Big Bang Theory has entered a merchandising orbit that we rarely see for a live-action television show. A combination of such a successful hit series and an impassioned fan base allows us to develop a consumer prod-ucts program, the likes of which we haven't seen in a long time," said Karen McTier, Executive Vice President of Domestic Licensing and Worldwide Marketing, Warner Bros. Consumer Products. "We've established a strong and growing products program in the U.S. and are now in the midst of expanding our international program for fans around the world." (Warner Bros Backstage 2012)[3]

The marketing of TV series in the contemporary transnational media environ-ment includes a wide variety of corporate activities, including but not limited to the creation of merchandise (cultural goods such as the *BBT* T-shirts). In Jenkins's words: "Such marketing strategies promote a sense of affiliation with and immersion in fictional worlds. The media industry exploits these intense feelings through the marketing of ancillary goods, from *T-shirts* to games, with promises of enabling a deeper level of involvement with the program content" (Jenkins 2006a: 147, my italics). As we will see later, such ancillary goods also offer consumers different *styles* of fandom, and different resources for *styling* the body and the self. In terms of mediatization, the consumption and display of merchandise is one important way in which media content influences social practices and social life and is circulated and recirculated among transnational television fan communities. Before looking more closely at these (re)circulation processes in T-shirts, it is worth providing some background on how sociolinguists have previously addressed media engagement in the context of television series.

Media engagement and (re)circulation processes

Media engagement studies in interactional sociolinguistics and linguistic anthropology have looked at different ways in which audiences deal with media language, especially in relation to young people, face-to-face interaction, and transnational or minority communities (cf. Androutsopoulos 2014: 9, 18–25; Georgakopoulou 2014). Such studies do not necessarily focus on TV series, although there are some that examine films (in Androutsopoulos 2012). Coupland (2007: 171–176) discusses the transportability of television talk more generally and with a focus on accent and dialect. In relation to TV series, Gregoriou (2012) studies viewer comments on an official message board for *Dexter*, but most pertinent to this chapter is Richardson's (2010) sociolinguistic exploration of audience responses to TV series: Richardson focuses on online audience responses to television drama, and finds that such responses may either focus on meaning and performance or focus on dialogue (of the respective TV series), but even where dialogue is not explicitly focused on, it helps to create understanding and interpretations (Richardson 2010: 85). Where dialogue *is* the focus, it can be used in different ways by audiences: they can cite dialogue to support an interpretation, criticize it or quote it as a tribute (I will call this 'tribute quoting'); they can appropriate catchphrases and create new dialogue inspired by TV series (i.e. fan fiction).

In addition, Richardson's particular interest is in the writing persona or authorial voice, where she distinguishes between different voices and stances. For her:

> It is in its online *voices* that the writing audience identifies itself— that members of the viewing public constitute themselves as ordinary viewers, fans, or critics. Stances are variously offered by writers to their readers. At one end of the spectrum viewers provide unarguable expressions of personal taste at the level of "I never liked *ER* as much after George Clooney left," whereas at the other end there are lengthy and highly articulate accounts of strengths and weaknesses (Richardson 2010: 92, italics in original).

Building on Richardson (2010), I distinguish four ways of responding to TV series—four key processes of (re)circulation:

- (re)circulation of the narrative
- (re)circulation of the dialogue
- (re)circulation of the production
- performative (re)circulation

Under '(re)circulation of the narrative' I include any reference to the narrative world (characters, plots), which does *not* cite dialogue; under '(re)circulation of dialogue' I include any partial or complete citing of TV dialogue; under '(re)circulation of the production' I include any references to or comments on the production or broadcast of the narrative world (performance, actors, directors, channel, network), and under 'performative (re)circulation' I include the impersonation of television characters (e.g. through role playing).[4] In this chapter I am not concerned with fan fiction or fan art, which (re)circulate TV series in yet another way. Importantly, the term '(re)circulation' is not meant to imply mere repetition, replay, or rebroadcasting of mass media content and mass media language; rather, the label serves as a reminder that these practices can ultimately be traced back (in different ways) to a fictional TV series. (Re)circulation *may* include mere rebroadcasting (for instance, retweeting an exact quote from a TV series with no added information), but (re)circulation processes often go beyond this (for instance, adding an evaluative comment or an image). Since the original content (the televisual narrative) is located in a specific context and transmitted via a particular medium, and the (re)circulated content has a different context and may be transmitted via a different medium, we are concerned here with processes of remediation and/or resemiotization (Iedema 2003). This also means that (re)circulation processes can be multimodal (e.g. combining language and visuals).

Further, it is clear that different (re)circulation processes are not entirely separate from each other. For example, (re)circulations of dialogue may be embedded in plot comments, and insofar as they can be traced to a particular scene in the narrative they also function to (re)circulate the narrative. Performative (re)circulation also functions to (re)circulate the narrative, because it can only be understood in relation to it. Further, different types of (re)circulation have the potential to occur together, as in this invented example:

Sheldon is so funny. [(re)circulation of the narrative: comment on character]

I love how he uses 'bazinga.' [(re)circulation of dialogue: citing of dialogue]

Jim Parsons is a brilliant actor! [(re)circulation of the production: comment on actor]

Here a comment on a character is combined with citing of dialogue (*Bazinga* is Sheldon's "signature interjection" [Bednarek 2010: 131], which is introduced in season 2 and is a signal that he has made a joke or played a prank) and a comment on the actor's performance.

In my analysis of *BBT* fan T-shirts, I will first simply classify them according to the (re)circulation processes identified above, and then comment on how they are associated with different styles of fandom, and means for identity and community negotiation. The notion of decoding will become important here, too—how much knowledge is necessary to understand these various types of (re)circulations, and what does that mean for identity and community negotiation? I have already noted that styles can be multimodal, and while my discussion will not include a comprehensive multimodal analysis (i.e. analysis of all meanings made in all modes and of all relations between these modes), I will nevertheless make some pertinent points on the visuals where relevant. For this case study I analyzed all 64 different T-shirts that were available for purchase on February 26, 2012 on the official merchandise website http://the-big-bang-theory.com/shop/Official-Clothing.[5]

(Re)circulation processes in *BBT* fan T-shirts

First, the *BBT* T-shirts can (re)circulate parts of the narrative without citing any dialogue. Such (re)circulation often proceeds via visual representation of the TV characters, as ensembles or individuals, which can be more naturalistic (Figure 6.3, though in black/white) or less so (Figure 6.4, a comic-style drawing). To understand these (re)circulations, only limited knowledge of *The Big Bang Theory* is necessary—recognition of the characters. As Figure 6.3 shows, some T-shirts explicitly express the wearer's positive stance (here multimodally through a combination of words and symbol)—these introduce an explicit affective component. This seems to be an offline analogue to what Richardson calls "unarguable expressions of personal taste" (Richardson 2010: 92) in relation to linguistic online audience responses.

FIGURE 6.3 'I love Leonard'

FIGURE 6.4 *BBT* ensemble

FIGURE 6.5 Mee Krob Mondays

FIGURE 6.6 Sheldon's spot

FIGURE 6.7 Wesley Crushers

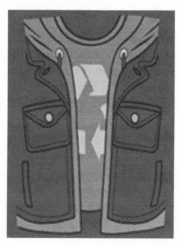

FIGURE 6.8 Leonard's outfit

(Re)circulations of the narrative may also refer to specific plot elements (Figures 6.5 and 6.6). These texts feature oblique visual-verbal references to the character Sheldon and his preferences: he only sits on a specific spot on the sofa (visually represented, with included verbal text "Reserved for Sheldon") and on Mondays he always eats Mee Krob (represented visually through the take-away carton with included verbal text "Mee Krob Mondays"). These T-shirts are very difficult to decode for outsiders and require more than basic familiarity with the televisual narrative.

Interestingly and perhaps surprisingly, some of the T-shirts also allow for performative (re)circulation. I refer here to recreations of a T-shirt that the TV characters *actually* wear in the show: In one episode Sheldon designs a T-shirt for his bowling team *The Wesley Crushers* (a reference to the *Star Trek Next Generation* character Wesley Crusher). The T-shirt that can be bought via the official website is a recreation of this bowling shirt (Figure 6.7). The other type of recreation is for a T-shirt to represent the clothes that characters typically wear in the show (Figure 6.8

FIGURE 6.9 Howard's quote

features Leonard's regular outfit). In wearing these T-shirts, fans can 'become' one of the characters, playfully performing 'being Leonard' as well as being a *BBT* fan.[6]

Several of the T-shirts do single out TV dialogue explicitly, in tribute quoting. Most often, the T-shirt represents an image of the character together with his/her quote. As these texts explicitly link the dialogue with the character by juxtaposing words and images, they do not require much effort in decoding. For instance, the multimodal T-shirt text in Figure 6.9 clearly links Howard with a quote.

Somewhat more effortful in terms of decoding are those T-shirt texts that do not include an image of characters but simply present the quote, together with an image or typographical features (Figure 6.10). Usually these T-shirts do not have information on who utters the quote; rather, they rely on the viewer to recognize and attribute it.

Interestingly, some T-shirts (re)circulate dialogue but change it for humorous purposes. Thus, one T-shirt features the line *Keep Calm and Bazinga*, a reference to both *BBT* and *Keep Calm and Carry On,* a heavily commercialized British World War II poster. Such play is similar to how audiences appropriate and play with catchphrases *themselves* (rather than through the wearing of a pre-designed T-shirt as is the case here). For example, Coupland (2007: 174) notes how school children produce innovative utterances based on a TV catchphrase, including syntactic play.[7]

(Re)circulation of TV dialogue can include fragments, rather than whole utterances. Thus, Figure 6.11 quotes a nickname that Penny gives to Sheldon in one

FIGURE 6.10 'Bazinga'

FIGURE 6.11 Shel-bot

FIGURE 6.12 'Purr'

episode, and Figure 6.12 is a fragment of a song, which Sheldon likes to have sung to him when he is ill. Another version of this T-shirt only features the cat without accompanying dialogue; here it is up to the viewer to supply the cited dialogue—the dialogue is indexed through a semiotic resource other than language. These texts require close familiarity with the televisual narrative to decode and associate them with a particular character.

Finally, those T-shirts where text is presented in first person (e.g. "*Our* children will be smart and beautiful"; "*I'm* a falcon *I* hunt better solo") or where a character is presented with a label that can also potentially be applied to the wearer (e.g. "*Engineers* do it with precision"; "Ladies Man") exhibit a dual layer of meaning, even when a pictorial representation of the character is present. These texts can simultaneously be read as a simple television quote/categorization of a televisual character *and* as originating with/labeling the wearer him/herself. Such instances could perhaps be interpreted as stylized utterances. While the notion of stylization is usually applied to spoken language (e.g. Blommaert 2005, Coupland 2007; Rampton 1995), it seems to be equally applicable here in the Bakhtinian sense of a 'multi-voiced utterance' where "ownership of voice is . . . complex and interesting" (Coupland 2007: 150). With these T-shirt texts it remains unclear whether the linguistic text represents the voice of the wearer, the voice of the character or a mixture of both. In the case of the T-shirt in Figure 6.13, readers familiar with the show will know that the character Raj is in fact *not* a 'ladies man' but only able to talk to women when drunk. For insiders, the wearer of such a T-shirt (who would presumably be male) thus makes an ironic, self-deprecating identity judgment, if the label is applied to himself, rather than projecting a macho image of success (cf. also Coupland's 2012: 18 point on multiple voicing and metaparody in metacultural T-shirt displays).

In sum, by providing T-shirts with a multitude of options for (re)circulating the TV series, corporations offer consumers different *styles* of fandom and different resources for *styling* the body and the self in this regard. Displayed on the body, the T-shirts are ways of activating meaning that is at the same time stylistic and social, hence "styling" the self (see Coupland 2007: 2). As shown previously, different categories of T-shirt texts can be distinguished, or, in Coupland's terms, different aesthetic "assemblage[s] of design choices" (Coupland 2007: 1). These make available a variety of distinct ways of (re)circulating media content—and thereby a variety of distinct ways of 'doing being a fan.' These styles differ not

FIGURE 6.13 'Ladies Man'

just in terms of intertextuality, playfulness, stylization, and multimodal design; they also differ significantly in terms of the effort they demand in relation to the knowledge needed to decode the connection to *BBT*. In Bourdieu's (1986: 47–48) sense, these T-shirts are commercial "cultural goods" (instances of cultural capital in the 'objectified' state) which demand access to different degrees of 'embodied' cultural capital—that is, respective cultural knowledge—to be appropriated and used properly.[8]

For corporations, these T-shirt texts clearly function to ensure the TV narrative's presence in the world and contribute to its reception and consumption. T-shirt texts are hence 'wearable paratexts,'[9] so to speak; the marketing for the TV series is done by the wearer. As Johnstone's (2009) Pittsburgh T-shirts do for local speech, these T-shirts put TV dialogue on display, online, on bodies, and in shops. Corporate intertextual play also functions "to bond with, build and retain loyal audiences" (Caple 2010: 128). However, the styling and stylization potential of T-shirts (for wearers) is more multifaceted than their commercial value (for corporations), which is largely the same irrespective of the different styles on offer.

For the wearers of these T-shirts, they are a means of making an aspect of their identity particularly salient and claiming community membership. Androutsopoulos notes that "the ability to recognize and recontextualize media quotes creates common ground and enables people to construct themselves as members of a community" (Androutsopoulos 2014: 24–25). The T-shirt texts that appear to require the least effort are those that feature a naturalistic representation of the character together with a quote, whereas T-shirts with more indirect representations take more effort and cultural capital to be decoded. There are thus more 'insider' and more 'outsider' T-shirts—the first category demonstrates expert status (being a serious viewer) to the fan community in the know, whereas the second category demonstrates fan status to both insiders *and* outsiders. Regardless of the style chosen, these T-shirts allow the wearer to index their membership of a *Big Bang Theory* community. Johnstone calls this function "identity-badging" (Johnstone 2009: 168). This identity-badging may arguably be ancillary to whatever identity work is going on in the current speech event, without necessarily disrupting it (other than perhaps eliciting a 'knowing' smile). But at other times, this styling of the body and the self may result in discourse about this fan identity or occasion other talk, acting as a point of orientation or departure for small talk. Such instances would be examples where "media resources of different kinds constitute increasingly common points of orientation for the establishment and management of social interaction" (Androutsopoulos 2014: 24). In other words, the sociocultural changes that are exemplified by these T-shirts (the rise of transnational television and its marketing) may be associated with an increased influence of the mass media on social practices and social life (mediatization).

(Re)circulation processes and new media

So far, we have considered processes of (re)circulation in the context of fan T-shirts, which are cultural products that are embedded in wider contexts of sociocultural change that has been happening since the late 1970s or even earlier. However, we have not touched upon a more recent sociocultural change: the rise of new technologies and their impact on discursive practices. A discussion of (re)circulation processes and socio-cultural change would be incomplete without at least briefly touching upon new media.

It is clear that both audience members and corporations use such media, but for different reasons: again, corporations are ultimately motivated by a desire for commercial profit (as in the case of the T-shirts), whereas fans may use them for multiple styling and stylization purposes, identity negotiation, and community building. However, most of the research on new media and television series focuses on audiences rather than corporations, and most of this research is nonlinguistic in its disciplinary origin using concepts such as participatory cultures and fan communities (Gorton 2009; Hills 2009; Jenkins 1992, 2006a, b; Jenkins, Ford and Green 2013). Again, sociolinguistic research by Richardson (2010) is an exception, with one chapter (Chapter 5) including a discussion of online audience responses to TV series. However, that chapter only describes threads, blogs, review columns, and fan fiction in more detail, and only discusses English-language contributions. It also does not consider the role of corporations in stimulating audience responses and in producing their own responses to television series. While my discussion only scratches the surface, I will therefore focus on additional types of new media texts (especially tweets), cite examples from various languages (though limited to those languages that I can understand—all translations in this chapter are mine) and also briefly comment on corporations. It must be emphasized that each of these aspects deserves extended analysis and there is no implication that the processes I discuss here are the only ways in which new media are used by audiences and corporations. I will continue to use *BBT* as my source of examples, but I will also add examples from other TV series, structuring this brief discussion according to types of (re)circulation processes.

First, it is easy to find examples where new media are used *to (re)circulate the televisual narrative*, for example through tweeting (live and otherwise). This includes instances of tweeters providing explicitly evaluative commentary (italicized by me)

- on characters:
  "If Sheldon wasn't on the big bang theory *it wouldn't be the same*; Sheldon from the Big Bang Theory is *Funny as Hellllll*"[10]
- on episode/plot:
  "*El major capitulo* de The Big Bang Theory *jajajajajaja* Sheldon en la piscine de Pelotas *jajajjajajajaja*" ['The best episode of *BBT* hahahahahaha Sheldon in the ball pit hahahahahahah']; "This big bang theory is *definitely the best one ever*, Sheldon touches penny's boob and raj, howard and leonard get stoned *hahaha*);

- or on both in one tweet:

   "*Jamas me habia reido tanto* con un capitulo de The Big Bang Theory, Sheldon *es unico, ese ser mata de risa a cualquiera*" ['Never before have I laughed as much as with this episode of *The Big Bang Theory*, Sheldon is unique, he's making anyone die of laughter'].

There are also less evaluative references and queries, which still include emotional expression via emoticons, typography, or hashtags (":o:o is that sheldon's girlfriend from the big bang theory??; The Big Bang Theory >>>#hahaha; Watching the big bang theory! Sheldon is talking!"). The importance of expressions of positive stance and personal taste becomes apparent again here, allowing television audiences to bond around their shared pleasure (see Zappavigna 2012 on the general potential of Twitter for affiliating and bonding).

Second, with regard to *(re)circulations of dialogue*, tweets also offer users means for incorporating catchphrases and playing with them. For instance, Zappavigna (2012) identifies social media memes involving phrasal templates with slots that can be modified, "allowing the meme to 'mutate' as users add their own elements to the slots" (Zappavigna 2012: 106). Such memes include templates based on fictional TV series: Zappavigna mentions the *I for one welcome our [ ] overlords* meme originating in *The Simpsons*. In her discussion of a fan website and a blog Richardson (2010) notes that catchphrases in the form of templates enhance audience creativity, but that more fixed catchphrases are also "played around with" (Richardson 2010: 102). Richardson further proposes that the fragmentation of audiences in the contemporary media environment means that "[t]he catchphrases of the future are less likely to achieve the distribution that those of the past were able to do" (2010: 101). However, it is clear that catchphrases take on life as hashtags, which may in fact help to distribute them more widely than in the past. Figure 6.14 shows examples of two catchphrases from US TV series used as hashtags on Twitter—the classic 'D'oh' (Homer Simpson, *The Simpsons*) and the contemporary 'Bazinga' (Sheldon Cooper, *The Big Bang Theory*).

Will new technologies such as Twitter compensate for the fragmented media landscape or not? Will TV catchphrases achieve more or less distribution than in the past? The jury is still out on these matters, but the searchable digital environment will allow researchers to approach these and other questions confidently, drawing on large-scale empirical analysis.

Tweets can also be used for tribute quoting: "Sheldon on the big bang theory saying 'booze cruise'"; "'Oh my God. You're about to jibber jabber about jibber jabber'—Penny to Sheldon, 'The Big Bang Theory.'" Corporations such as distributors or networks may also use tweets in a similar way but with commercial motivation. In these and other mediatization processes, commercial entities try to initiate and harness audience discourses for commercial purposes, as there is an apparent correlation between the amount of live tweeting and TV ratings (New Study Confirms Correlation Between Twitter and TV Ratings 2013).[11] Figure 6.15 shows a corporate tweet about the US TV series *Nurse Jackie*, with the hashtags #Zoeyism and #NurseJackie.

9h It's finals week at Troy. UAB football had its final week seven days ago. #Bazinga	*9h* It's over?!? Already??? Now I guess I have to watch hockey... #doh Wait! I PVR'd it!!! #woohoo!
1d "Out of the basement readiness" = A great education keeps kids out of your basement - @ #ties14 #bazinga!	*1h* Then, 15 minutes later, "Oh! It's Friday tomorrow!!!" #doh
2d sitcom idea: group of insecure men hang out, make sexist jokes, and bully their one other friend who has autism #ohwait #bazinga	*1h* What on earth is the current member thinking suggesting a working Supreme Court be the high school? WTF? #doh #nswpol
2d No way I could have someone like Sheldon Cooper in my life!! LOL #bazinga	*2h* That time when you are texting your boyfriend about a gift for someone but text that someone instead of your boyfriend. #Doh
2d There are only 10 types of people in the world: those who understand binary, and those who don't. #Bazinga	*3h* My brave attempt to recreate an appetizer. Who has two thumbs & forgot to salt the foie before searing? #doh pic.twitter.com/udLT9kgzak
	3h Wow. Dallas anthem singer forgets a word or two of O'Canada. #doh #jetsvsstars
3d I get so embarrassed every time walk through the tool aisle at work. All the stud finders keep going off. #Bazinga	*3h* First viewed our house during epic storm and basement was dry; a point in its favor. But I guess 2.5in of rain'll break the sump pump. #doh
3d Anyone else got a beef with the price of meat? #bazinga	*6h* #5amwakeupcall and a walk with this little stud!! #Kaleo #doh #nuts teamgfc #gfc instagram.com/p/wZ1HuVk-jv/
4d #Bazinga 🎄 RT @ I already posted a christmas song :)	*9h* Vaz feeds a 'Bobby Tax' line to the Fed and they fail to run with it. #Doh #HASC
5d This has to be my favourite ever scene while being on the show!! #Bazinga pic.twitter.com/En0ysgoInv	*20h* Listening to iTunes radio and debugging with Network Link Conditioner, wondering why iTunes keeps breaking :) #doh #iosdev
5d On @KBCChannel1 Jim McFie "The man responsible for sinking Mumias is now busy sinking Nairobi" > #Bazinga	*1d* Aaaaand I've locked myself out of my house #doh. I guess I'm going on a walk until @zacrbryant gets home. Good thing it's warm.

FIGURE 6.14 Catchphrases as hashtags (Twitter handles obscured)

Nurse Jackie ✓
@SHO_Jackie

"Ugh, I hate you. I love you." - Zoey
#Zoeyisms #NurseJackie

FIGURE 6.15 Corporate tweet

It is easy to imagine the same post coming from a fan, rather than the official Showtime *Nurse Jackie* account. There is nothing explicitly promotional about this tweet; rather it engages in a form of tribute quoting that is virtually identical to that produced by viewers if we compare it to the *BBT* tweet above (" 'Oh my God. You're about to jibber jabber about jibber jabber'—Penny to Sheldon, 'The Big Bang Theory' "). One could argue that this is a form of double stylization where the corporation (re)circulates the 'voice' of the character through the 'voice' of the typical fan. When corporate institutions engage in linguistic practices that can be associated with ordinary viewers or fans, we can speak of *corporate mimicry*. In so doing, these corporations mimic or imitate fan behavior as a marketing strategy to promote their product and to create "a sense of affiliation with and immersion in fictional worlds" (Jenkins 2006a: 147).

YouTube is another new media platform that is used to (re)circulate dialogue: A search for "The Big Bang Theory greatest quotes" results in many compilations of dialogue from the sitcom with titles such as

- *Sheldon BEST TOP TEN quotes—Big Bang Theory*;
- *Sheldon Cooper—40 Best Screams, Knocks, BaZingas, Freak-outs*;
- *Penny's Big Bang Moments*;
- *The Big Bang Theory—Shenny quotes* [quotes featuring both Penny and Sheldon];
- *The Big Bang Theory—Best of Raj*;
- *The Big Bang Theory—Wolowitz Funniest Scenes,*

and many more. While Richardson briefly mentions YouTube as an example of "*nonverbal* commentary on media texts . . ., in which contributors draw attention to scenes and images they find significant . . ., to share the pleasure" (Richardson 2010: 86, italics in original), it is clear that the produced videos are in fact multimodal and include crucial verbal text. The titles of such videos often make the producer's positive stance explicit through evaluative language such as *best (of), top ten, highlights, funny/funniest, sweetest, fave*. Similar to the T-shirt text in Figure 6.3 and other linguistic online audience responses, they are again expressions of personal taste. At the same time, in their role as *curators* of selected media content, the video producers arguably construct themselves as 'serious' or 'expert' fans.

Fan websites and Facebook pages also provide ample examples of tribute quoting. When we consider sites based in countries such as Germany and France, we see that European fans may quote the dialogue in its dubbed version (where available) or in the original English. Extract 2 comes from a French website dedicated to *Nurse Jackie*. The example is from a forum discussion regarding the question "What's your favorite episode?"

Extract 2: Discussing Nurse Jackie

> Je vais pas dire "épisode préféré," mais "scène favorite"! Cette où Coop chante comme un imbécile heureux: "I have a gun-shot ! I have a gun-shot!"!

> ['I'm not gonna go with "favorite episode" but with "favorite scene." The one where Coop crows like a happy idiot: "I have a gun-shot! I have a gun-shot"']

> (http://nurse-jackie.hypnoweb.net/forums/serie.163.7/episode-prefere-3.1.html, September 4, 2013)

The fan who answers the forum question points to his or her favorite scene from *Nurse Jackie*, simply by citing memorable dialogue from the scene in English ("I have a gun shot! I have a gun shot!"). The writer does not find it necessary to explain what is happening in this scene in terms of plot or to translate the cited dialogue, constructing both themselves and their audience as highly *Nurse Jackie* literate and serious viewers. Reviewing previous research into media engagement,

Androutsopoulos concludes that "media engagement clearly transcends the mono-lingual context" (2014: 21), for example through code-switching. Extract 2 is an instance of code-switching, but limited to multilingual reporting, where the reporting clause is in French, but the reported clause is in English.

Richardson argues that fans construct themselves as "serious" viewers, for example through their detailed critical engagement and familiarity with characters and plots (2010: 95). European fans can construct themselves as serious viewers by quoting the *original* (English) rather than dubbed dialogue. Thus, citing dubbed dialogue seems to be a less preferred option for fans (although a large-scale empirical analysis would need to confirm this), but it does occur, as Figure 6.16 from a German *Castle* Facebook page illustrates.

The first post is another (re)circulation of TV dialogue, this time in the form of tribute quoting of *dubbed* dialogue and accompanied by the writer's explicit positive stance, expressed through an emotive interjection and an emoticon. Code-switching does occur, however, through the English emotive interjection "aawww". This is in line with other expressive interjections that German speakers borrow from American English and TV series (Androutsopoulos 2014: 23). In contrast, the writer of the second post (" 'Hang up or I'll kill you.' and then an ad break—really @Channellname???") cites the dubbed dialogue ([re]circulation of dialogue) simply in order to criticize the television channel broadcasting the series ([re]circulation of production).

FIGURE 6.16 Facebook posts (https://www.facebook.com/CastleGerman)

Finally, new media offer users (whether fans or corporations) a medium for *performative (re)circulation*, for instance Twitter, which enables the creation of accounts for television characters. For example, there are at least three 'Dr. Sheldon Cooper' Twitter accounts, with profile pictures of Sheldon (as played by Jim Parsons) and profile descriptions that sometimes mix stylized utterances (utterances by 'Sheldon') with disclaimers originating in the 'true' voice of the user. The first two account descriptions that follow illustrate this mixing of voices (note the disclaimers *not affiliated with Jim Parsons or TBBT; Parody; Parodia*), while the third has no disclaimer:

- Dr. Sheldon Cooper (@username) Possibly the most intelligent human being on the planet. *not affiliated with Jim Parsons or TBBT. Parody*. I enjoy Halo, Guitar Hero and a warm beverage. Bazinga [248,000 followers on June 17, 2015]
- Dr. Sheldon Cooper (@username) Comunidad Friki. El primer Homo Novus. Con un Cociente Intelectual de 187, pocas palabras puedo escribir aqui que entendais. *(Parodia)*['Geek community. The first Homo Novus. With an IQ of 187, there are few words that I can write here that you will understand. (Parody)'] [178,000 followers on June 17, 2015]
- Dr. Sheldon Cooper (@username) I'm a Caltech Theoretical Physicist with a B.S., M.S., M.A., Ph.D., And an Sc.D. OMG Right? Bazinga! [523,000 followers on June 17, 2015]

Conclusion

Any analysis of sociolinguistic change needs to consider both similarities and differences. Comparing (re)circulation processes in the T-shirt texts and in new media, there are in fact many similarities: an original TV series includes a variety of distinctive stylistic resources (e.g. as used by specific characters such as Sheldon or Raj) which then become available for (re)circulation—by audience members or corporations. Different (re)circulation processes rely, exploit, iterate, and consolidate these resources in new contexts, enabling users to blur boundaries between mediated and 'real-life' identities, for example, through stylization. This is the case both for T-shirt texts and new media texts.

In relation to discursive practices of (re)circulation, both show ample evidence of tribute quoting (on T-shirts, in tweets, in YouTube compilations) and play with catchphrases (T-shirt texts such as *Keep calm and Bazinga*; mutated social media memes); both often incorporate expressions of positive stance or personal taste (T-shirt texts such as *I* ♥ *Leonard*, evaluative and emotional tweets and Facebook posts, YouTube 'best of' compilations); and both allow for "performative enactments" (Georgakopoulou 2014: 221) via recreated T-shirts or Twitter accounts. In terms of style and stylization, both allow for different styles of fandom—different ways of using and combining semiotic modes and of performing 'being a fan.' For instance, more oblique ways of (re)circulating media content on T-shirt texts can be used to construct an identity of a 'serious' or 'expert' fan, and the same can be achieved through curating a YouTube compilation or through quoting of original rather than dubbed dialogue in web or facebook posts. Both also enable stylized utterances with complex ownership of voice (T-shirt texts such as *"Our* children will be smart and beautiful;" TV character Twitter accounts) and both show a high level of corporate intrusion and commodification.[12]

With regard to the latter point, Barker (1997) notes that television is dominated by multinational conglomerates and "needs to be understood ... in the wider context of the globalization of capitalist modernity" (p. 3). Corporations are aware of the importance of audiences, and may try to stimulate fan activities. They also actively (re)circulate television content themselves, so that we can distinguish *corporate (re)circulation* from *citizen (re)circulation*—the latter term coined in analogy to the term *citizen journalism* and not meant to imply that these 'citizens' are state-bound. The motivations of corporations and 'citizens' for (re)circulating content differ crucially: Corporations are ultimately interested in commercial gain, although an intermediate aim might be to promote audience affiliation, immersion, and involvement. For audience members, on the other hand, (re)circulation processes have a huge potential for styling, stylization, identity, and community building. There is also pleasure in the act of (re)circulation and sharing itself, in the 'decoding' of intertextual references, and (as I have mentioned several times already) in the feeling of belonging to a community (Bednarek 2010: 31–33; Caple 2010; Zappavigna 2012: 113, 117). This pleasure and its resultant styles and identities are exploited by corporations so that we can speak of a commodified sociality—although this does not necessarily detract from the benefits that users gain.

These similarities in (re)circulation processes are in line with Jenkins's claim that new media platforms are "sites where multiple *existing forms of participatory culture*—each with its own historical trajectory, some over a century old—come together" (Jenkins et al. 2013: 30, my italics). At the same time, there are differences in relation to speed, variety (of perspectives), sharing, and reach (Jenkins 2006a: 141–142). To give just one example, it would take a long time for the wearer of a fan T-shirt to be seen by hundreds of thousands of people, whereas a user with a TV character Twitter account may reach 248,000 followers in one instant, once he or she has gained such a large following.

Further, Richardson claims that new technologies have lowered the barrier for engagement with TV series (Richardson 2010) and Jenkins argues they have moved fandom towards the mainstream, "with more Internet users engaged in some form of fan activity" (Jenkins 2006a: 142). Importantly, the digital environment permits users to connect through searches, allowing them to find particular topics or communities— whether via web searches or hashtag searches on Facebook or Twitter. Twitter, for instance, has been called "*searchable talk*, a change in social relations whereby we mark our discourse so that it can be found by others, in effect so that we can bond around particular values" (Zappavigna 2012: 1, italics in original). The practice of using a catchphrase such as *Bazinga* as hashtag does not appear to have a non-digital analogue, at least not in T-shirt texts. This 'searchability' also means that processes of recirculation have now become easily *traceable*. In the digital environment, (re)circulation processes that also occur elsewhere are hence able to move at great speed and with transnational reach, to multiply and mutate, to extend beyond the private to the public and to become searchable and traceable. It is for these reasons that I have elsewhere called them *hyper-mobile* (Bednarek 2013). Thus, new media allow fans to forge transnational communities, but they also give unprecedented power to international conglomerates to manage and distribute discourse to create and retain loyal audiences. This power may also be associated with an increased influence of the mass media on social practices and social life (mediatization). Although I have contrasted T-shirt texts with new media here, it is worth keeping in mind that they themselves exemplify sociocultural change in relation to the rise of transnational television and marketing, which in itself intensified mediatization.

To conclude, Androutsopoulos (2014) mentions "four ways in which the recontextualization of media resources is relevant to sociolinguistic change" (23): processes of conventionalization (e.g. catchphrases); processes of large-scale circulation of media phrases; the constitution of points of orientation for social interaction; and the mediation of communities. In this chapter, I have only scratched the surface as far as the recontextualization of television series is concerned, but it has become clear that audience and corporate practices may play a role in all four processes. I have also argued that (1) more attention needs to be paid to particular platforms; (2) the recontextualization of TV series is a transnational phenomenon, undertaken by both audiences and corporations; (3) marketing activities constitute important processes of mediatization and often mimic fan activities in a process that I have called *corporate mimicry*. It is a matter for future research to determine the extent to which the (re)circulation processes that I have examined in this chapter differ from media engagement through informal language use in private or other face-to-face settings.

Acknowledgements

I am very grateful to the editors for their highly useful and constructive comments on an earlier version of this chapter.

Notes

1. Interview with *BBT* fans, Wissenschaft mit Knalleffekt. Warum die Fans die TV-Serie "The Big Bang Theory" lieben Von Sebastian Felser, Deutschlandfunk, http://www.dradio.de/dlf/sendungen/corso/1704187/ (August 23, 2013); with thanks to Friederike Tegge for alerting me to this interview.

2. While other merchandise is also worthy of consideration (games, calendars, etc.), this is beyond the scope of this chapter. Fans may also design and produce their own T-shirts, although I will focus on official merchandise here. I am also not claiming that fan T-shirts are a new phenomenon; compare, for example, the wearing of football jerseys or band T-shirts.

3. Available at http://www.warnerbros.com/studio/news/warner-bros-consumer-prod-ucts-and-warner-bros-television-blast-future-merchandise (last accessed August 3, 2016).

4. Georgakopoulou talks about "performative enactments" in everyday classroom peer-talk, where pupils may imitate TV characters (Georgakopoulou 2014: 221).

5. I did not count a T-shirt as 'different' if it only used a different color scheme but retained the same elements.

6. This is comparable to wearing a Star Trek uniform to a convention. In some shops it is also possible to buy a mask with Sheldon's face, allowing wearers to dress up as 'Sheldon,' again becoming a TV character.

7. In addition, the T-shirt also mimics the war poster's general design (color schema, etc). This is an example of T-shirt texts making *multiple* intertextual connections, not just to the original narrative of *BBT*, but to other texts. Johnstone (2009: 166), citing Miller (2002), suggests that there is a tradition of playful T-shirts which involve borrowed or recontextualized images, and this also occurs in the Pittsburgh T-shirts she analyzes. The complexity of intertextual relations in T-shirt texts thus allows a lot of room for further analysis. Resemiotization (Iedema 2003) also plays a role and multimodal analysis of intersemiotic shifts is clearly an area worthy of future research.

8. While Bourdieu (1986) talks about cultural capital in the sense of educational knowledge, this concept has also been applied to subcultures (Thornton 1996). In other words, we can also talk about cultural capital in the context of *other* kinds of cultural knowledge. Media engagement in peer talk has been seen as carrying symbolic capital for participants (Georgakopoulou 2014).

9. For Genette, the term *paratext* refers to material that accompanies a literary work, such as prefaces, advertisements, press releases. These paratexts surround and extend the literary text "precisely in order to *present* it, in the usual sense of this verb but also in the strongest sense: to *make present*, to ensure the text's presence in the world, its 'reception' and consumption" (Genette 1997: 1, italics in original). The term can be extended to non-literary narratives such as fictional TV series, because such narratives are also surrounded by paratexts with similar functions (Bednarek 2014).

10. These examples are presented as they originally appeared and are based on a ran-dom selection of tweets automatically extracted from http://www.tweetarchivist.com/ using the search term *'Sheldon' The Big Bang Theory*. Without additional research, it is not appar-ent where the tweeters are based—for instance, the Spanish tweets could originate in the United States or outside the United States. English and Spanish could be the first language of users or not.

11. http://www.nielsen.com/us/en/insights/news/2013/new-study-confirms-correlation-between-twitter-and-tv-ratings.html (last accessed August 3, 2016).

12. Sociolinguistic research has paid a considerable amount of attention to the intru-sion of corporate institutions into linguistic practices, but primarily in relation to the commodification of everyday or institutional talk and linguistic varieties. An overview of relevant research is provided in Johnstone (2009), and includes studies of the commodifica-tion of conversation and intimate talk, speech styles and scripted utterances in consumer

service, linguistic styles, language varieties, and bilingualism. In relation to television, Coupland (2007: 174) briefly mentions the marketing of a catchphrase from a BBC sketch series, and Bednarek (2010: 2014) examines DVD cover blurbs for TV series, albeit not from a sociolinguistic perspective.

References

Androutsopoulos, Jannis (ed.). 2012. *Language and Society in Cinematic Discourse*. Special issue of *Multilingua* 31, 2–3.

Androutsopoulos, Jannis. 2014. Mediatization and sociolinguistic change. Key concepts, research traditions, open issues. In Jannis Androutsopoulos (ed.) *Mediatization and Sociolinguistic Change*. Berlin: De Gruyter. 3–48.

Barker, Chris. 1997. *Global Television: An Introduction*. Oxford: Blackwell.

Bednarek, Monika. 2010. *The Language of Fictional Television*. London: Continuum.

Bednarek, Monika. 2012. Constructing 'nerdiness': Characterisation in *The Big Bang Theory*. *Multilingua* 31: 199–229.

Bednarek, Monika. 2013. Mobile narratives. Paper given at the *Poetics and Linguistics Association Annual Conference* (PALA), University of Heidelberg, Germany, July 31–August 4, 2013.

Bednarek, Monika. 2014. "An astonishing season of destiny!" Evaluation in blurbs used for advertising TV series. In Geoff Thompson and Laura Alba-Juez (eds.) *Evaluation in Context*. Amsterdam: John Benjamins. 197–220.

Berry, Sarah. 2001. Marketing and promotion. In Roberta E. Pearson and Philip Simpson (eds.) *Critical Dictionary of Film and Television Theory*. London: Routledge. 264–267.

Blommaert, Jan. 2005. *Discourse: A Critical Introduction*. Cambridge: Cambridge University Press.

Bourdieu, Pierre. 1986. The forms of capital (trans. Richard Nice). In John E. Richardson (ed.) *Handbook of Theory of Research for the Sociology of Education*. New York: Greenword Press). 241–258.

Caple, Helen. 2010. Doubling-up: Allusion and bonding in multi-semiotic news stories. In Monika Bednarek and James R. Martin (eds.) *New Discourse on Language: Functional Perspectives on Multimodality, Identity, and Affiliation*. London: Continuum [now Bloomsbury]. 111–133.

Cohen, Jonathan. 1999. Favorite characters of teenage viewers of Israeli serials. *Journal of Broadcasting & Electronic Media* 43, 3: 327–345.

Coupland, Nikolas. 2007. *Style: Language Variation and Identity*. Cambridge: Cambridge University Press.

Coupland, Nikolas. 2009. Dialects, standards and social change. In Marie Maegaard, Frans Gregersen, Pia Quist and Jens Normann Jørgensen (eds.) *Language Attitudes, Standardization and Language Change*. Oslo: Novus. 27–48.

Coupland, Nikolas. 2012. Bilingualism on display: The framing of Welsh and English in Welsh public spaces. *Language in Society* 41: 1–27.

Genette, Gerard. 1997. *Paratexts: Thresholds of Interpretation*. Cambridge: Cambridge University Press.

Georgakopoulou, Alexandra. 2014. 'Girlpower or girl (in) trouble?' Identities and discourses in the (new) media engagements of adolescents' school-based interaction. In Jannis Androutsopoulos (ed.) *Mediatization and Sociolinguistic Change*. Berlin: De Gruyter. 217–244

Giles, David C. 2002. Parasocial interaction: A review of the literature and a model for future research. *Media Psychology* 4, 3: 279–305.

Gorton, Kristyn. 2009. *Media Audiences: Television, Meaning and Emotion*. Edinburgh: Edinburgh University Press.

Gregoriou, Christiana. 2012. 'Times like these, I wish there was a real Dexter': Unpacking serial murder ideologies and metaphors from TV's *Dexter* internet forum. *Language & Literature* 21: 274–285.

Hermes, Joke. 2005. *Re-reading Popular Culture*. Malden: Blackwell.

Hills, Matt. 2002. *Fan Cultures*. London: Routledge.

Iedema, Rick. 2003. Multimodality, resemiotization: Extending the analysis of discourse as multi-semiotic practice. *Visual Communication* 2, 1: 29–57.

Jenkins, Henry. 1992. *Textual Poachers: Television Fans and Participatory Culture*. London: Routledge.

Jenkins, Henry. 2006a. *Convergence Culture: Where Old and New Media Collide*. New York: New York University Press.

Jenkins, Henry. 2006b. *Fans, Bloggers, and Gamers: Exploring Participatory Culture*. New York: New York University Press.

Jenkins, Henry, Sam Ford and Joshua Green. 2013. *Spreadable Media: Creating Value and Meaning in a Networked Culture*. New York: New York University Press.

Johnstone, Barbara. 2009. Pittsburguese shirts: Commodification and the enregisterment of an urban dialect. *American Speech* 84, 2: 157–175.

Landay, Lori. 1999. Millions "Love Lucy": Commodification and the Lucy phenomenon. *Feminist Formations* 11, 2: 25–47.

Miller, Sylvia J. 2002. Phish Phan Pholklore: Identity and community through commodities in the Phish parking lot scene. *Midwestern Folklore* 28: 42–60.

NOTA International TV Trends. 2011/2012 season. *Médiamétrie*. http://www.mediametrie.com/eurodatatv/.

Pennycook, Alastair. 2007. *Global Englishes and Transcultural Flows*. London: Routledge.

Rampton, Ben. 1995. *Crossing: Language and Identity among Adolescents*. London: Longman.

Raugust, Karen. 1996. *Merchandise Licensing in the Television Industry*. Boston: Focal Press.

Richardson, Kay. 2010. *Television Dramatic Dialogue: A Sociolinguistic Study*. Oxford: Oxford University Press.

Scripted Series Report. 2010/2011 season. *Médiamétrie*. http://www.mediametrie.com/eurodatatv/.

Selby, Keith and Ron Cowdery. 1995. *How to Study Television*. Basingstoke: Macmillan.

Sinclair, John, Elizabeth Jacka and Stuart Cunningham. 1996. Peripheral vision. In John Sinclair, Elizabeth Jacka and Stuart Cunningham (eds.) *New Patterns in Global Television*. Oxford: Oxford University Press. 1–32.

Stuart-Smith, Jane. 2011. The view from the couch: Changing perspectives on the role of the television in changing language ideologies and use. In Tore Kristiansen and

Nikolas Coupland (eds.) *Standard Languages and Language Standards in a Changing Europe*. Oslo: Novus. 223–239.

Tagliamonte, Sali and Chris Roberts. 2005. So weird; so cool; so innovative: The use of intensifiers in the television series *Friends*. *American Speech* 80, 3: 280–300.

Thornton, Sarah. 1996. *Club Cultures: Music, Media and Subcultural Capital*. Hanover: University Press of New England.

Zappavigna, Michele. 2012. *Discourse of Twitter and Social Media*. London: Continuum [now Bloomsbury].

PART III

The Art of Mediated Style

BLURRING THE BOUNDARIES BETWEEN
'ORDINARY' AND 'ELITE'

7

Styling the 'ordinary': Tele-factual genres and participant identities

Joanna Thornborrow

Introduction: Shifting forms of public participation

Watching 'ordinary' people on television is now ubiquitous in contemporary forms of reality show programming around the world. It is commonplace to see on our TV screens not actors but people who are drawn from the general population and placed within what Jack Bignell (2005) has referred to as the 'middle spaces' of tele-factual broadcast genres. These participants, who are neither media professionals nor celebrities or public figures, increasingly provide the staple materials for a vast range of reality TV shows, from game-shows, competitions, and documentaries to the lifestyle and makeover programs which have contributed to the emergence of these reality genres as some of the most popular media formats in recent years.

This proliferation of tele-factual genres globally over the last decade and a half has also generated a great deal of theoretical debate about the shifting nature of the mediated public sphere, where the boundaries between public and private discourses, and public and private identities, are becoming increasingly blurred, as well as about the relationship between television and its audiences. Reality TV contributes to this blurring by putting the spotlight on what would otherwise have been backstage behaviors, bringing ordinary, everyday mundane situations front-stage, blending the observational documentary with the scripted soap opera to produce hybrid genres which have given rise to new conceptualizations of mediated performance. At the core of these debates is the concept of an ordinary person whose private self is repackaged through a mediated public performance as a reality TV participant. For instance, John Corner (2002) has argued that in tele-factual genres, the private self is transformed into what he refers to as a public 'self-in-performance,' either through interactions with other participants or through sequences of more reflective, more monologic, direct-to-camera talk. One such

143

Style, Mediation, and Change. Edited by Janus Mortensen, Nikolas Coupland, and Jacob Thøgersen
© Oxford University Press 2017. Published 2017 by Oxford University Press

example is participants' diary room talk in the *Big Brother* series. These sequences, produced entirely for the camera/audience, away from other participants, have often been described as a form of mediated confessional discourse (Tolson 2006)—a private, backstage performance in one sense, away from the primary public frame of interaction in the *Big Brother* house, that becomes a frontstage performance in its own right, delivered directly to the camera and the viewing audience.

In this chapter I begin with an account of the theoretical positions around what being a supposedly ordinary participant involves, and how ordinariness has been theorized in relation to the role of people who are not media professionals in media discourse, particularly in the light of what Graeme Turner (2010) has called 'the demotic turn' in tele-factuality. Then, in the second part of the chapter, I analyze some data taken from two highly successful reality show series, *WifeSwap* (UK and US) and *Come Dine With Me* (UK), paying close attention to the ways in which these broadcasts provide a site for the construction of ordinary identities in three main dimensions of discursive practice: through the representation of participants' individual lifestyles manifested in their linguistic and other behaviors; through the production style (i.e. the editing choices and processes in which these lifestyles are represented and packaged within the broadcast); and through situated rhetorical performance styles—sequences of talk and interaction which are shaped as routine discourses of ordinary participation in these contexts. In the final part of the chapter I argue that the styling of ordinary identities is consistently at work through these three distinct but interwoven dimensions and that, whatever participants are shown to be doing in these series, it is rarely about being ordinary and much more about being 'different' from the other (ordinary) participants, and often problematically so.

What is ordinariness?

The concept of ordinary television (Bonner 2003) has been used as a way of describing and analyzing the ever-increasing presence of people who are non-media professionals on our TV screens. This presence has, however, changed from the early years of audience participation in television talk show and discussion/debate formats. In such programs members of the public were either, as some argued, being given a legitimated voice within the mediated public sphere, or alternatively, labeled 'trash,' generating a moral panic in relation to television's depiction of a social underclass whose chaotic lives in need of so-called therapeutic intervention provided much of the material for prime-time viewing across the United States and the United Kingdom, as well as the rest of Europe, in the 1980s and 1990s (Livingstone and Lunt 1994; Richardson and Meinhof 1999). Reality TV, on the other hand, involves participation in a wide range of different scenarios in which members of the public from many different social backgrounds are engaged in a performance of being their ordinary selves. But as I have just noted, to participate in a reality TV show seems to involve doing something other than being ordinary, and begs the question of what ordinariness is and how an ordinary identity is accomplished in this context.

In their seminal work on media discourse and audience participation Livingstone and Lunt (1994) distinguished between two categories of participant in discussion-based talk shows: the category of "lay" refers to ordinary members of the public without any institutional status, as opposed to the category of "expert" which refers to a participant with attributed institutional status and knowledge. They identified a set of what they called particular discourse "styles" for each category: lay speaker style was "narrative" and "authentic," while expert speaker style was "alienated" and "fragmented."[1] This work formed the basis of a raft of subsequent discourse analytic studies on the language and participatory frameworks involved in television talk shows (see, e.g. Lorenzo-Dus 2001; Thornborrow 1997, 2001; Tolson 2001). However, in recent research focusing on the tele-factuality of lifestyle and reality program genres in which public participation is increasingly located, the notion of ordinary rather than 'lay' is now foregrounded as a defining category for the participants who are not actors or media professionals. The ordinary person is at the heart of the demotic turn in popular television programming which draws many of its protagonists from members of the general population, and who can thus be seen as 'people like us' (i.e. like the viewing audience who watch them) (Bignell 2005; Bonner 2003; Turner 2010). But at the same time, these participants are 'not like us' and in this context not ordinary at all, since they are positioned in a broadcast performance role in which they have to do something other than being ordinary. For instance, participants in *Big Brother* were selected because of their individual personality traits and social backgrounds, which the producers considered would have interesting viewing potential (and thus boost audience ratings) when brought into contact with other different personalities and backgrounds within the social context of the house (Bignell 2005). So how then does ordinariness become watchable through these contexts of mediation?

The early series of *Big Brother* were in many ways seen as a prototype for the way that reality TV formats were styling social interaction and social identities, through the construction of mediated contexts where participants competed with each other not just in terms of the challenges set for contestants, for example, but, more importantly, in terms of what the audience seemed to be looking for in their choice of who to vote out of the house. Andrew Tolson (2006) argues that it became clear that the participants for whom *Big Brother UK* audiences voted were not the competitive game players nor those who displayed some kind of ordinariness in terms of being just like everyone else but the participants who were seen to be performing convincingly as 'themselves' both within the frame of sociable interaction with others in the house and in the confessional frame with *Big Brother* and the audience of the diary room.[2]

As the reality TV genre has developed and mutated—as media genres usually do—in search of new, popular, and marketable formats for reality TV, the production of watchable characters is becoming increasingly 'storied.' In early British docu-dramas of the 1990s, such as *Airport* or *The Cruise*, generally seen as the precursors of 21st-century reality TV genres, storylines were developed around the experiences of specific participants who were selected to become leading characters in the series (Dovey 2000). In current reality shows, more and more scripted and edited versions of what may have started life as a form of 'the real' are appearing on our screens. Second-wave reality genres like *The Only Way Is Essex, Made in Chelsea*, or *Jersey Shore* are good examples of this, where participants become characters in mediated performances of their own lives.

agree

To return to my initial question, then, how does ordinariness become a watchable performance? Or to put it another way, how does reality television *style* ordinariness for its audience? On close examination, what seems to be happening in the middle-space performances in the final edited broadcasts of many reality TV shows is primarily the construction of specificity on the one hand and difference on the other. In his often-quoted essay Harvey Sacks (1984) pointed out that "doing 'being ordinary'" is work that people routinely do to display that they are just like everyone else. Goffman too, in his work on self presentation and performance (1959, 1963), considers ordinary identity to be a social achievement where, although what constitutes ordinary will shift according to the social context and interactional situation, to be ordinary is essentially to fit in, to behave in such a way as to not be noticeable, to not draw any particular attention to oneself. Ordinariness is thus not generally deemed to be watchable (except by an ethnomethodologist); in fact, quite to the contrary, ordinariness is about avoiding drawing attention to one's behavior. Participants' performance of an ordinary identity in tele-factual genres, where their primary role is, as Mark Andrejevic (2002, 2004: 195) aptly described it, to engage in "the work of being watched," often involves constructing noticeable difference and drawing explicit attention to that difference.

Reality TV participants are mainly shown to be engaged in the performance of a categorizable social identity, based on marked, recognizable characteristics and behaviors, which are then brought into contact with one or more other categorizable social identity(ies). The point of contact is often conflictual or problematic in some way, and is thus made dramatic, creating watchable performances for the audience. This audience may, or may not, recognize participants as ordinary in the sense of being (as noted earlier) 'just like them,' but, perhaps more importantly, they are being invited to recognize the construction of specific social identities. The production choices that are made on the level of participant selection and combination, the editorial selection and combination of specific discursive performances for the broadcast, and the way these are foregrounded in close editing and voice-over processes, all contribute to the styling of one participant as being different from (i.e. 'not like') the other(s). The construction of ordinariness and ordinary identities within these formats is thus being accomplished in particular ways which, as I will argue in the following section, often depend more on performances of being 'not like someone else' than of being ordinary. This often generates trouble or conflict of some kind, since in the middle-space performance context of reality TV, these ordinary identities can be set against each other and made noticeable, problematic, and watchable for viewers.

Ordinariness, difference, and watchability

In this section I draw on approaches from interactional sociolinguistics and conversation analysis in order to establish what displaying an ordinary identity involves, in order to develop a microlevel discussion about ordinariness. The point is to show how the mediated performances of social selves worked up in tele-factual contexts are primarily performances of identities that are highly specific, and discursively marked as such. In the social interactional sense of ordinariness, as observed and documented by Goffman (1959, 1963) and Sacks (1984), being ordinary is a social accomplishment, something that has to be worked on. In ordinary, everyday social encounters people are generally concerned with maintaining social relationships that depend on their displaying shared understandings of the situation and its routine, ordinary nature. Sacks points to the ways in which being ordinary is a routine social activity whereby social interactions and situations can be habitually and jointly construed as 'usual':

> [T]he cast of mind of doing "being ordinary" is essentially that your business in life is only to see and report the usual aspects of any possibly usual scene. That is to say, what you look for is to see how any scene you are in can be made an ordinary scene, a usual scene, and that is what that scene is. (1984: 416)

According to Sacks, it is through our shared understandings of what constitutes being ordinary that everyday actions are accomplished, unremarkably, routinely, and unproblematically. However, being on reality TV frequently involves noticing and reporting on the scene you are in as in some way *not* usual. It is these participant noticings and reportings of the unusual (for them) that then become available for subsequent identity framing within the broadcast's generic structures and through the editing processes. Different types of behaviors become domestically, socially, and culturally styled, as we will see in the analyses that follow. It is here that style becomes crucial in the display of difference which is at the heart of reality television's routine production of social identities.

Whether or not the participants in reality shows might be 'just like us,' the viewers, what we tend to see in these tele-factual contexts is a participant identity that is built up within the program through the discursive foregrounding of particular social categories. Establishing difference is crucial to these performances, as in the categories referred to in the following trailer for an episode of *WifeSwap* (*WifeSwap* US, Season 6, Episode 3): "A family of Goths who dance ballet and commune with the dead swap with an ultra-competitive hockey-playing family." In this summary statement category work is done in the initial framing of participant identities as well as within the episode, when participants explicitly comment on differences between their own behaviors and those of others. It is therefore through situated *difference* rather than generic forms of *ordinariness* that public participation is being discursively packaged for the tele-factual audience, and programs like *WifeSwap* and *Come Dine With Me* contain routine sequences in which participants are shown displaying these identities in rhetorically styled and structured ways. In the next part of the chapter, using examples taken from these two series, I examine how tele-factual genres produce performances of being different by mobilizing conflicting discourses of social categories and lifestyles. But first, a brief word about style.

The concept of style that I work with here is based on two core notions from sociolinguistics that seem most pertinent in the context of analyzing these programs. The first is that genres and styles are intrinsically linked, and that a particular media genre is recognizable and interpretable by audiences in part because of the styles (or ways of speaking) and other discursive practices that become most closely associated with it (Coupland 2007). In documentary programming, from which tele-factual broadcasting is an offshoot (see Corner 2002), voice-over commentaries, interactions shown on-screen between participants, and talk directly to camera for the audience (which can be in the form of more extended video diaries or 'v-logging,' or presented as short monologic segments extracted from what may have initially been a dialogic sequence) are the principal forms of talk through which this genre is constituted. Moreover, there are program-specific, routine sequences in which these forms of talk are arranged and embedded which recur in each episode of a reality TV series, as we will see in the two analytic subsections that follow. The second is the relationship between style and social meaning, through which specific linguistic forms and discursive actions come to index specific social categories and cultural values, and (re)contextually construct situated identities of class, gender, or lifestyle choices (Silverstein and Urban 1996). These are then made relevant, foregrounded, and brought into opposition with other identities through the recontextualization processes of selection and editing (van Leeuwen 2008).

I have selected data from two popular programs on the UK broadcasting channel, Channel 4. *WifeSwap* and *Come Dine With Me* are both highly successful, long-running series in which participants are brought into someone else's domestic environment (for an evening in the latter, for a fortnight in the former). As illustrated in the trailer quoted above, in *WifeSwap* distinct social categories for the participants are already inscribed from the start of the broadcast, and each carries its own set of social meanings. Goths and hockey players, one is to assume, do not usually mix well. However, the participants themselves also have to take up positions in relation to this new context, and with their transposition into a different social environment comes an evaluation of that environment. This is achieved through various generically specific activities and routine sequences. In *WifeSwap* one of these is in the first encounter with the new home, another is reading the other wife's household 'manual'—an account of the family's management systems, or, to borrow an expression from theories of organizational culture, "how things are done around here" (Handy 1993). In *Come Dine With Me* reading the proposed menu for the evening and commenting on the food served after the meal also provide occasions for evaluation. The voice-over text in this program also plays a crucial evaluative role and is produced with its own particular tongue-in-cheek, mocking style.

DISCOURSES OF DIFFERENCE IN *WIFESWAP*

The first set of examples, Extracts 1 through 3, illustrates one of the routine opening sequences from *WifeSwap*, the moment when each woman encounters her new domestic environment for the first time and has a look around the house that will be her home for the duration of the episode. In each case, the participants are filmed and recorded as they react to and comment on what they find there, with a voice-over (VO) introduction and some occasional direct-to-camera (TC) segments. Within this particular sequence, which occurs right at the beginning of each episode, there is a discursive realization of difference—what I call the 'not me'— routinely produced by each of the women in turn. These initial differences index social and cultural styles which can then be brought into opposition, and are frequently the cause of conflict later in the program. In each of the following extracts, I have reproduced the program's initial description of the participants after their names. Transcribing conventions are set out in an appendix to the chapter.

Extract 1: Susan and Debbie

Debbie has a large house and is married to a successful businessman; Susan is a Christian freegan who lives in a caravan.

VO: before they meet their new family, Susan and Debbie have a chance to explore their new homes

1	Debbie:	oh makes me feel sick just looking at it
2	Susan:	oh boy (.) and just one family lives here
4		gee (.) oh my goodness this is the bathroom
5		it's wa::y too big for (.) just a couple of people
6	Susan TC	you could probably have (.) you know probably
7		thirty people living in a house this big
8	Debbie:	eeow presume I'm sleeping up here which is a bit weird
9		oh it's really damp it's really cold ugh
10	Susan:	so who lives in here (.) the clothes (.) I see
11		my wardrobe's probably smaller than that
12	Debbie:	they probably stuff their clothes in (.)
13		that's all you <u>can</u> do in here

14 Susan: they've got ~an even bigger TV down here~

15 Susan TC: Jesus said to sell everything you have and give your money

16   to the poor it doesn't seem fair (.) that- that some people

17   should have so much and other people should have so little.

18 Debbie: what's this then. is this school uniform.

19 Debbie TC: starting to feel a bit upset really (.) that people live like this

20   when they clearly um (3.0) ((looks down away from camera))

21   have high standards you know they still do school

22   and you know ((crying)) I'm upse↑t by it

Extract 1 is a structured, bounded sequence showing the women's initial reactions to their new domestic situation. It starts in line 1 with an evaluation, "it makes me feel sick", and ends with another one in line 22, "I'm upset by it." The camera shots vary between showing the women reacting to what they find, expressing surprise (line 2), disgust (lines 8–9), disapproval (lines 15–17), and shock (lines 19–22) as they touch, open doors, look at things, and occasionally directly address the camera. We find a similarly structured sequence in Extract 2, where participants Cara and Anna are filmed exploring their new home and expressing their surprise at what they find there, again with occasional talk direct to camera:

Extract 2: Cara and Anna

Ex-pats Marbella socialites Anna and her husband Chris swap places with 'back-to-nature' Dan and Kara, who live on an eco-friendly boat in Spain.

1   Anna: oh my god they live on a boat they live on a boat

2   they live on a boat (.) so cool

3   Cara: ((looking around))

4   one two three four five six seven eight nine cars

5   Anna TC: my new home (.) wow

6   ((climbs on board))

7   Anna TC: minimalistic is the word I think I would use for this (.)

8   at first it's a bit like (.) wuow

9   Cara: oh my god it's like a swimming pool inside isn't it

10   ((opens door)) ((lifts hand over open mouth))

11 Cara TC: it would be a bit like going shopping

12   every time you went inside your wardrobe you know

13   ((on floor looking at shoes))

14		o::h go::d she's gonna be in stilettos on the boat
15		((doubles up – bleep))
16	Anna:	((looking round lifting things up))
17		but there's got to be a secret panel or something
18		where she keeps her clothes
19	Anna TC:	she must have clothes ((arms stretched down and open palms))
20		~they can't just disappear~
21	Cara:	((looking at boiler)) to heat up (.)
22		they have a fire in the bathroom?
23		the money they must have spent on this place (.)
24		they could have got themselves a- a farm
25	Anna:	she's got a white pot here saying ladies ((chewing sun glasses))
26		which is rea::lly throwing me (.) it couldn't be that ladies have
27		to pee in there that wouldn't be possible

We can note here the matching pairs of TC sequences where the new home is critically evaluated by each woman, the boat is "minimalistic" (line 7) while the clothes
closet is too big, "like going shopping every time you went inside your wardrobe"
(lines 11–12). These comments serve to construct the foundations of two very
different social identities for the two participants, whose lifestyles and values are
marked as 'other' from the very start.

Furthermore, the emergence of a particular rhetoric of performance can be
identified in these two sequences in which first the expression of surprise, then
the evaluation of the other family or wife (often directed to the camera and thus
the viewing audience), are accomplished. This performance is generally produced
through sets of verbal actions accompanied by similar camera shots as the women
are filmed walking around the house, occasionally turning to address the camera
directly. There is first of all an expression of surprise, "oh my God; oh boy; oh my
goodness," and a series of 'noticings': "they have a fire in the bathroom; what's this
then (.) is this school uniform; she's got a white pot here saying ladies." There is
usually some directly expressed evaluative inference about the other's behavior or
practice: "she must have clothes; o::h go::d she's gonna be in stilettos on the boat";
sometimes there is more mitigated conjecture: "you could probably have (.) you
know thirty people living in a house this big; the money they must have spent on
this place." There is explicit subjective self-positioning in terms of the expression of
an emotional state either directly, as in "I'm upset," or surprise and astonishment
through marked laughter and smiley-voice utterances: "~they can't just disappear~;
"they've got ~an even bigger TV down here~". There is also explicit negative evaluation: "ugh it's damp; it's way too big for just a couple of people". These discursive

actions of displaying surprise, of noticing and of negative evaluation are edited together to form routine and predictable sequences which are reproduced in each new episode, and within which specifically different social identities become established through a construction of the other as 'not like me.'

One last example, this time taken from UK series 5, will serve to demonstrate the routine nature of this rhetorical performance of a social identity which is based on difference:

Extract 3: Carrie and Bridget

Carrie and John live on an estate in Lancashire; Bridget and Mike live on a farm in Northamptonshire.

VO: before they meet their new families the women have a chance to explore their new homes

1	Carrie:	I'll tell you what they want to get a bit fucking more modern
2		don't they well look at the state of her hairdo
3		you know what I mean
4	Bridget TC:	you know I like open I like air I feel really enclosed
5		((lifts her shirt collar))
6		I feel myself all in a bit of a hot sweat uhuhuhuh
7	Carrie:	((running hands along window ledge))
8		it's not as clean as I'd have it but I mean
9		the beds are just not properly made
10		there's clothes everywhere
11		there's just shit been left everywhere
12	Bridget:	((rubbing the door))
13		it's like everything needs painting
14		needs cheering up a bit doesn't it
15		things look so unfinished
16		this would absolutely send me mad
17	Carrie:	I mean is that a real mouse and a real owl that's been stuffed
18		I mean what's wrong with sticking a nice vase of fresh flowers
19		or or on the side why why d'you have to put-
20		put a dead owl you know what I mean
21	Bridget:	aaahhh hundreds of kids' videos watching telly all the time
22		that's a waste of time that is
23	Carrie:	there is no way I'm gonna get on with these people
24		it seems boring old fashioned they want to get to reality

25		you know what I mean people don't live like this
26	Bridget:	oh my god ((opens door)) there's a dog (.) fat?
27	Bridget TC:	you could saddle him up and ride him hahahahaha
28	Carrie:	((looking out of window))
29		you look out for miles and there's just
30		fields and grass and trees you know what I mean
31		I feel like I'm stranded in the middle of nowhere
32		((turns to look over shoulder at camera))

Extract 3 contains similar displays of surprise to those in the first two. In what are shown on-screen as edited monologic segments, Bridget and Carrie nevertheless appear to be addressing their talk to someone, using dialogic markers such as "you know" and "I mean," the tag question in line 14 and the question in lines 17 and 18, as well as talking directly to camera when expressing their emotional state (lines 4–6, 29–31). There are noticings (lines 2, 9–11, 26), and explicit negative evaluations (lines 22, 24, 26–27). The social and cultural identities being brought into opposition here are explicitly indexed through these discursive actions: on the one hand 'someone who' doesn't do mess, dust, old stuff, or open spaces, and on the other, 'someone who' doesn't do TV, minimal décor, fat dogs, or enclosed spaces. There are class-based categories of social identities being constructed here too—middle-class versus working-class, also rural versus urban—which are also strongly indexed by the women's accents. (I have not focused on these here, although for UK viewers the accents in question would be heard as marked northern English [Lancashire] and more standard midlands English [Northamptonshire].) There are also, inevitably, some stereotypical female gender identities being given off in these performances—one is blonde, a bit 'rough,' a bit obsessive, while the other is brunette, an outdoorsy farmer's wife, not very house-proud.

Turning now to another routine activity in *WifeSwap*, reading 'the other wife's household manual,' further rhetorically structured performance styles emerge through which a specific social identity category is foregrounded and made 'other.' In the next two examples, lifestyle choices and cultural values are again set against each other as socially incompatible identities.

Extract 4: Reading the manual—Anna and Cara

VO: each wife has written a manual as a guide to the running of their home

1	Anna:	this is going to be so:: interesting
2		"my husband Dan and I have gone back to basics"
3		yeah ((laughing)) telling me hah hah hah

```
 4   Cara:      "I have a housekeeper" oohh
 5              ((mouth wide open then covered with hands))
 6   Anna:      "we believe that men and women have different aptitudes
 7              and that as a wife ~my role is to take on the domestic
 8              and maternal duties~"
 9              ((puts both hands up to each side of face laughing)) aarghhh
10   Cara:      "the nanny looks after Hilton three (2.0) and I don't want
11              to be running around after him all day every day"
12   Cara TC:   her nanny may know him better than (.) he- she does you know
13   Anna:      "we also collect our (2.0) wee >in a big container
14              to pour over vegetables for fertilizer"<
15              ((lifts arms up behind head))
16   Anna TC:   I knew I shouldn't have opened that bucket and I was right
17   Cara:      "Chris is a workaholic and I believe that our marriage works
18              precisely ~because we see each other so little~"
19              ((puts one hand up to side of face laughing))
20   Cara TC:   oh this is so different hey?
```

Extract 5: Reading the manual—Debbie and Susan

VO: each wife has left a manual as a guide to the running of their home

```
 1   Debbie:    "as freegans" ((raises both arms up and out from elbow))
 2              never heard that before (.) "we reject materialism capitalism
 3   Debbie TC: and consumerism" ((looks up)) oh Christ (.) OH:: CHRI::ST.
 4   Susan:     "our food is always fresh, and mostly organic (.) we don't
 5              eat any processed food as a healthy diet is a basis
 6              ((smiling)) for a healthy life (.) I think it's irresponsible
 7              ~to eat rubbish ~" huh huh huh huh huh huh
 8   Debbie:    o::h no please tell me what I'm not reading now
 9              "we get practically everything we need to survive from the bins
10              (1.0)
11              bin raiding (.) can be quite messy as you have s- to sometimes
12              dig deep in the bin and s:ift through the spilt food items"
13   Debbie TC: this is shocking
14   Susan:     "last Christmas we spent" (3.0) ~wh:at~ "last Christmas
```

15   we spent ten thousand pounds on the kids"

16   Susan TC: quite immoral (.) to be honest

17   Debbie: "in our community we don't celebrate (.) birthdays"

18   Debbie TC: what has this child got to look forward to apart from

19   rummaging through bins

These sequences, in which each woman reads aloud a segment from the other's manual and then reacts with an explicitly negative comment followed by an evaluation, are equally structured rhetorical performances of being different. Nonverbal expressions of surprise, such as covering the mouth with the hands, raising the arms, as well as verbally expressed dismay—for example, "oh Christ," "oh no," or amusement (Extract 4, line 3, 19; Extract 5, line 7—are followed by a TC explicit evaluation of the other's lifestyle choice (Extract 4, lines 12, 16, and 20; Extract 5, lines 13, 16, and 18–19), spliced together in the broadcast to form these recurringly patterned, discursive constructions of difference. Once again, style emerges here in the process of noticing and evaluating different domestic practices and behaviors, which in turn index contrasting social identities, gender roles, and parenting choices.

RECONTEXTUALIZING SOCIAL STYLE IN *COME DINE WITH ME*

I now turn to another UK reality TV series which has been successfully exported and localized around Europe and beyond, and which, like *WifeSwap*, uses a domestic setting as the site for the evaluation of social practice through generically structured routines for establishing difference between its participants. Channel 4's *Come Dine With Me* (*CDWM*) is a competition format, where, over the course of a week, four participants living in the same geographical area take turns to host a dinner party for the others, planning a menu, cooking and serving the food, and entertaining their guests. At the end of the evening they are then evaluated and given a numerical score out of ten by each of the other participants. The winner at the end of the week is the person with the highest number of points.

Style in this series is once again central to the production of generically specific discursive routines, as well as to the indexing of social meanings. As in *WifeSwap*, there is a routine sequence of discovery, for example when participants are given the opportunity to read, react to, and comment on the proposed menu for the evening, but these sequences are shot with participants situated within their own familiar environments, rather than in a new, unfamiliar one. However, as in *WifeSwap*, this routine sequence of reading the menu in *CDWM* functions to index different social meanings and to construct identity categories which can then be reframed as potentially problematic within the context of the upcoming social event—the dinner party.

A crucial feature in this series is the way the VO commentary is used to evaluate the performance of the participants throughout the program. The voicing of the commentary is in itself a highly styled verbal text. Rather than being delivered in the matter-of-fact key generally heard in the descriptions of activities in reality shows like *Big Brother* or *WifeSwap*, where typically the VO text is used to report on actions and situations, such as "shortly afterwards Anna decides to talk to Big Brother" or "Mel is talking to Tom in the garden" (*Big Brother UK*, Season 1). In *CDWM* the commentator adopts a highly ironic, mocking, and evaluative style designed to ridicule some of the selected behaviors and character traits of the week's participants. This is achieved through the production styling of the VO commentary which is much more participative than in other reality shows, as it is frequently edited into a participant's stretch of talk to produce a dialogic effect. This means that, as well as providing information about what is seen on-screen for the viewing audience, it is also dialogically styled as talk that is addressed directly *to* the participant, rather than, as is usual in conventional VO commentary, talk that is *about* them. On a metapragmatic level, this intervention by the commentator creates an alignment between viewers and the commentator, whereby the audience is invited to share the same stance as him as he engages in poking fun at the participants. Extract 6 illustrates this dialogic style, as Linda expresses some skepticism about a fellow contestant's ability to cook Caribbean food:

Extract 6: *CDWM* (Leeds)

Linda: he's not cooking this

VO: he is

Linda: he's getting this brought in

VO: he's not

Linda: if he cooks this an' he pulls this out the bag
         I'll give him money myself

VO: might hold you to that 'cos he's cooking it
         even the fish stock's from scratch

In *CDWM*, as we saw in the extracts from *WifeSwap*, particular social categories for participants are often inscribed from the outset of the program, and these are often linked to its geographical location. Setting an episode in Basildon, Essex, for instance, is to already index (ironically, with the epithet "classy") negative cultural stereotypes associated with that area.

VO: tonight we're in Basildon (.) classy
      ((on-screen shot of neon sign saying "bar," and a bottle pouring into a glass))

For a UK audience, the labels 'Essex man' or 'Essex girl' connote a set of attributes that are frequently characterized in jokes about the kind of cars they drive, the amount of alcohol they consume, the way they dress, and their sexual behavior, none of which index being 'classy' in the above sense. Essex is also the setting for another reality series *The Only Way Is Essex* (mentioned earlier, in the section *What is ordinariness?*).

The styling of ordinary identities in *CDWM* is produced by the selection and manipulation of what the participants actually say and do, and the way their talk to camera is reframed and recontextualized by the editing and the voice-over text. As will be seen in Extracts 7–12 taken from this program, selected behaviors and social practices are edited into sequences that rearticulate these identities and frame some of them as stereotypically 'Essex.' The participants are generally introduced by the VO at the start of the program by their profession, for example:

> business coach Andy
> business owner Antonia
> hairdresser Vicky

but professional designations rapidly become replaced throughout the broadcast by other distinguishing categories and characteristics, for example:

> self-confessed loud mouth and hairdresser Vicky
> motor mouth Vicky
> flesh hunter Andy
> gym junkie Ryan

Reading the menu for the coming evening is a routine activity in each episode which shows the participants' reactions to the food they are going to be served, and it is a particularly productive resource for this kind of identity work in the broadcast. In these often very short, highly edited sequences, individual participants are given the menu to read, generally in an identifiable setting (in this episode from Basildon these settings include a pub, a gym, a tanning salon, a beauty salon, and a tattooing parlor). The setting provides the frame for their verbal reactions spoken to camera as we can see in the following extracts from the first dinner of the week:

Extract 7: *CDWM* (Basildon)—Reading Antonia's menu

In the gym

Ryan:	I'd eat mushrooms and I'd eat chestnuts
	but I'm not too sure whether I'd (.) put them in a soup
VO:	bad luck fella

In the pub

| Andy: | it's nice to see somebody's got a- a- |
| | a good grasp of- of menus it sounds interesting, |

> (.) I love beef anyway I love all food >but I love beef<
>
> uh fantastic

VO: you should be easy to please then

In a hairdressing salon

Vicky: I will try it but I am not a dessert person

In each case, the participant makes an explicit statement about his or her own eating habits "I'd eat mushrooms," "I love all food," "I am not a dessert person," in relation to what he or she sees on the menu. Again, as in *WifeSwap*, these sequences function to index a specific identity category emerging for each participant as 'someone who …,' a category which will subsequently be used as a motif for building his or her 'character' during the week. The VO commentary contributes to this construction of character through evaluations and mockery, as in "you should be easy to please then," a character trait which is developed over the week as Andy is consistently represented as someone who is rather undiscerning, smarmy, and an easy target for sexual innuendo and teasing.

Extract 8: *CDWM* (Basildon)—Reading Ryan's menu

In a pub

Andy: I'm not gonna talk about vajazzling on

               on national television

VO: you big tease

Andy: ((laughing)) I'm sure that Ryan will be able to explain that

In a men's clothes shop

Andy: I always like a bit of fruity stuff

VO: you all right Andy

Ryan is represented as a tattooed, pierced, and artificially tanned 'gym bunny' who likes taking his top off at the dinner table. Prior to the foregoing extracts, Ryan had just been filmed only managing to do eight press-ups in the gym, and putting on fake tan at home. He is subsequently filmed reading menus in a tanning salon and while getting a tattoo. In the following examples, the VO teasingly picks up on these characteristic activities:

Extract 9a: *CDWM* (Basildon)—Reading Antonia's menu

In the gym

Ryan: quite excited about the chocolate orange fondant

               I must say ((laughs))

VO: must be hungry from all them press-ups

Extract 9b: *CDWM* (Basildon)—Reading Andy's menu

In tanning salon

Ryan: maybe it's uh (.)

          little rack of ribs or something who knows

VO: fake tan didn't work then

However, he is also constructed as someone who is a bit naïve with questionable tastes, and whose attempts to impress go very wide of the mark. His choice of dishes for his evening's menu reinforces this identity: homemade "turkey twizzlers" (banned from school canteen menus for containing no turkey), "fromage and frites in a beef jus" (which turns out to be grated cheese, oven chips, and gravy granules), and the "vajazzled spotted dick" pudding, which are constructed to be, then put down by the VO as, all very 'Essex.'

Vicky's character on the other hand is consistently represented as an unsophisticated loud mouth, and the editing focuses on her constant repetition of "I'm not a dessert person":

Extract 10: *CDWM* (Basildon)

VO: Antonia makes a basic chocolate and orange cake mix

          then moves on to her pistachio custard

In hairdressing salon

Vicky: eeuow sounds hideous

In the taxi

Vicky: I'm not a dessert person at all I hate desserts

VO: stop talking now

In pet shop

Vicky: I probably won't like the dessert I don't like desserts much

VO: yeah you mentioned

The intervention of the VO text here uses her repeated expressions of dislike for dessert (edited to increase the perceived extent of the repetition) to draw attention to and make fun of her depicted character as a loudmouth who never stops talking.

In the next set of examples, Antonia and Vicky comment on Ryan's proposed menu in two short sequences that are nonetheless saturated with social meaning. Vicky's pronunciation of the word *frites* as *frights* is corrected by the VO, while Antonia's question, "that surely isn't cheese chips and gravy is it," is answered as follows in Extract 11.

Extract 11: *CDWM* (Basildon)—Reading Ryan's menu

In a café

Vicky:	fromage and frights=
VO:	=frites
Vicky:	in a beef jus (.) don't really know
	what that is

In a beauty salon

Antonia:	that surely isn't (.) cheese chips and gravy is it
VO:	yep
Antonia:	surely not

In these sequences we are invited with the commentator to laugh at Vicky's lack of sophistication and her pronunciation of the French word *frites* and at Antonia's pretensions to be knowledgeable about food.

Extract 12: *CDWM* (Basildon)—Reading Andy's menu

Antonia:	done properly (.) it'll be lovely
VO:	oh
Antonia:	done wrong (1.0) it's gonna be horrible
VO:	thought so

The recontextualization of verbal actions as a social practice "makes them pass through the filter of the practices in which they are inserted" (van Leeuwen 2008: 12) and this filter is often evaluative. In this series, the VO, as we have seen, intrudes as a dialogic participant in, as well as an external observer of, the proceedings, and functions not only to comment on what is happening on-screen, as for instance in the cooking scenes (Extract 10), but to evaluate these behaviors through irony, overt teases, and intervention in the talk-to-camera sequences (e.g. in Extracts 11 and 12). The actions in the VO 'turns' are often highly face threatening, such as the other correction of Vicky's pronunciation: *frites*, or the unmitigated directives: "stop talking now" or "put your shirt on." The participants as 'characters' are thus developed over the week's episodes through the recontextualizing practice of selection and editing of these middle-space performances—that is, a particular behavior within the context of the cultural event of the 'dinner party' in which forms of sociability and choices in the preparation and cooking of food can then be 'sent up' by the VO text. These indexes of social style are foregrounded in the program, made noticeable, and then evaluated as inept, or undesirable, or in terribly bad taste, and quite often all of these at once. *CDWM* thus offers its viewers watchable performances of social identities, designed to be specifically 'someone who does X,' where doing X is often presented as ridiculous rather than as ordinary (see also Thornborrow 2015).

In conclusion: Style and ordinary performance

Through the discussion of the extracts I have argued that the notion of style becomes salient on several levels. First on the macrolevel of a display of 'lifestyle' (Giles 2002; Lorenzo-Dus 2009)—the variety of choices, habits, and practices around working, parenting, managing relationships, food, health, and money, in which particular sets of social values and identities are indexed by a social category, label, or 'style' (e.g. *Goths* or *Freegans; Essex*). Second, style can be seen at work in the program's filming, editing, and voice-over commentary practices, which recontextualize and generically reproduce the sequences within which these social identities are routinely framed. Here, the use of voice-over and selected direct-to-camera shots of one participant's comments and reactions to 'the other' are examples of a particular style of production. And third, style also comes into play at the microlevel of rhetorical performance, the routine discursive display of the 'not me,' or the 'someone who' is problematically indexed as 'being *not* like' the other participant(s). These performances which occur in the early part of an episode are crucial to the development of a potentially dramatic clash or conflict between characters later on in the program. These routine sequences become styled performances in their own right, reproduced in series after series, and instantly recognizable as one of the key discourses of tele-factuality.

The difference between contemporary generic contexts for ordinary participation in broadcast media and earlier forms of broadcasting that involved members of the public is striking in many ways. Ordinary people have been seen and heard on air for decades in a whole range of genres, from the early radio broadcasts documented by Scannell and Cardiff (1991) to the many popular quiz programs and competitions of the 1960s and 1970s—for example, *The Generation Game* or dating shows such as *Blind Date* in the United Kingdom. However, the mediated frames of participation in these shows were clearly demarcated as public spaces and maintained for the duration of the broadcast, while in tele-factual programming, the boundaries between public and private domains of discourse are becoming less and less clearly defined. As the 'reality' lens pushes further into domestic spaces where social identities and lifestyles can be scrutinized, packaged, and offered up for our entertainment, it is in these middle-space performance roles that participants' actions and interactions are being recontextualized through metapragmatic discourses of production, editing, and voice-over, and that ordinary people can be made watchable as they are brought into dramatic collision through the situated context of the broadcast for its audiences.

Transcription conventions

The following transcription conventions have been used in the process of transcribing talk for use as data:

equals sign	=say	latching, no break between turns
numbers in round brackets	(0.5)	timed pause to nearest .5 second
dot in brackets	(.)	very brief pause
underlining	say	emphasis or stress
colons	sa:::y	stretching of prior sound
up and down arrows	↑say↓	indicate marked pitch movement
full stop	say.	falling intonation
comma	say,	continuing intonation
capital letters	SAY	very loud talk, shouting
degree signs	°say°	quiet talk
'greater' than	<say>	slowed-down speech
'less' than	>say<	speeded-up speech
. preceding h	.hhhh	marked in breath
no. preceding h	hhhh	marked out breath
laughter particles	huh huh huh	laughter
tilde each side of word	~say~	'smiley' voice
parentheses with xxxx	(x x x x)	stretch of untranscribable talk
double parentheses	((sits down))	contextual information
TC	Anna TC:	direct address to camera
VO	VO	voice-over segments

Notes

1. It should be noted that Livingstone and Lunt were not sociolinguists; therefore, their conceptualization of style does not correspond to the overall understanding of style in the context of this chapter/book.

2. Tolson attributes the success of a participant called Nadia in *Big Brother UK* 2005 to this type of performance: the series was won by a participant whose social identity was in many ways not ordinary at all, and who thus was highly watchable as a tele-factual character. Unknown to the other housemates, but known to the viewers, she was at a critical moment of social and sexual self-transformation from man/male to woman/female, a moment where restyling her identity and performing an 'authentic self' within the context

of the house was particularly problematic. Viewers clearly warmed to her both in the house and in the diary room and voted for her consistently.

References

Andrejevic, Mark. 2002. The work of being watched: Interactive media and the exploitation of self-disclosure. *Critical Studies in Media Communication* 19, 2: 230–248.

Andrejevic, Mark. 2004. The webcam subculture and digital enclosure. In Nick Couldry and Anna McCarthy (eds.) *MediaSpace: Place, Scale and Culture in a Media Age*. London: Routledge. 193–208.

Bignell, Jonathan. 2005. *Big Brother: Reality TV in the Twenty-First Century*. London: Palgrave.

Bonner, Frances. 2003. *Ordinary Television: Analyzing Popular TV*. London: Sage.

Corner, John. 2002. Performing the real: Documentary diversions. *Television & New Media* 3: 255–269.

Coupland, Nikolas. 2007. *Style: Language Variation and Identity*. Cambridge: Cambridge University Press.

Dovey, Jon. 2000. *Freakshow: First Person Media and Factual Television*. London: Pluto.

Giles, David Clifford. 2002. Keeping the public in their place: Audience participation in lifestyle television. *Discourse & Society* 13, 5: 603–628.

Goffman, Erving. 1959. *The Presentation of Self in Everyday Life*. New York: Doubleday Anchor Books.

Goffman, Erving. 1963. *Behaviour in Public Places: Notes on the Social Organisation of Gatherings*. New York: The Free Press.

Handy, Charles. 1993. *Understanding Organizations* (4th ed.). London: Penguin Books.

Livingstone Sonia and Peter Lunt. 1994. *Talk on Television: Audience Participation and Public Debate*. London: Routledge.

Lorenzo Dus, Nuria. 2001. Up close and personal: The narrativisation of private experience in media talk. *Studies in English Language and Linguistics* 3: 215–148.

Lorenzo-Dus, Nuria. 2009. *Television Discourse: Analysing Language in the Media*. London: Palgrave Macmillan.

Richardson, Kay and Ulrike Meinhof. 1999. *Worlds in Common? Television Discourses in a Changing Europe*. London: Routledge.

Sacks, Harvey. 1984. On doing 'being ordinary.' In J. Maxwell Atkinson and John Heritage (eds.) *Structures of Social Action: Studies in Conversation Analysis*. Cambridge: Cambridge University Press. 413–429.

Scannell, Paddy and David Cardiff. 1991. *A Social History of British Broadcasting: Serving the Nation 1923–1939*. Oxford: Blackwell.

Silverstein, Michael and Greg Urban (eds.). 1996. *Natural Histories of Discourse*. Chicago: University of Chicago Press.

Thornborrow, Joanna (ed.). 1997. Broadcast Talk. *Text*, 17, 2. Special issue.

Thornborrow, Joanna. 2001. 'Has this ever happened to you?': Talk show narratives as mediated performance. In Andrew Tolson (ed.) *TV Talk Shows: Discourse, Performance, Spectacle*. Mahwah, NJ: Erlbaum. 117–137.

Thornborrow, Joanna. 2015. *The Discourse of Public Participation Media: From Talk Show to Twitter*. London: Routledge.

Tolson, Andrew (ed.). 2001. *Television Talk Shows: Discourse, Performance, Spectacle.* Mahwah, NJ: Erlbaum.

Tolson, Andrew. 2006. *Media Talk: Spoken Discourse on TV and Radio.* Edinburgh: Edinburgh University Press.

Turner, Graeme. 2010. *Ordinary People and the Media: The Demotic Turn.* London: Sage.

van Leeuwen, Theo. 2008. *Discourse and Practice: New Tools for Critical Discourse Analysis.* Oxford: Oxford University Press.

8

Art on television: Television as art

Adam Jaworski

Introduction: Elite and democratizing values of artistic styles

For Gombrich, style is "any distinctive, and therefore recognizable, way in which an act is performed or an artifact made or ought to be performed and made" (Gombrich 2009 [1968]: 129). Whether considered a primary tool of periodization of art—the style of an era (Panofsky 1995)—or a contemporary artist's individual *modus operandi*, style is the way people project their identities and values in the context of specific communicative contexts (Fairclough 2003; van Leeuwen 2005).

The meaning potential of style has its origins in the associations we make with specific classes of speakers and situations, whereby semiotic items are linked to social values. The recognition of style is based, in part, on making intertextual connections—how earlier texts, or their features, have been incorporated into new texts (Bakhtin 1981; Fairclough 2003). In this chapter, I focus on some aspects of mediatizing art style on television. More specifically, I examine how three opening sequences in an art documentary program are multifunctional—they are not simply 'introductions' informing the viewers of 'what is to come.' Rather they are constructed as individual pieces of performance art in their own right designed to capture and hold the attention of the viewers. They draw on and intertextually echo the distinctive styles of the individual artists. This presentation of the segment introductions has two potential effects on the program's audiences. On one hand, for a knowing audience to appreciate this intertextuality positions them as elite art aficionados. On the other hand, making the introductions accessible to a less knowing audience has a democratizing effect.

I draw on sociolinguistic and art-historical approaches to style to suggest that these televisual acts of mediatization of individual artists' styles are consequential "for the social construction of everyday life, society, and culture as a whole" (Krotz, 2009: 24, cited in Androutsopoulos, 2014: 10). In particular, I suggest that

165

Style, Mediation, and Change. Edited by Janus Mortensen, Nikolas Coupland, and Jacob Thøgersen
© Oxford University Press 2017. Published 2017 by Oxford University Press

the recognition and uptake of a personal artist style in these segments is a key element of creating engagement between the program and its target audience, the construction of a 'knowing viewer' and an imagined community of art lovers/experts, or a mediated community of 'art connoisseurs.' As I argue in my discussion, these particular instances of the mediatization of art can be positioned as the program makers' attempt to resolve the tension between the apparent egalitarian status of television as a mass medium and the relative perception of contemporary art as elitist.

Art on television

The seven-season Public Broadcasting Service (PBS) *Art in the Twenty-first Century* series (*Art:21*, 2001–2014 http://www.pbs.org/art21/) features profiles of approximately 100 artists grouped into three to four episodes around loosely titled segments such as "Place," "Identity," "Consumption," "Spirituality," "Time," "Loss & Desire," "Stories," "Time," and so on. Each of the four segments in Season 1 is introduced by a vignette created by an artist other than those appearing in the program interviews.[1] Each introduction contains specific tropes that can be traced back to the contributing artist's style referencing their own work. In other words, the artists use devices, themes, and stylistic features that they are known for, their textual and visual 'trademarks,' or, to use Agha's (2003) term, *features* that have been enregistered as indexing their practice. In this chapter I analyze three such introductions for the following segments from Series 1: (1) "Place," by Laurie Anderson; (2) "Identity," by William Wegman with Steve Martin; and (3) "Consumption" by Barbara Kruger with John McEnroe.

In contrast to Wegman and Kruger, Anderson appears as the sole host in her segment. Despite her numerous collaborations with other artists, she is predominantly known for her solo projects as a multimedia performance artist, as well as for her drawings, paintings, sculpture, films, and music. One of her preferred self-designations is 'storyteller.' Many of her shows consist of sequences of semi-autobiographical or fantastical stories, which she typically narrates herself in a multitude of stage personas, styles, and visual and vocal guises.

Wegman's and Kruger's openings are hosted by Martin and McEnroe, respectively, and neither artist appears in person. Although Wegman does cast himself in his video art pieces, he is better known for his photographic work in which he has repeatedly photographed his Weimaraner dogs, at times featuring in the photographs himself. The Weimaraner photographs are highly staged, poetic, humorous, or surreal. Wegman often uses different props, such as clothes and accessories, to anthropomorphize his dogs, blurring the distinction between the canine and human. Kruger's work is predominantly text-based, consisting typically of relatively short slogans, often with feminist overtones, that act as commentaries on different aspects of social life: politics, consumer culture, sexism, war, religion, corporate greed, and so on. Some of the work involves large-scale installations with text in block Helvetica UltraCompressed font in white, red, and black, entirely covering gallery walls and floors. Her collages juxtapose red bands with white text in Futura Bold Oblique overlaid on black and white photographs. Her work does not involve self-portraiture. These may be some of the reasons why, in the three examples selected for analysis, only Anderson self-hosts the introduction to "Place." Anderson and Wegman are both credited as writers and directors of their segments. The end credits for the "Identity" segment include no mention of either Kruger or McEnroe.[2]

The reason for choosing the three introductions for analysis here is that, of all the segment introductions, they were devised by visual artists in the style of their own practice.[3] The other filmic openings (up to Season 3) were introduced by various other celebrities (actors, a dancer/choreographer, a professional basketball player) and directed by Charles Atlas. From Season 4 onward the introductions featured simply the segments' titles and names of the featured artists with audio excerpts from the following interviews. The art format of the introductions from Season 1 was, then, eroded in subsequent seasons to fade from view completely in Season 4. This was probably due to budgetary concerns. The ultimate paring down of the elaborate art format of the openings gives an impression that they were originally conceived of as somewhat extravagant 'winks and nods' at the viewing public, attempts to entertain as well as to inform, some of them being particularly humorous.

Imagined media communities

Art:21 takes a resolutely popularizing (egalitarian) stance evidenced by its website, where educational guides accompanying each series are clearly framed as teaching resources. For example, the *Educator's Guide to the 2001 Season*[4] (Season 1) emphasizes aspects of learning centered around a common goal of "communication and conversation about issues that are important to students," and making connections with students "in your community," seeking out local artists, museums, and public works of art. The artists profiled in the program are referred to in the *Guide* as "real people" of different ages, with different ethnic backgrounds, and using a wide range of media in their work. With a strong US bias typical of "banal nationalism" (Billig 1995), the *Guide* adds: "Collectively, the artists look like the diverse populations of our schools," where "our schools" refers to the schools in the USA. Finally, the program's egalitarian ethos is emphasized in the *Guide*'s comment addressed at the teachers: "You do not need to be an expert on art to use the series as a teaching resource … Join in exploring new ideas alongside your students." In other words, watching and enjoying the program is not positioned as the prerogative of a narrow group of 'art experts' but as a shared pursuit of discovery by teachers, students and the 'general public.'

One of the affordances of television in general is, arguably, its widespread, democratizing reach. Television, like radio before it and the internet on an even greater scale today, creates a sense of 'bringing in' public figures, bringing them 'into people's living rooms,' and creating a sense of involvement between viewers and presenters, often blurring the boundaries between the 'public' and 'private' spheres (e.g. Hartley 1996; see also Thornborrow, Chapter 7, this volume). Scannell (1989) discusses this process under the term *sociability*; Fairclough's (1995) term is *conversationalization* (see Lorenzo-Dus 2009 for a useful overview). In his discussion of DJ radio talk, Montgomery argues further that radio (and by extension television) "also manages simultaneously to dramatise the relation of the audience to itself: as listeners we are made constantly aware of other (invisible) elements of the audience of which we form a part" (Montgomery 1986: 103).[5]

In their analysis of changing formats in newspapers and TV news programs, Machin and Polzer (2015) give numerous examples of how different media organizations compete to attract audiences by altering their presentation (e.g. layout, font, and color) and modes of addressing readers/viewers. With regard to TV news programs, they comment on how the BBC, for example, has responded to market research findings that their viewers found the programs 'formal and boring' by introducing a number of measures to capture and hold the viewers' attention. Some of these include elaborate and spectacular opening sequences with dramatic visual effects such as animated globes spinning at unusual angles, bursting and flying beams of light (signifying breaking news transmitted across the world), raising and lowering the lights in the studio at the openings and endings of the news bulletins, or speedy digital clock countdowns, often accompanied by rhythmic music or clock chimes. In news features, involvement is created by studio presenters' direct gaze at the viewers (Kress and van Leeuwen's [1996] "demand images" that require addressee's response or involvement), frequent use of inclusive pronouns ('we,' 'us'), and, in on-the-spot reporting, correspondents walking toward the camera gesticulating and frowning, as if trying to work out a problem, even though their text is scripted (see also Ellis 2000).

The segment introductions analyzed in this section rely on the verbal track in delivering their educational, proselytizing message about the accessibility of contemporary art and its themes. This is particularly evident in Anderson's introduction, in which she delivers a mini-lecture on place, and in Kruger's introduction, in which McEnroe poses a number of questions about art and consumption. The visual track veers toward the humorous, the fantastical, or the extravagant. Such division of labor between the two modalities is consistent with recent developments in print media (Machin 2004), broadcast news (Machin and Jaworski 2006), or natural history programs (Darley 2003), where the still or moving image has shifted away from its predominantly denotative function as evidence or witness to a predominantly connotative, symbolic, or entertainment function. Yet, the visual and digital theatrics (cf. Ekström 2000) in the *Art:21* introductions add up to more than simple edutainment. They function as autonomous pieces of video art that require from the audience a degree of recognition, intertextual knowledge, and understanding of the artists' prior work and their individual styles to grasp their 'hidden' meanings and cultural references. Artists recontextualize elements of their practice and imagery and insert them into the segment introductions, drawing viewers' attention to these acts of representation as poetic, comical, or ironic self-stylizations.

No doubt, much of media organizations' effort to create mass following for their outputs is economically driven. To use loosely Bell's (1984) term, the *audience design* features aimed at increasing the viewers' loyalty and fostering a sense of group identity may also create an awareness and solidarity with other viewers/listeners (see Montgomery 1986), or construct a group *habitus* (Hjarvard 2013). Of course, television is not a monolithic medium and the public's viewing choices are clearly motivated by a number of individual and group values, tastes, dispositions, and class allegiances. Our habitus determines our viewing choices as much as it is shaped by them. Different programs, entire channels, and even modes of transmission (e.g. satellite vs. cable vs. online) can be considered either 'egalitarian' or 'elitist,' typically reflected by their viewing figures.

Art:21 faces a paradox. While it deals with a theme that is typically considered as elitist—contemporary art—it aims to reach a broad and potentially new audience—educationalists and students of various ages (including adults)—as "a window through which to view numerous contemporary themes" (*Educator's Guide to the 2001 Season*, as introduced at the beginning of this section). The way this paradox is managed is most clearly demonstrated by the introductory vignettes, such as those transcribed in Extracts 1–3. They are arguably redundant in the structure of the program, as each new segment ("Place," "Identity," "Consumption") could be introduced with just a written title sequence, a 'talking head,' or a voice-over by an anonymous announcer, or a combination of these more traditional, simpler, and less expensive options (as the program indeed does in later seasons, as discussed in the previous section *Art on television*).

The chapter, then, focuses on the introductory sequences understood here as instances of Goffman's "brackets," that is, sequences that are "often marked off from the ongoing flow of surrounding events by a special set of boundary markers or brackets of a conventionalised kind" (Goffman 1974: 251; see also Androutsopoulos 2010: 228). As opening brackets, the section introductions contextualize the artists' profiles but can be viewed as information-and-entertainment-media events in their own right. In fact, the explanatory and educational ethos of PBS is skewed here in favor of the esoteric, poetic, and humorous. However, this is not an entirely new development in the case of the PBS, which has collaborated with artists such as Laurie Anderson and William Wegman before, folding art into its educational mission.

To borrow Luginbühl's (2014) terminology from his analysis of the US and Swiss TV news program formats, the introductory vignettes in *Art:21* belong to the *presentation genres* (Goffman's brackets, above), which in the case of news programs include headlines, greetings and good-byes, program notices, program previews, story previews, and lead-ins/lead-outs. According to Luginbühl's diachronic analysis spanning the period 1968–2005, other things being equal, news presentation genres have come to be more prominent both in his US and Swiss data. Their proliferation makes the structure of the programs more explicit and demonstrates, he suggests, "a more intense orientation towards the audience" (Luginbühl 2014: 322), possibly to break up or embellish their news bulletins by ever more dramatic sequences aimed at capturing and holding viewers' attention (see Machin and Polzer 2015). Likewise, in the context of *Art:21*, audience members are not only informed about the contents of the next segment (its theme, names of the profiled artists, etc.) but also entertained, potentially mystified, and 'tested' on their familiarity with the work of various contemporary artists.

Thus, the segment introductions punctuate the program by separating its units and by introducing the themes and the names of profiled artists. In this sense, they perform Halliday's (1978) *textual* (organizational, cohesive) and *ideational* (referential, informative) functions. However, the theatrical, playful, and aestheticizing aspects of the introductions constituted as original video art pieces perform also, if not predominantly, Halliday's *interpersonal* function by fostering through the televisual medium an imagined relationship between the program producers and their target audience. In their analysis of the newspaper format, which can be extended to other genres, Barnhurst and Nerone suggest that the form of a medium "includes a proposed or normative model of the medium itself . . . [or] the way the medium imagines itself to be and to act. In its physical arrangement, structure, and format, a newspaper reiterates an ideal for itself" (Barnhurst and Nerone 2001: 3). The three segment introductions in *Art:21* are, then, framing devices signaling or contextualizing the cultural presuppositions and assumptions about participants' communicative roles, their goals, communicative genres, and norms of interaction (Coupland 2012; Goffman 1974). They are the locus of the ideological work "representing 'the imagined relationship of individuals to their real conditions of existence'" (Althusser 1971: 162; cited in Barnhurst and Noble 2001: 3).[6] In a TV series on 'art,' the opening vignettes contextualize its content through being conceived of as stand-alone pieces of television art. The ideological work they are tasked with, I argue, is to demystify or demythologize art as inaccessible, esoteric, and elitist.

In the following section, *Television as art*, I introduce the data examples with the three artists' self-referential, intertextual links to their work, which, I suggest, turn the opening segments into pieces of performance art on television. I analyze them in three sections with a focus on how they manage the tension between the egalitarian and elitist stances of the program, namely, how they reconcile the educational remit of *Art:21* appealing to a broad audience with its 'highbrow' subject matter (contemporary art). As I proceed, I will introduce some aspects of the three artists' individual styles and practices to explain their origins and effects. The first (sub)section, *Creating a 'knowing' viewer*, orients to the predominantly visual, self-referential semiotic resources that the artists insert into the openings. It is this aspect of their "high performance" that "requires an acculturated audience able to read and predisposed to judge the semiotic value of a projected persona or genre" (Coupland 2007: 154); in this case, the viewers are positioned as 'art experts.' The other two sections, *The host's persona as 'ordinary'* and *The host as engaged with the viewer*, focus on balancing the 'elitist mode' (Meinhof 2004) of artists' (self-) stylization with their (or their hosts') rearticulation of their own personas, and art generally, as mundane and egalitarian. To be clear, this rearticulation is taking place in the (high) performance, mediatized frame within a powerful institution (PBS). However, following Coupland (2007: 154), these acts of stylization engage viewers in processes of social (moral and aesthetic) re-evaluation of speakers' (principals') and viewers' actual and metaphorical identities, stances, goals, and values, interrupting ongoing situational frames, adding to them new layers of social context, and introducing new and dissonant identities and values.

Television as art

The styling and self-styling work that goes on in the data examples takes place in the visual track, and, to an extent, in the verbal track. A degree of ironic distance is created between the two tracks, as hosts, in their deadpan (Anderson, Martin) or earnest (McEnroe) delivery of their scripts, do not make any overt references to the visual track. To use Barthes's terminology, the verbal track does not act as the visual track's *anchorage*—an explanation of the visual, the way it does, for the most part, in the artists' profiles. Rather, the relationship between the two is that of *relay*, the visual and verbal tracks elaborating on one another (Barthes 1977). The visuals are in fact somewhat distracting in that they contain much detail that is either very intrusive or requires viewers' concentration to be noticed and fully appreciated. Their illusory, surreal, or otherwise stylized character adds elements of playfulness, humor, and diversion. Sometimes, the visual track acts as *illustration* (i.e. extension and a particular instantiation of the verbal track).

CREATING A 'KNOWING' VIEWER

In their introductions the three artists (Anderson, Wegman, and Kruger) use stylistic elements that involve visual imagery and spoken or written texts that make intertextual reference to their earlier practice and artworks. For example, Laurie Anderson begins her introduction to Place with the words "I dreamed that I was living in a billboard" (still 1-3), where variants of the phrase 'I dreamed that . . .' begin a number of her stories and where 'dreams' is a common theme running through her performances, songs, and drawings. This gambit acts both as an orientation and abstract (in the sense of Labov and Waletzky 1967) to the brief, suitably surreal story that follows: "and I was living there because the city had become <u>so</u> crowded that billboards were the only places left (.) but it was great I had an <u>amazing</u> view of downtown and plenty of time to just sort of look around and (.) figure out what

Extract 1
PBS *Art:21* series, Season 1, 2001—Introduction to Place[7]
Created and directed by Laurie Anderson
Time: 2'08"

Personnel
Laurie Anderson

I dreamed that I was living in a billboard (.) and I was living there

because the city had become <u>so</u> crowded

that billboards were the only places left (.)

but it was great I had an <u>amazing</u> view of downtown and plenty of time to just sort of look around:

and (.) figure out what to do to next

(5) [gentle, nostalgic music]

the most of the work that I do as an artist (.)

whether it's music or: images or: stories (.)

begins with the place (.)

a room (.) a road (.)

the city (.) a country (1) [sound of fog horn]

and these places become jumping-off points for my imagination

(2) [various traffic noises]

[quiet Chinese music starts playing]

but why do we fall in love with the place? sometimes it's because it's exotic and full of energy (.) and other times

because it's (.) <u>huge</u> and <u>empty</u> and full of possibility (1)

the kind of place where almost anything could happen

(.)

(3) I think

we fall in love with places for the same reason that we fall in love with people (.) and our reasons

are irrational and

passionate and hard to explain (.) [soft sound of train passing] and sometimes when we fall in love with a place it becomes part of us (.) forever

(10) [soft marimba music] you know art about places is often

about how we mo:ve through space (.)

it's about point of view (.) and perspective (.)

and scale (.) and exploration (.)

but it's also about how we track these places

and make them into works of art (.) I am Laurie Anderson

and in a minute we'll be looking at the works of several artists

who reinvent the way we see places and space (.)

and they're Richard Serra (.) who makes sculpture on a very large scale (.)

Sally Mann (.) who is rooted in her southern landscape (.)

Margaret Kilgallen and Barry McGee (.) who do street art and murals (.)

and Pepón Osorio (.) who is known for large-scale installations that evolve from interactions with neighborhoods and people

to do next" (1-3–1-7). The story is accompanied by a visual sequence of Anderson speaking from various billboards, some masquerading as fictitious advertisements for different 'services': "Feeling lost?," (1-5–1-6) "Going nowhere?," (1-8) "Need a change?" (1-9), complete with made-up telephone numbers. The relationship between the verbal and visual tracks here is, as I noted earlier, that of *relay*; she is the storyteller and the story's main character in both. The words "because the city had become <u>so</u> crowded" (1-4) are accompanied by a shot of a crowded street at night adding a visual dimension to the story's orientation. In Barthes's terms, the visual here *illustrates* the verbal.

The remaining part of the verbal track is Anderson's personal account of her view of *place* as a key inspiration for her work, and the relationships people develop with places (the mini-lecture alluded to above). This shift to a more down-to-earth theme and style is marked by a five-second pause and gentle, nostalgic music in the soundtrack. In the visual track, however, the imagery remains for the most part equally surreal, except for several close shots of Anderson speaking directly

Extract 2
PBS *Art:21* series, Season 1, 2001—Introduction to Identity
Created and directed by William Wegman with Steve Martin
Time: 2'20"

Personnel
Steve Martin (sole speaker)
Jason Burch
Chip
Chundo

hi (.) I am Steve Martin

and welcome to my home (1)

as you look around my house you can see that it is filled with many (.) beautiful art objects (.)

but we don't have a lot of time tonight (.) to look around

the house and examine each object (.) <u>tonight</u>

we are going to be looking at the work of

(2)

also (3)

we also are going to examine the work of

(2) and

(2)

you're probably wondering why I (.) Steve Martin (.) am hosting a show on contemporary art (.)

you probably know me as

an actor and comedian (.) but I am so much more (.) I am a writer (.) I am (.) a (.) playwright (.) a novelist (.) and: sometimes I am just

Steve (.) a named being (.)

so rather than talk about that (.) just pick a card (.) and just

concentrate on it and do not tell me what it is [selects card from deck (4♠); whirring of lawnmower motor starts]

(4) [looks at card]

so we'll put it back in the deck (.) and we are going to shuffle the cards

(2) [shuffles cards]

I am now going to find your card (.)

concentrate on it (.) and voilà

(2) [whirring of lawnmower motor stops]

well I am sure you have a lot to think about in terms of (.) contemporary art (.) and see that as an exciting and challenging field (1)

can you excuse me for just a moment? (12)

[puppeteer leaves]

[puppeteer returns]

anyway (.) [whirring of lawnmower   without any (1) further ado (.)
motor starts]

let's start our show and take a   one (.) two (.)   one (.) two (.) three (.) four
look at four   (.) important contemporary
                                                         artists [starts drawing and
                                                         counting four cards from deck]

[looks down at 'his' hands] who   deal in (2)   notions of [whirring of
all <u>deal</u> in (2)   lawnmower stops]

identity

to camera (1-14; 1-26; 1-34). Even then, however, after she says "anything could happen," she creates an aura of mystery by covering part of her face behind a large Chinese, red fan (1-22), previously and subsequently seen as a prop used by a group of dancers in the park (1-19–1-20; 1-23).[8]

Apart from the shots of Anderson on billboards, the fantastical and dreamlike visual imagery is conjured up by Anderson sitting in an oversized or miniature white armchair in various locations, for example, on a rooftop (1-13), against the background of the Hudson River with the Statue of Liberty in the distance (1-15), or in a park (1-24–1-25). Sometimes she is seen riding on the giant chair, for example, alongside the Hudson River (1-17–1-18) or in a supermarket (1-28–1-31). These two props (chairs) have appeared in a number of Anderson's shows, for example *Songs and Stories from* Moby Dick (1999–2000). The same performance is probably referenced when she is shown riding on the oversized chair, emerging from a

Extract 3

PBS *Art:21* series, Season 1, 2001—Introduction to Consumption

Created and directed by Barbara Kruger with John McEnroe

Time: 1'20"

Personnel

John McEnroe

(6) [sound of tennis ball being hit twice]

hi I'm John McEnroe (.) you probably know me

as a tennis player (1)

but did you also know I love art?

(2)

you know what the greatest compliment I ever received was?

that I play like an artist in a tennis court (.)

that I took chances (.) went out in a limb (.) people sometimes think myself included that art and tennis are too expensive and out of their reach

but anyone can walk into a
tennis court

(1)

(1) [sound of tennis ball being
hit once]

and anyone can walk into a
gallery or a museum [car horn]

you don't have to buy the art or
buy into it

(2)

even if we don't consume art
(.) we all consume (.) <u>food</u>

(2) [tennis ball x 1]

<u>sex</u>

(3) [tennis ball x 3]

<u>money</u>

(3) [tennis ball x 3]

culture

yeah that'd be (.) cool [tennis ball x 1]

and finally (.) what is consumption anyway

(3)

the four artists you'll meet tonight

Michael Ray Charles

Matthew Barney

Andrea Zittel

and Mel Chin

all raise questions about the things we consume every day [tennis ball x 2]

(.) now enjoy the show

(1)

car wash tunnel of "New Gentle Touch Car Wash" bearing the tagline "Whale of A Wash" (1-10), a possible reference to a number of her whale songs from the *Moby Dick* show and her album *Life on a String* (2008).

Much of Anderson's work is situated in New York (Yee 2011) or is *about* New York and New Yorkers (e.g. *New York Social Life*, 1979). In one of her interviews, Anderson declares: "First, I am an artist, second, a woman, and third, a New Yorker" (Dery 1991: 797). Thus, the choice of New York as the identifiable location of her segment introduction (e.g. the image of the Statue of Liberty) allows the 'knowing' viewer to 'read' her introductory segment as another autobiographical performance.

Finally, in her closing, Anderson states the names of the four artists featured in the segment "who reinvent the way we see places and space" (1-35). This is followed by necessarily brief but more informative than the other two introductions' characterization of each artist's practice. In the visual track this is accompanied by the display of the artists' names and some related imagery on billboards (1-36–1-39), which acts as a fantastical visual coda alluding to the introduction's beginning.

William Wegman's introduction to Identity is a self-parody based on his video *Ordinary Deck* (1998) and his numerous photographic and film pieces that since the early 1970s have featured his Weimaraner dogs. In *Ordinary Deck*, Wegman pretends to perform a card trick wearing an oversized jacket, 'his' hands being animated by a puppeteer hidden behind him. In other films, Wegman's place is taken by one of his dogs dressed in a jacket with human arms. The Identity opening segment was filmed on a soundstage designed as an interior of a 'typical,' or 'nondescript' middle-class, American house almost identical to that in *Ordinary Deck*. The program end-credits list, apart from Steve Martin as host, the puppeteer Jason Burch and two Weimaraners, Chip and Chundo. Martin faces the camera sitting at a table covered with a purple cloth. To his right stands a lit floor lamp and a sofa with a sleeping Weimaraner (2-3). Behind him is a panoramic window overlooking a garden. Later in the segment, a Weimaraner dressed in a check shirt can be seen and heard riding on a lawnmower across the lawn from left to right (2-19–2-21; 2-23–2-25) and back (2-34–2-39). In the middle of the segment, Martin starts rather inexpertly and deceitfully (2-20) performing a card trick, shuffling, dealing, and choosing cards from his deck (2-18–2-25). At one point his head is replaced for two seconds by the head of a Weimaraner (2-22). His hands are animated by a puppeteer, which the viewer realizes when the puppeteer 'takes a break' (2-28) and leaves Martin for 12 seconds without 'his' arms, speechless and motionless (2-29), after which the arms 'return' back to Martin (2-30–2-31).

Martin's script throughout appears somewhat rambling. He rapidly shifts between topics: his house, himself, art, and card tricks, often without any particular reason or explanation, e.g. "so rather than talk about that (.) just pick a card" (2-18); "well I am sure you have a lot to think about in terms of (.) contemporary art (.) and see that as an exciting and challenging field" (2-26). Towards the end of the segment, he puns on the word 'deal' meaning 'distributing cards' and 'being engaged in the process of art making': "anyway (.) without any (1) further ado (.) let's start our show and take a look at four … important contemporary artists who all deal in (2) deal in (2) notions of identity" (2-32–2.34 … 2.36–2-40). This is interrupted when Martin draws four cards from the deck and starts counting: "one (.) two (.) three (.) four (.) important contemporary artists" (2-36). Thus, rather than talking about identity (the way Anderson talks about place, for example), Martin *plays* with identity, baffling and confusing his audience, in both verbal and visual tracks.

This is consistent with much of Wegman's work, in which dogs are anthropomorphized, people are metamorphosed into dogs, and different body parts appear to act outside of their owners' control. Ironic, funny, ridiculous, and sublime, the images let us see familiar situations, stances and personas in new ways. In his opening segment analyzed here, Wegman similarly plays with notions of identity, for example, when a Weimaraner rides the lawnmower, when Martin's head is replaced by that of a Weimaraner (2-22), or when 'his' right hand 'spontaneously' scratches his chin, by which time we know it's not *his* hand (2-33). These apparent incongruities can be seen as a source of humor to all the viewers but, in contrast to those who are not, only those who are acculturated consumers of Wegman's earlier work can be rewarded with a sense of distinction for their ability to access the lamination of the segment with another generic frame: a self-stylized and self-parodic piece of video art.

In Barbara Kruger's introduction to Consumption, John McEnroe's script and accompanying visuals are interspersed with the artist's slogans: "Love *art* Buy *art* Sell *art*" (3-7–3-12; 3-22–3-27), "Money talks" (3-16–3-17), "Feed *me* Love *me* Buy *me* Need *me*" (3-37–3-44), and "Want the show Crave the show Consume the show" (3-51–3-53). The four artists in the segment are introduced by McEnroe's voice-over and four red bands with their names in white Futura superimposed on the footage of a tennis court (3-46–3-49). The slogans, which fill up the whole screen, are reminiscent of Kruger's artworks covering entire gallery walls. The bands of text with the artists' names are stylistically linked to her photographic and textual collages, which originated, in turn, from Kruger's experience as an artistic director of *Mademoiselle*, a graphic designer for various *Condé Nast* publications, and a designer of book covers. By bringing the visual and linguistic imagery from the commercial sphere to her art, Kruger appropriates, displaces and recasts these discourses in unsettling, subversive, and ironic ways. Her introduction, specifically to the theme of consumption and art, adds a layer of metacommentary on the relationship between these two areas of social life and, additionally, on her own role as an artist and entrepreneur, both critiquing and colluding in the production and commodification of art. Without prior knowledge of Kruger's work, the viewers may find the textual elements in the visual track somewhat puzzling if not downright redundant. Those 'in the know' are likely to see them as yet another example of Kruger's artistic practice and an auto-ironic poke at her own role in the art market.

THE HOST'S PERSONA AS 'ORDINARY'

All three introductions discussed here establish, directly or indirectly, the personas of their presenters as 'ordinary.' That is, despite the surreal, fantastical, or extraordinary circumstances created in each segment, they are all presented as utterly unexceptional or mundane (Sacks 1984).

As has been stated, in her introduction to Place (Extract 1), Laurie Anderson opens the segment as a cross between an autobiographical and fantastical story. But the fantasy is couched in terms of the mundane, everyday experience that is common to anyone who has wandered round any city, a modern-day flâneur strolling in a leisurely manner across the streets, or sitting in a park, and 'taking in' the sights: "but it was great I had an <u>amazing</u> view of downtown and plenty of time to just sort of look around: and (.) figure out what to do to next" (1-6–1-7). This common and familiar experience acts for Anderson as a departure point for self-presenting as an 'artist of the everyday,' firmly rooted in and drawing inspiration from her locality: "the most of the work that I do as an artist (.) whether it's music or: images or: stories (.) begins with the place (.) a room (.) a road (.) the city (.) a country (1) and these places become jumping-off points for my imagination" (1-10–1-16). Again, such 'rootedness' in place is likely to resonate with many viewers who can imagine themselves in similar circumstances.

In William Wegman's introduction to the Identity segment (Extract 2), the host, Steve Martin, appears as himself. The apparent blandness and ordinariness of the domestic setting created for the introduction is emphasized by Martin's greeting and welcome: "hi (.) I am Steve Martin and welcome to my home" with Martin extending his right arm and holding it still momentarily, palm up, in an 'offering' or 'inviting' gesture (2-3–2-4). The invitation cannot certainly be accepted by the viewers, yet it works as a democratizing device. Then, rather unexpectedly, Martin confounds this initial sense of the ordinary when he continues to describe the house as extraordinary: "as you look around my house you can see that it is filled with many (.) beautiful art objects" (2-5). This is unexpected as none of what is visible onscreen can be considered as an art object in a conventional sense. This is possibly the first puzzle in the segment that will remain unresolved for any viewer without sufficient references to Wegman's art, where Weimaraners are central to his iconography.

Next, Martin shifts viewers' attention from the idea of exploring his 'home' to presenting the names of the artists in the Identity segment ahead: "but we don't have a lot of time tonight (.) to (.) look around the house and examine each object (.) <u>tonight</u> we are going to be looking at the work of [names of the four artists featured in the program start to appear on the screen]" (2-6–2-13). As each artist's name appears on-screen, the doorbell chimes as if the artists were at the door popping in to Martin's house (and the viewers' houses) for a chat (2-9; 2-10; 2-12; 2-13). Then, Martin creates another diversion and continues his self-presentation beyond the persona of a comedian that the public associates him with the most: "you're probably wondering why I (.) Steve Martin (.) am hosting a show on contemporary art (.) you probably know me as an actor and comedian (.) but I am so much more (.) I am a writer (.) I am (.) a (.) playwright (.) a novelist (.) and: sometimes I am just Steve (.) a named being" (2-14–2-17). The last still in this sequence shows Martin in a two-second close-up, smiling broadly and wearing a casual, check shirt, in contrast to a more formal, open-neck shirt and jacket in the rest of the video. The apparent sincerity of his ordinariness is emphasized by the intimate proxemic distance (close up), his casual attire, and the first name caption "Steve."

Likewise, John McEnroe in the introduction to Consumption (Extract 3) balances his public persona with that of an ordinary or average person. He starts with a self-introduction—using, similarly to Martin, a greeting and direct, second person address—that positions him as both a (sport) celebrity and an art collector/ art lover: "hi I'm John McEnroe (.) you probably know me as a tennis player (1) but do you also know I love art?" (3-4–3-6). However, he questions the assumption that both these pursuits—playing tennis and love of art—are accessible only to the chosen few: "people sometimes think myself included that art and tennis are too expensive and out of their reach (1) but anyone can walk onto a tennis court (1) and anyone can walk into a gallery or a museum (1) you don't have to buy the art or buy into it" (3-15–3-21). In the visual track, this is accompanied by brief shots of someone's (McEnroe's?) feet walking across a tennis court (3-19) and McEnroe in a baseball cap and casual clothes walking in the street, as if to an art gallery (3-20). Finally, McEnroe suggests that art is an object of consumption just like any other commodity or pursuit and lists several activities that are shared by 'everyone,' turning all the people into 'consumers': "even if we don't consume art (.) we all consume (.) food (2) sex (3) money (3) culture" (3-28–3-34). As he lists these common areas of consumption, 'ordinary' people appear on the screen eating a doughnut (3-29), kissing (3-31), handing over money (3-33), and talking on the telephone (the last scene acted by McEnroe himself) (3-35). The sequences captured in stills 3-29, 3-31, and 3-33 appear to come from—or were shot in the style of—stock footage that is highly stylized, decontextualized (uniform white background, unidentifiable models), and symbolic of the ideas of consumption rather than documenting any specific people, events, or situations (Machin and Polzer 2015). Such imagery, possibly considered recognizable and appealing to 'everyone' due to its generic and aestheticizing qualities, may have been chosen as another device in creating a democratizing effect.

THE HOST AS ENGAGED WITH THE VIEWER

In the visual track, involvement between the artists/hosts and the viewers is established through interpersonal distance and gaze. The hosts appear mostly in close or medium-close shots corresponding to the kinesic zones of intimate or personal communicative contact (Hall 1966). Some exceptions include long shots of Laurie Anderson (Extract 1), possibly motivated by creating enough orientation shots to establish New York as a specific location (e.g. 1-12, 1-15). McEnroe (Extract 3) is shown in long shot on the tennis court to establish his identity as tennis player (e.g. 3-3).

In contrast to the main interviews in *Art:21*, in which the artists usually speak off-camera or to an off-screen, silent interviewer, the hosts in the segment introductions address the camera directly, creating a sense of involvement with the viewer and conflating their 'voice as person' and their 'voice as character' (or as 'artwork') (see Coupland 2011; also Kress and van Leeuwen 1996 on *demand* vs. *offer* images). However, the use of hosts' gaze in the introductions is not uniform. This is particularly notable in Anderson's segment, in which she sometimes appears as a character that she herself narrates with an off-screen voice-over (e.g. 1-5, 1-9, 1-11, 1-30). Switching between offer and demand images, Anderson seamlessly oscillates between the *host* and *character* personas, for example, turning her face toward the viewer in the sequence captured in 1-5–1-6, or turning it away in 1-21–1-22. Such conflation of her 'real-life' and 'artistic' personas is not untypical of Anderson's other public appearances or interviews, one critic observing: "Like Pee-Wee Herman, Ronald Reagan, and Michael Jackson, she is *always* in character: her onstage and offstage personae are virtually inseparable" (Dery 1991: 791).

Martin and McEnroe, for the most part, maintain eye contact with the viewer by looking directly at the camera. The few exceptions involve sequences in which Martin engages in a visual byplay (Goffman 1981) looking at the watch on 'his' left hand saying "but we don't have a lot of time tonight" (2-6), and when he looks down at 'his' hands to 'prompt' them to deal a deck of cards they are holding (2-37–2-39). McEnroe looks away from the camera when he is shown playing tennis (3-5), walking in the street (3-20), and speaking on the phone (3-35). Martin's redirection of the gaze has a comic effect as part of the performance of his multiple personas, when we realize that his hands are actually those of the puppeteer. McEnroe's averted gaze indicates a shift from the *host* frame to *performance* frame, in which he acts out the role of an 'ordinary guy' playing tennis, 'consuming' culture, or apparently walking to a gallery.

In all three segments the hosts use viewer-centered and inclusive modes of address. Halfway through her introduction, Anderson shifts from considering the role of place from her personal point of view, "the most of the work that I do as an artist" (1-10), to a more inclusive stance marked by the use of 'we,' "but why do we fall in love with the place?" (1-19). This is maintained throughout the rest of her script including her announcement of the Identity segment in terms of a joint activity, "in a minute we'll be looking at the works of several artists" (1-34). Martin and McEnroe are equally viewer-centered with their use of the 2nd person pronoun 'you' and inclusive 'we', creating a sense of involvement and joint action, e.g. "you're probably wondering" (2-14), "let's start the show'"(2-34), and "did you also know I love art?" (3-6).

REASSESSING ART STYLE THROUGH STYLIZATION

The foregoing data discussion suggests that the three segment introductions function as invitations and encouragement for the general public to engage with the world of contemporary art. But they are also conceived as instances of performance art styled by their creators with elements (visual and/or spoken) from their artistic practice accessible only to a narrow segment of potential viewers. With reference to vocal stylization, Coupland suggests that acts of social semiosis of this general sort may bring "conflicting identities and realities into contact with each other, making them available for reassessment" (Coupland 2010: 110). This point is extended to all verbal performance by Bauman and Briggs (1990), who have argued that "performances move the use of heterogeneous stylistic resources, context-sensitive meanings, and conflicting ideologies into a reflexive arena where they can be examined critically" (Bauman and Briggs 1990: 60).

In *Art:21*, the mundane and typically unremarkable genre of a segment introduction in a documentary TV program is elevated to become a piece of performance art. The three segment introductions alter their expected 'talking head' or 'voice-over' format into autonomous broadcast pieces blurring the boundaries between the peripheral and focal parts of the program, and between 'popular' (TV) culture and 'high' (visual) culture. In the remaining part of the chapter, I aim to reassess the three artists' self-stylizations in the segment introductions by opening up a dialogue with some insights about the ideological meanings of style in art history, the sociolinguistics of stylization, and Bolter and Grusin's (1999) approach to remediation.

STYLE AND IDEOLOGY IN ART

Art historians have long appreciated that a new *zeitgeist* enforces a new style—individual style, school style, national style, or period style—conceived of as "expression of the temper of an age and a nation as well as expression of the individual temperament" (Wölfflin 1950 [1932]: 10). Gombrich (2009 [1968]) warns against the "physiognomic" approach to style treating it as an easy window into a person's or a social group's psyche. Yet, different styles are imbued with specific social and political meanings, which can be durable if not immutable (Agha 2003). In visual arts, for example, painterly abstraction was practiced in the revolutionary Russia as a manifestation of a new, progressive ideology, yet, by the 1960s, it was denounced in the Soviet Union and replaced by Socialist Realism. At that time, in the 1950s, American art was dominated by Abstract Expressionism. The painterly style favored by each of the superpowers at the height of the Cold War became one of the instruments of ideological struggle.

But the 'meaning' of artistic style is never devoid of the specific historical and material conditions of viewing a work of art (Bal and Bryson 1991). As my analysis demonstrates, mediatization techniques, alongside art historical debates, can relativize the potential durability of artists' performance styles, in the sense that they can actively reframe artists' styles as open to question and to ideological reinterpretation (Androutsopoulos 2014; Johnstone and Baumgardt 2004). It is in this sense that the recontextualization of performance art pieces in *Art:21* can be seen as having a democratizing effect.

Elite and democratic art styles: Mantegna and Leonardo

Ideological debates over the suitability and 'meaning' of stylistic choices in art and literature go back even further. For example, Bolland (2014) gives a fascinating account of how, toward the end of his life, the Italian Renaissance painter Andrea Mantegna adopted a painterly style that can be described as 'hard' or 'stony.' The human figures painted by him acquire a statue-like quality, as if chiseled in marble, as is the case of his *St Sebastian* at Ca'd'Oro, Venice (see Figure 8.1). In the lower right of the painting, a warning is affixed to the candle: NIHIL NISI DIVINUM STABILE EST CAETERA FUMUS, 'Nothing but the divine is stable, the rest is

FIGURE 8.1 Andrea Mantegna, *St Sebastian*, c.1500. Tempera on canvas, 213 x 95 cm. Venice: Ca'd'Oro.

Source: www.aiwaz.net. Licensed under Public Domain via Wikimedia Commons—https://commons.wikimedia.org/wiki/File:St_Sebastian_3_Mantegna.jpg#/media/File:St_Sebastian_3_Mantegna.jpg

smoke.' The inscription, together with Mantegna's depiction of Sebastian's body as carved out of stone rather than covered with soft flesh, combines the idea of a classical sculpture and a living body. The heavenly and the earthly, the stable and the evanescent are juxtaposed or joined up. "The painting puns on the relationship between *durus* (hard) and *durabilis* (lasting), or, to return to the painting's inscription, between *stabilis* and *statua*" (Bolland 2014: 355).

Mantegna's style worked against some of the ideas of how to best represent the human body advocated by other prominent Renaissance artists and humanists. For example, in his *De pictura* (1435), Leon Battista Alberti praises artists like Leonardo da Vinci for their attempts to imitate nature, especially in representing human flesh. He is critical of some of his contemporaries for copying earlier artists leaving overt traces acknowledging their sources and retaining elements of their artifice. Leonardo considered painting to be a kind of natural rather than conventional language with a transparent relationship between the represented object and the seen object. For him, such painting style should have a universal appeal. In contrast, Mantegna's late style of painting based on the artful permanence of stony statues, which relied on references to ancient sculpture, may have been intended for a more specialist audience. The Marchesa of Mantua and a patron of the arts, Isabella d'Este, characterized Leonardo's style as *suavità* ('soft') and *dolcezza* ('sweet'), in opposition to Vasari's description of Mantegna's style as *asprezza* ('harsh') and *durezza* ('hard') (Bolland 2014: 362). Mantegna's 'hard' style may not have easily appealed to the mass viewer, the way the 'soft' and 'sweet' style of, say, Leonardo's might have done, with his splendid *sfumato* evocation of the transient body. In this respect, Mantegna is resolutely elitist, although elitism is not for him an end in itself. Rather, he offers a counterpoint to Leonardo's democratic and universalizing stance. As argued by Bolland, Mantegna's art presents something of a paradox that embodies an enduring message.

The painting's inscription claims that all earthly things are volatile, although its visual language seems to qualify this statement. Neither ancient art style nor Latin has evaporated like smoke, and probably will not do so in the future, despite some loss of their transparency or legibility. And the figure of Sebastian is sculptural but not lifeless. His open mouth and appearance of stepping forward from the shadows of the niche create both emotion and motion. St Sebastian's body, which is almost the same height as the canvas, is set against a dark niche—rather than against the landscape of Rome as in Mantegna's earlier depictions of the saint—which makes him appear to exist outside historical time.

> Through a series of careful overlaps, Mantegna depicts the saint's body as partially passing through the plane defined by the bands of patterned stone surrounding the niche. That stone marks the forwardmost boundary of the (fictive) niche, and serves (at least on three sides) as a frame for the (actual) painting. Mantegna's Sebastian is thus poised not only between the realms of

transience and eternity, shadow and light, but at the very border separating life and art. (Bolland 2014: 372)

I return to this point at the end of the concluding section.

IMMEDIACY AND HYPERMEDIACY IN *ART:21*

The difference between Mantegna's 'stony' and Leonardo's 'sfumato' styles, as well as that between the broadcasting style of the segment introductions and the artist profiles in *Art:21* can be accounted for in terms of Bolter and Grusin's (1999) continuum of 'immediacy'–'hypermediacy.' Transparent, perceptual immediacy aims at erasing or diminishing the element of mediation from the viewer's experience of interacting with objects in mediated space. Bolter and Grusin discuss three aspects of achieving transparency in Renaissance painting: (1) the invention of linear perspective and the illusory representation of three-dimensional space on a two-dimensional canvas; (2) the use of oil paint to 'conceal' the surface of the canvas, to erase and deny the process of painting; and (3) automatization of the technique of linear perspective, first through the use of *camera obscura* and subsequently in photography, film, and television.

The practice of hypermediacy, on the other hand, is a visual style that "privileges fragmentation, indeterminacy, and heterogeneity and ... emphasizes process or performance rather than the finished art object" (Mitchell 1994, cited in Bolter and Grusin 1999: 31). Examples include webpages with multiple text and graphic windows, interface icons and buttons, hypertext links, menu items, and so on. Other manifestations of hypermediacy in which the mixing and fascination with different media is dominant include "such diverse forms as medieval illuminated manuscripts, Renaissance altarpieces, Dutch painting, baroque cabinets, and modernist collage and photomontage" (Bolter and Grusin 1999: 34). To cite just one example, following Greenberg (1973) and Lanham (1993), Bolter and Grusin consider collage and photomontage as central to 20th-century art. These art forms are created by rearranging existing photographic and textual forms by detaching them from their original contexts and recombining them into heterogeneous spaces that "make viewers conscious of the act of representation" (Bolter and Grusin 1999: 39), which is closely related to Coupland's (2001, 2007) interpretation of stylization.

The artist profiles featured in *Art:21* (see note 1 in this chapter) tend toward the immediacy end of the continuum. They are shot in a 'straight' documentary style that minimizes the experience of the mediational space. Artists usually speak to an off-screen, silent interviewer, or off-screen with the visual track focusing on their artworks. Most interviewers' questions are edited out and artists do not look directly at the camera. Sometimes, when they are looking at the interviewer positioned next to the camera, the interviewees appear to be 'missing' the gaze of the viewer only minimally, though the effect is that of looking *past* rather than *at* the viewer.[9] The interviews are conducted in various locations: studios, galleries, artists' homes, or outdoors. All the locations are usually made relevant to the artists' practice, biography, or display of their work. Occasionally, artists appear with other people—studio assistants, family, and friends—who may be interviewed briefly or are shown in 'spontaneous' interactions with the artist. Roughly half the time given to each artist's interview involves footage of his or her artworks with the artist's commentary in voice-over. The profiles are imaginatively constructed, with their settings, structure, and filming techniques adapted to the style and/or theme of each artist's work. For example, photographs are shown as slide shows, sculptures are filmed from various angles, and performances are *staged as* performances. In this way, the artworks are objectified, or remediated without "repurposing" (Bolter and Grusin 2000: 45), unlike in the segment introductions, where elements of artists' styles are recycled to be consumed as performance pieces with new purposes and meanings (cf. Bolter and Grusin 2000: 65; see also Banda and Jimaima, 2015).

No doubt, the documentaries give the viewing public a unique access and insight into the lives and work of many contemporary artists. However, the artists appear far more distant and aloof than, say, Anderson, or the hosts in Wegman's and Kruger's opening sequences. The viewers of the profiles are precluded from symbolic interaction with the artists; they remain 'flies on the wall,' in contrast to the segment introductions, where hosts draw viewers into some form of engagement and participation. Somewhat ironically, the egalitarian ethos of the program breaks down precisely where the promise of meeting the artists as 'real people' could have (or should have) been staged with *a more intense orientation toward the audience* (to use the phrase from Luginbühl, 2014, quoted earlier).

Paradoxically, the segment introductions, with their scripted monologues delivered against the backdrop of highly staged visual tracks, with elaborate theatrical or cinematic sets, extras and props, special effects, and graphics, deliver a greater degree of involvement between the program and its viewers than its core material. But the paradox is only apparent. As has been suggested, the opening sequences are instances of high performance, and it is precisely in those moments that the distant and aloof world of 'high' art is invited to introduce new dissonant identities and re-evaluations of social relations (Coupland 2007: 154). Artists and their celebrity friends deauthenticate themselves as 'ordinary' through self-parody of their own artistic styles. They invite the audiences to laugh *with* them not *at* them (Coupland 2007: 175). Following Bakhtin (1981), after Rampton (1995), Coupland considers metaparody as instances of *uni-directional multi-voicing*, as opposed to *vari-directional multi-voicing*, where the former refers to the stance of ideological alignment with preceding utterances/speakers and the latter to deliberate misalignment with the source.[10] Anderson, Wegman, and Kruger repurpose their artistic practices as illustrative, educational, humorous or reflexive 'takes' on the program themes allowing the audience, not only to view their artworks on television but to experience television as art.

Conclusion: Stylistic coherence, mediatized performance, and the democratization of art

Van Leeuwen (2004) suggests that multimodal texts such as posters or display advertisements should be considered single communicative acts in which the stylistic unity between the image, the typography, and the layout enhances the text's cohesion. However, the degree of perceived cohesion is likely to depend on the reader's/viewer's ability to 'read' the stylistic resources deployed in the various 'tracks' of the text. The multimodal affordances of television allow its different 'tracks' to work in numerous, creative ways.

The opening segments in *Art:21* have been conceived as performance art pieces in which communicative focus goes "above and beyond its referential content" (Bauman 1975: 293). The visual and textual references to the artists' imagery serve as keying devices for the audience to recognize the introductions as *performances*, or as hypermediated patchworks of artists' archetypal themes, visual tropes, and symbols. Otherwise, Laurie Anderson's surreal imagery would be simply baffling, William Wegman's momentary trick of replacing Steve Martin's head with that of a Weimaraner completely out of place, and Barbara Kruger's slogans intrusive. Surely, the theme of each segment, the names of the represented artists, even some rudimentary contents of the segments are introduced, but providing this information is only of secondary concern (each artist in the program is also introduced by a separate title sequence). The introductions are offered to the viewers as mediatized recontextualizations of the artists'/hosts' earlier works, activities and personas thematically related to each segment's focus. They are presented to entertain and to educate the viewing public, or in the words of Bauman (1975), they are "available for the enhancement of experience" (293).

There is a tension here between the three introductions' egalitarian and elitist stances. On one hand, the introductions rely on some of the most archetypal imagery (e.g. direct gaze) and text forms (e.g. pronoun 'you') that hail, or appellate (Althusser 1971) the viewer as a 'knowing' subject and invite him or her to participatory involvement (Burke 1968 [1931], cited in Bauman, 2011). On the other hand, the artists deploy their unique, enregistered artistic styles that have been imbued with certain sociocultural values and positioning. However, as Bell has observed, "[e]nregisterment requires a style to be exposed more widely than just the individual performer, for example through repetition, pastiche or parody" (Bell 2011: 646). In the data examined here, this is achieved with a degree of metaparody by the artists themselves. This self-referencing and its presumed recognition by the audience is a key element of positioning the viewers as the art world 'in-group' members, or as art connoisseurs, even if only as novices among the art aficionados. Here, there is the link with Andrea Mantegna's hard or stony painterly style; to repeat, Mantegna's style may have been elitist but it was not an end in itself. It was a means to conveying a more subtle message of the transience of human life. Nor is the deployment of the relatively elitist styling of the segment introductions in *Art:21* an end in itself. To relatively unacculturated viewers they may appear obscure, irrelevant and redundant, while those 'in the know' may see these sequences as poignant or humorous commentaries on the unsettled and ambivalent role of art in contemporary life. Here, artists (or their proxies) appear as 'real people' whose role is not only to bridge the gap between life and art but, through the medium of television, to bring art—and, at least symbolically, its makers—closer to the life of a mass audience. And this, I believe, is how the tension between the apparent egalitarian status of television as a mass medium and the relative perception of contemporary art as elitist is resolved by the program makers.

Acknowledgements

I thank Nik Coupland and Janus Mortensen for their most helpful comments on the earlier versions of this chapter. I have also benefited from discussions with Crispin Thurlow, Alaina Janack, Marcel Burger, Gilles Merminod, Liz Stokoe, Richard Fitzgerald, and from Indra Kupferschmid's advice on Kruger's typography. All caveats apply. The verbal and visual tracks of the extracts are reproduced under 'fair use' standards.

Notes

1. I do not analyze the interviews here. However, I draw some contrasts between the (self) presentation of the artists in the segment introductions and the representation of the artists featured in the profiles, especially in the section on *Immediacy and hypermediacy in Art:21*.

2. All artists and hosts are credited in the title sequences for each of the segments (see the second still of each of the Extracts included later in the section on *Television as art*).

3. The fourth segment introduction to 'Spirituality' was created by the video artist Beryl Korot and hosted by S. Epatha Merkerson. I do n't discuss it here for reasons of space.

4. Available at http://www.art21.org/files/uploads/pdf/art21_season_one_guide.pdf (last accessed June 10, 2016).

5. A growing literature on interactivity in online newspapers and news blogs suggests that journalists and other blog authors rarely respond to readers' comments (e.g. Bolander 2013). Freeman, who provides a useful review of this research area, comments that if not fully successful, "news comments and blogs at least provide cultural tools that potentially foster interactivity" (Freeman 2014: 99).

6. I take 'imagined' in the Althusser quote to mean 'ideological.'

7. The three extracts are presented in two tracks, visual and verbal. The text under each still, when present, corresponds to the text spoken in the particular sequence of the video footage. In-text quotations from the transcripts are referenced by the corresponding still numbers, prefixed by the extract number. So, (still 1-2) refers to Extract 1, still 2, (still 3-23) refers to Extract 3, still 23, and so on. The transcription conventions are as follows:

[word]   additional information about the soundtrack and visual track

<u>word</u>   emphasis

word   louder than surrounding talk

word: lengthening

?   rising intonation

(.)   untimed pause shorter than 1 second

(1)   timed pause measured in seconds

8. Anderson used fans as masks in some of her earlier performance pieces, for example, in her *Songs and Stories for the Insomniac* (1975).

9. McEnroe's gaze creates the same effect when he is reading his script from an autocue (Extract 3, stills 14, 18).

10. I discuss some examples of varidirectional multivoicing in text-based art in Jaworski (2014).

References

Agha, Asif. 2003. The social life of cultural value. *Language & Communication* 23, 2–3: 231–273.

Althusser, Louis. 1971. *Lenin and Philosophy*. New York: Monthly Review Press.

Androutsopoulos, Jannis. 2010. Localizing the global on the participatory web. In Nikolas Coupland (ed.) *The Handbook of Language and Globalization*. Oxford: Wiley-Blackwell. 203–231.

Androutsopoulos, Jannis. 2014. Mediatization and sociolinguistic change: Key concepts, research traditions, open issues. In Jannis Androutsopoulos (ed.) *Mediatization and Sociolinguistic Change*. Berlin: De Gruyter. 3–48.

Bakhtin, Mikhail M. 1981. *The Dialogic Imagination*. Austin: University of Texas Press.

Bal, Mieke and Norman Bryson. 1991. Semiotics and art history. *The Art Bulletin* 73, 2: 174–298.

Banda, Felix and Hambaba Jimaima. 2015. The semiotic ecology of linguistic landscapes in rural Zambia. *Journal of Sociolinguistics* 19, 5: 643–670.

Barnhurst, Kevin G. and John C. Nerone. 2001. *The Form of News: A History*. New York: Guilford Press.

Barthes, Roland. 1977. *Image, Music, Text*. London: Fontana.

Bauman, Richard. 1975. Verbal art as performance. *American Anthropologist, New Series* 77, 2: 290–311.

Bauman, Richard. 2011. Commentary: Foundations in performance. *Journal of Sociolinguistics* 15, 5: 707–720.

Bauman, Richard and Charles L. Briggs. 1990. Poetics and performance as critical perspectives on language and social life. *Annual Review of Anthropology* 19: 59–88.

Bell, Allan. 1984. Language style as audience design. *Language in Society* 13, 2: 145–204.

Bell, Allan. 2011. Falling in love again and again: Marlene Dietrich and the iconization of non-native English. *Journal of Sociolinguistics* 15, 5: 627–656.

Billig, Michael. 1995. *Banal Nationalism*. London: Sage.

Bolander, Brook. 2013. *Language and Power in Blogs: Interaction, Disagreements and Agreements*. Amsterdam: John Benjamins.

Bolland, Andrea. 2014. Artifice and stability in late Mantegna. *Art History* 37, 2: 352–375.

Bolter, Jay D. and Richard Grusin. 1999. *Remediation: Understanding New Media*. Cambridge, MA: MIT Press.

Burke, Kenneth. 1968. *Counter-Statement*. Berkeley: University of California Press. (Original work published 1931).

Coupland, Nikolas. 2001. Dialact stylization in radio talk. *Language in Society* 30: 345–375.

Coupland, Nikolas. 2007. *Style: Language Variation and Identity*. Cambridge: Cambridge University Press.

Coupland, Nikolas. 2010. The authentic speaker and the speech community. In Carmen Llamas and Dominic Watts (eds.) *Language and Identities*. Edinburgh: Edinburgh University Press. 99–112.

Coupland, Nikolas. 2011. Voice, place and genre in popular music performance. *Journal of Sociolinguistics* 15, 5: 573–602.

Coupland, Nikolas. 2012. Bilingualism on display: The framing of Welsh and English in Welsh public spaces. *Language in Society* 41, 1: 1–27.

Darley, Andrew. 2003. Simulating natural history: *Walking with Dinosaurs* as hyper-real edutainment. *Science as Culture* 12, 2: 227–256.

Dery, Mark. 1991. Signposts on the road to nowhere—Laurie Anderson, crisis of meaning. *South Atlantic Quarterly* 90, 4: 785–801.

Ekström, Mats. 2000. Information, storytelling and attractions: TV journalism in three modes of communication. *Media, Culture & Society* 22, 4: 465–92.

Ellis, John. 2000. *Seeing Things: Television in the Age of Uncertainty*. London: I.B. Tauris.

Fairclough, Norman. 1995. *Media Discourse*. London: Edward Arnold.

Fairclough, Norman. 2003. *Analysing Discourse: Textual Analysis for Social Research*. London: Routledge.

Freeman, Danyal J. 2014. *A Vernacular Rhetoric of Anti-Politics*. Unpublished PhD Dissertation, City University of Hong Kong.

Goffman, Erving. 1974. *Frame Analysis: An Essay on the Organization of Experience*. New York: Harper & Row.

Goffman, Erving. 1981. Footing. In Erving Goffman, *Forms of Talk*. Oxford: Blackwell. 124–157.

Gombrich, Ernst. 2009. Style. In Donald Preziosi (ed.) *The Art of Art History* (2nd ed.). Oxford: Oxford University Press. 129–140. (Original work published in 1968, in *International Encyclopaedia of the Social Sciences*, 15. New York: Macmillan).

Greenberg, Clement. 1973. Modernist painting. In Gregory Battcock (ed.) *The New Art: A Critical Anthology*. New York: E. P. Dutton. 66–77.

Hall, Edward T. 1966. *The Hidden Dimension*. New York: Anchor Books.

Halliday, M. A. K. 1978. *Language as Social Semiotic: The Social Interpretation of Language and Meaning*. London: Edward Arnold.

Hartley, John. 1996. *Popular Reality: Journalism, Modernity, Popular Culture*. London: Arnold.

Hjarvard, Stig. 2013. *The Mediatization of Society*. London: Routledge.

Jaworski, Adam. 2014. Metrolingual art: Multilingualism and heteroglossia. *International Journal of Bilingualism* 18, 2: 134–158.

Johnstone, Barbara and Dan Baumgardt. 2004: "Pittsburghese" online: Vernacular norming in conversation. *American Speech* 79: 115–145.

Kress, Gunther and Theo van Leeuwen. 1996. *Reading Images: The Grammar of Visual Design*. London: Routledge.

Krotz, Friedrich. 2009. Mediatization: A concept with which to grasp media and societal change. In Knut Lundby (ed.) *Mediatization: Concept, Changes, Consequences*. New York: Peter Lang. 19–38.

Labov, William and Joshua Waletzky. 1967. Narrative analysis: Oral versions of personal experience. In June Helm (ed.). *Essays on the Verbal and Visual Arts: Proceedings of the 1966 Annual Spring Meeting of the American Ethnological Society*. Seattle: University of Washington Press. 12–44.

Lanham, Richard. 1993. *The Electronic Word: Democracy, Technology, and the Arts*. Chicago: University of Chicago Press.

Lorenzo-Dus, Nuria. 2009. *Television Discourse: Analysing Language in the Media*. Basingstoke: Palgrave Macmillan.

Luginbühl, Martin. 2014. Genre profiles and genre change: The case of TV news. In Jannis Androutsopoulos (ed.) *Mediatization and Sociolinguistic Change*. Berlin: De Gruyter. 305–330.

Machin, David. 2004. Building the world's visual language: The increasing global importance of image banks in corporate media. *Visual Communication* 3, 3: 316–336.

Machin, David and Adam Jaworski. 2006. Archive video footage in news: Creating a likeness and index of the phenomenal world. *Visual Communication* 5, 3: 345–366.

Machin, David and Lydia Polzer. 2015. *Visual Journalism*. Basingstoke: Palgrave Macmillan.

Meinhof, Ulrike H. 2004. Metadiscourse of culture in British TV commercials. In Adam Jaworski, Nikolas Coupland and Dariusz Galasiński (eds.) *Metalanguage: Social and Ideological Perspectives*. Berlin: De Gruyter. 275–288.

Mitchell, W. J. T. 1994. *Picture Theory*. Chicago: University of Chicago Press.

Montgomery, Martin. 1986. DJ talk. *Media, Culture & Society* 8, 4: 421–440.

Panofsky, Erwin. 1995. *Three Essays on Style*. Cambridge, MA: MIT Press.

Rampton, Ben. 1995. *Crossing: Language and Ethnicity among Adolescents*. London: Longman.

Sacks, Harvey. 1984. On doing 'being ordinary.' In J. Maxwell Atkinson and John Heritage (eds.) *Structures of Social Action*. Cambridge: Cambridge University Press. 413–429.

Scannell, Paddy. 1989. Public service broadcasting and modern public life. *Media, Culture & Society* 11, 2: 134–166.

van Leeuwen, Theo. 2004. Ten reasons why linguists should pay attention to visual communication. In Philip LeVine and Ron Scollon (eds.) *Discourse and Technology: Multimodal Discourse Analysis*. Washington, DC: Georgetown University Press. 7–19.

van Leeuwen, Theo. 2005. *Introducing Social Semiotics*. London: Routledge.

Wölfflin, Heinrich. 1950. *Principles of Art History: The Problem of the Development of Style in Later Art* [*Kunstgeschichtiche Grundbegriffe* (trans. M. D. Hottinger), 7th ed.]. Mineola, NY: Dover Publications. (Original work published in 1932).

Yee, Lydia. 2011. *Laurie Anderson, Trisha Brown, Gordon Matta-Clark: Pioneers of the Downtown Scene, New York 1970s*. New York: Prestel.

PART IV

Styles of Technologically Mediated Talk

WHAT'S NEW ANYWAY?

9

Talking for fun and talking in earnest: Two styles of mediated broadcast talk

Martin Montgomery

Introduction

Just as nature abhors a vacuum, so broadcasting abhors silence. Indeed, the professional term for unintended silence in broadcasting is *dead air*—eloquent testimony to its unwanted character.

Broadcasting, in its concept of dead air, inasmuch as it proscribes silence, seems in so doing to favor a certain kind of talk—one which we may characterize, following Tolson (2005), as marked by liveliness. One measure of liveliness might be the avoidance of silence, so much so that an informal communicative entitlement (Myers 2000) for speaking on air (while avoiding dead air) might well be the capacity to talk without hesitation, pause, or other forms of apparent dysfluency. This requirement, indeed, reaches its apogee in the long-running BBC Radio 4 panel game *Just a Minute*, in which the contestants are challenged to speak for one minute without hesitation, deviation, or repetition on any subject that comes up on the cards.

Nonetheless, even within broadcasting the tolerance of silence or pausing would seem to vary: for example, some genres (such as the experiential interview) show more tolerance for silence than others (such as the a interview) (Montgomery 2007). So much so that it is as if, across the array of genres that constitute broadcast talk, are distributed different styles of speaking, with liveliness at one end of a continuum occupied at its opposite end by something we may describe as 'talking in earnest.' If one marker of liveliness as a style is the avoidance of silence, then we should at least entertain the possibility of a contrasting style—talking in earnest— being marked by an increased tolerance of silence—and this despite the proscription against dead air. This chapter, therefore, will take as its focus the nature of silence in broadcast talk and suggest that particular occurrences of silence may

Style, Mediation, and Change. Edited by Janus Mortensen, Nikolas Coupland, and Jacob Thøgersen
© Oxford University Press 2017. Published 2017 by Oxford University Press

mark a comparatively under-investigated style of speaking encountered in some genres of broadcast mediated talk.

Silence in broadcasting and the concept of dead air

Regarding dead air *Wikipedia* (2014) offers a useful definition:

> The term is most often used in cases where program material comes to an unexpected halt, either through operator error or for technical reasons, although it is often used in cases where an individual broadcaster has lost their train of thought. Among professional broadcasters, dead air is considered one of the worst things that can occur.

Why should this be? Part of the answer lies in one of the particular values embodied in the broadcast experience. Although the technological affordances of real-time broadcasting have also had embodied within them the possibility of recording, the special promise of broadcasting, particularly at the outset and during its classic pre-digital phase, was to bring the remote event 'live' to the audience in the here and now—'live-to-air.' To no small degree, the elaboration of a broadcasting infrastructure and technological innovation within it have been driven by the search for enhanced ways of doing 'liveness' (see Marriott 2007; Scannell 2013).

At the same time the specific character of liveness, whatever the ways in which technological improvements deliver it, may vary in different domains of broadcasting. Certain kinds of broadcasting—the state funeral, the royal wedding, the inauguration of a president—make particular technological demands in the delivery of liveness which will differ from others—the sporting event, for instance, or disaster reporting (Scannell 2013).

If liveness has been the implicit promise of broadcasting for much of its history, then anything that breaks the circuit between the audience and the event is, almost by definition, a threat to its raison d'être. In short, the reason why "dead air is considered one of the worst things that can occur" (Wikipedia 2014) among broadcasters is because it undermines a fundamental premise of broadcasting—that of being live, 'on air.'

However, there is more to dead air in broadcasting than simply the sound of silence. Dead air in broadcasting is a public event. Although silence has received a fair amount of attention from ethnographers and sociolinguists (Basso 1970; Baumann 1983; Jaworski 1993; Tannen and Saville-Troike 1985), the conditions under which it has attracted comment are precisely those of relatively small-scale social interaction; and, where the events are public, they are limited to relatively small gatherings under clear conditions of co-presence. Dead air in broadcasting, however, assumes its special character precisely because it differs from everyday, co-present, talk-in-interaction in two crucial ways: first, in its 'produced' character and second in its audience design.

Broadcast talk depends on the significant deployment of technical apparatuses of recording and transmission, for the most part in purpose-designed studios, often requiring substantial capital investment and trained personnel—including speaking participants who have a professional or semi-professional status as 'talkers.' At the same time audiences come to the activity of experiencing or listening to broadcast talk with sets of expectations about the nature of the talk that they are hearing, structured in terms of time of day, channel (public service or commercial), topical interest, genre, and so on. Most significantly, we experience broadcast talk as members of a larger community of listeners or viewers. As listening and viewing participants, therefore, we are aware, as a condition of the broadcast event, that the same experience in which we momentarily share is being offered simultaneously to very large numbers of others. Both in terms of the effort that is expended on producing talk for the broadcast audience and in terms of the shared experience of receiving it, an audience can assume a warrantable status for the talk—that it will be in some way designed as of interest to others beyond its immediate interlocutors. This inevitably transforms the character of any breakdown or apparent interruption in its delivery. More specifically, where silences occur within talk in the broadcast setting they will attract attention and require or demand interpretation by the audience in ways that go beyond those applied in everyday co-present interaction precisely because of their candidate status as dead air.

Liveness and liveliness

Of course, although the liveness of broadcasting is most often understood in terms of its capacity to transmit directly the unfolding of an event as it happens in the 'here and now,' much of broadcasting is not so much predicated upon 'events' as such but on spoken reactions to them, and on unfolding commentary. Indeed, talk itself is often the primary focus of broadcasting, institutionalized in a complex array of genres, ranging from interview (with many subtypes), to phone-in, to commentary, to the ubiquitous talk show. If broadcast events (the NFL Super Bowl, the Royal Wedding, the Olympics) are often defined by their newsworthiness, broadcast talk is often justified by its liveliness—and it is this liveliness that is often identified as its prime warrant for being 'on air.' Indeed, we might further suggest that if, for the most part, live-to-air broadcasting abjures silence, then liveliness is the style of talk that embodies its avoidance. From this perspective, styles of broadcast talk, by drawing on clusters of features, constitute in part the appropriate key (in Hymes's term) for the performance of the genre.

By way of example, an extreme case of liveliness may be seen in the following episode from a well-known UK talk show *Parkinson*, broadcast on UK Independent Television (ITV) for a special Christmas Day edition in 2004. The eponymous interviewer, Michael Parkinson, has already interviewed a rock star, Rod Stewart, a comedian, Joe Pasquale, and a popular soap-star actress, Barbara Windsor, before

1al guest, *Lily Savage*, is introduced. *Lily*, the audience are well aware, is a
a adopted by her alter ego, the comedian Paul O'Grady. *Lily* enters the studio space of the interview by sashaying down a flight of stairs to the enthusiastic
applause of the studio audience. Parkinson stands to greet and welcome her and
Lily greets first Joe Pasquale and then Barbara Windsor. *Lily* is wearing a fur coat
and opens it wide as she approaches Parkinson in a frank gesture of availability that
is reinforced by her opening remark to him, "take what you like ... help yourself."

Extract 1: *Lily Savage*/Paul O'Grady on *Parkinson* (2004)

MP: Michael Parkinson

LS: *Lily Savage*

BW: Barbara Windsor

SA: Studio Audience

Link: http://www.youtube.com/watch?v=Ye2RdnIyerQ (Extract 00:10–03:39)
Transcription conventions are available at the end of the chapter.

1	LS:	take what you like
2	SA:	[laughter]
3	LS:	help yourself
4	SA:	[laughter]
5	LS:	oh come here gorgeous (.)
6		oh no tongues
7	SA:	[laughter]
8	LS:	[how are you Barbara
9	BW:	[(xxx) lovely thank you darling
10	MP:	now tell us about this comeback
11		the reason for it
12	LS:	comeback
13	MP:	comeback
14	LS:	comeback (.)
15		I hate that word (.)
16		it's return (.) return (.) to the people out there in the dark
17		who've never deserted me
18		sorry about that Michael a bit of Norma Desmond slipped in there (.)
19	SA:	[laughter]
20	LS:	weeell I thought you know
21		Barbara will tell you

22		the excesses of show business got the better of me (.) you know
23		and when you find yourself in a skip at five o'clock in the morning
24	SA:	[laughter]
25		with one of the Bay City Rollers on your back or a Mini
26	SA:	[laughter]
27	LS:	you know what I mean
28	SA:	[laughter]
29	LS:	you think Lily it's time to call it a day love
30		so I went back up to Liverpool for a bit (.)
31	MP:	right (.) and what did you do there
32	LS:	well I worked for a friend of mine who's got an agency (.)
33		big Rita her agency is,and ah
34		I was a sort of a social consultant really
35	SA:	[laughter]
36	LS:	and then then there was all that business with Wayne Rooney
37		you know what I mean and I thought I thought
38	SA:	[laughter]
39	MP:	I didn't know about that Wayne Rooney
40	LS:	it was me Michael it was me
41	SA:	[laughter]
42	LS:	I woke up I looked at this spotty forehead
43	SA:	[laughter]
44	LS:	two inches of pubic hair and I thought Lily you're too old
45	SA:	[laughter]
46	LS:	get off the game
47	SA:	[laughter]
48	LS:	now he's playin for Manchester
49	MP:	I know
50	LS:	fifty quid and he wasn't worth it believe you me
51	SA:	[laughter]
52	LS:	and the poor lad got a rash
53	SA:	[laughter]
54	LS:	yes well I didn't know [sniff]
55	MP:	anything else you been doing we should know about
56	LS:	[phphphph] I been doin lots well then I

57		decided I thought while you've still got a womb Lil I thought you know
58	SA:	[laughter]
59	LS:	cheap audience in here tonight haven't you
60	SA:	[laughter]
61	LS:	do anything to come in for a warm
62	SA:	[laughter]
63	LS:	I thought while I I'll carry another woman's eggs for her
64	SA:	[laughter]
65	LS:	I don't mean as a market stall you know what I mean no no
66	SA:	[laughter]
67	LS:	for lesbian couples who couldn't have children
68	SA:	[laughter]
69	LS:	I had eighteen yes
70	SA:	[laughter]
71	MP:	eighteen what
72	LS:	babies in a period of three years
73		oh I'm prolific what
74		I had to have my pelvic floor laminated
75	SA:	[laughter]
76	LS:	get over I'm tellin you
77	SA:	[laughter]
78	LS:	they shot out seriously
79	SA:	[laughter]
80	LS:	there's lesbian couples all over the country delighted because of me
81	SA:	[laughter]
82	LS:	sold two on ebay wherever you are yes
83	SA:	[laughter]
84	LS:	I tell you what
85	MP:	what
86	LS:	her video saved my life
87	MP:	did it
88	SA:	[laughter]
89	LS:	or what
90	MP:	what
91	LS:	I did the buttock clenchin exercises

92		I can pick a pencil up now with my bum
93	SA:	[laughter]
94	LS:	no one can look up my bum I can pick a table up I can show you later
95	SA	[laughter]
96	LS:	marvellous that Barbara
97	BW:	thank you dear thank you
98	MP:	now what's this rumour there is about Mr O'Grady killin you off
99	LS:	don't talk to me about that four-eyed fruit (.) I've had enough of him
100	SA:	[laughter]
101	LS:	I never watch the Paul O'Grady show
102		Barbara I know he's a pal of yours
103		and I don't want to speak ill of him
104		I'm a Richard and Judy girl
105	SA:	[laughter]
106	MP:	are you
107	LS:	oh yes
108	SA:	[laughter]
109	LS:	and I'll tell why
110	SA:	[laughter]
111	LS:	I am
112		I'm not watching that shite with somebody with a chicken and a dog
113	SA:	[laughter]
114	LS:	Richard and Judy because you can have a bevvie
115		no with the wine club
116		you know Judy can't wait until six o'clock to have one
117	SA:	[laughter]
118	LS:	with the wine club so
119	SA:	[laughter]
120	LS:	I sit there Michael six bottles of Blue Nun I'm unconscious by half six
121	SA:	[laughter]
122	MP:	let's talk a bit about the panto cos you are back in panto now
123	LS:	I am
124	MP:	this is your comeback now in panto
		so tell me is it an original panto

One index of liveliness is the response of the studio audience: there is a great deal of laughter (at lines 2, 4, 7, 19, 24, 26, 28, 35, 38, 41, 43, etc.). The talk is deliberately and self-consciously humorous and takes for granted the audience's knowledge of the two personae (*Lily Savage*, the fictional, assumed persona, and Paul O'Grady, the relatively stable identity behind the assumed persona) as well as the popular cultural contexts in which they operate (there are references, for instance, to the Bay City Rollers—the 1970s Scottish pop group—and Coronation Street—the Manchester-based television soap opera). Speaking in the persona of *Lily Savage*, O'Grady is referred to in the third person, "I never watch the Paul O'Grady Show," a show which *Lily* dismisses on the grounds that she, *Lily*, is a "Richard and Judy girl." In fact, O'Grady's show was in lighthearted competition with a popular UK daytime television chat show, *The Richard and Judy Show,* which ran on a rival TV channel. Other characteristics of this example of broadcast lively talk are truncated anecdote: for example, "the business with Wayne Rooney" (a star footballer with Manchester United, regarding whom tabloid newspapers had published allegations of consorting with prostitutes) and "carrying another woman's eggs for her." The anecdotes depend on (sexual) innuendo for their humor but also on a dense, interlocking set of references to aspects of popular (and tabloid or show business) culture in which *Lily* positions herself as often a central (and fictionalized) pivotal figure.

There is, in this respect, a highly performative character to the talk. While *Lily*'s supposed adventures provide a persistent point of reference for the talk, her performance clearly marks her as not a 'real' person. *Lily*'s mannerisms are highly exaggerated, even camp. Indeed, many of her mannerisms and some of her self-reference foreground aspects of female anatomy—for instance, "womb," "eggs," or "pelvic floor." In this way, the talk becomes an elaborate way of performing an assumed identity and the distance between *Lily* and the underlying person of O'Grady. In short, her performance is that of a 'man' self-consciously assuming the identity of a certain culturally constructed type of 'woman.' These features of the talk and its performative nature are not new, of course; they are well known to British television viewers in other examples such as *Dame Edna Everidge*/Barry Humphrys or *Mrs Merton*/Caroline Aherne, as well as in much older traditions of music hall and pantomime.

Most significant, however, the talk proceeds without interruption, at speed, with much exaggeration of gesture and intonation, all of which contribute to a sense of liveliness. There is no sense of the awkward pause and certainly no instance of dead air.

'Lively talk' versus 'talking in earnest'

If broadcast talk, by virtue of the act of broadcasting, can be said broadly to favor styles of talk where participants continuously perform in a lively fashion, routinely with a minimum of hesitation or pause, are there no occasions where silences can be a meaningful and significant part of the listening and viewing experience? The remainder of this chapter is devoted to arguing that, as well as styles of 'lively talk,' broadcasting also draws on a contrasting style of talk which I will call 'talking in earnest' where the tolerance of silence is perceptibly different and where silences may even be an essential quality or property of the performance.

Take, for instance, the following extract from an interview between Oprah Winfrey and Whitney Houston on American Broadcasting Company's nationally syndicated talk show *The Oprah Winfrey Show* (2009).

Extract 2: Whitney Houston on *The Oprah Winfrey Show* (2009)

OW: Oprah Winfrey
WH: Whitney Houston
Link: https://youtu.be/dxmqjoe9MlE?t=1m3s (Extract 01:03–02:01)

	1	OW:	I DON'T (.) KNOW (.) HOW (.) you live in a world
	2		(.) where (.) you are (.) Bobby Brown and REAlly (.)
	3		you're in the shadow (.)
	4	WH:	yeah (.)
	5	OW:	you're in the shadow
→	6	WH:	yeah (.) he supported me
→	7		(1.0)
	8		he loved me
→	9		(1.0)
	10		we fought (.) hard we loved hard
	11	OW:	mmhum
→	12		(1.0)
	13	WH:	hhhh an:d I think at some point in time (.)
	14		other things began to take place
	15	OW:	was he jealous (.) of you
→	16	WH:	(7.0) hhhh (4.0)
	17		he's not going to like this but yes
→	18	OW:	uhum (2.0) and then did you (1.5) try to overcompensate
	19	WH:	(.) I tried [to play down (.) all the [time (.) I did (.)
	20	OW:	[(bu) [yeah yeah
	21	WH:	hhhh I tried to play I'm Mrs. Brown everybody
	22		don't call me Ms. Houston
	23		I'm Mrs Brown

Overall, the extract is characterized by relatively high incidence of pausing. In the first turn of the extract, Oprah pauses at a rate approaching once every two words, combined with heavy emphasis for the segment "I DON'T (.) KNOW (.) HOW (.) you live in a world." The rhythm of talk and turn-taking is thus quite different from fast-paced lively talk. Indeed, there is a sense in which both participants can be heard as choosing their words with care. Take, for instance, Whitney Houston's turn, lines 6–10:

```
       6   WH:   yeah (.) he supported me
  →    7          (1.0)
       8          he loved me
  →    9          (1.0)
      10          we fought (.) hard we loved hard
```

With its parallel structures, punctuated by pausing, the overall effect is of talk taken seriously: not lively talk but talking in earnest.

Pause versus silence

Pausing is one thing; however, silence is another. At line 16 there is an extending gap of 11 seconds punctuated by an intake of breath following Oprah's question to Whitney Houston about her husband Bobby Brown, "Was he jealous of you?" This is very different in character from the pauses at lines 7, 9, 12, and 18, which generally seem to be within the boundaries of a speaker's turn. The gap at line 16 clearly comes at point of turn transition so that it is heard as belonging to Houston. It is Houston's turn to talk and she seems in some way to decline to do so. Interestingly the camera holds on Houston for the whole of the 11 seconds, reinforcing the notion that this is her turn.

While pausing may be a variable property of talk in interaction, marking a cline in broadcast talk between lively talk and talking in earnest, silences such as Houston's of 11 seconds are particularly noticeable—especially in broadcasting—to the extent that they may well attract explicit interpretation and comment. Are there any criteria, then, that can be used to distinguish a pause from a silence? Jefferson (1988) has suggested that there may well be a metric in ordinary conversation by which the upper limit for pausing may be 0.9–1.2 seconds. Beyond this length, gaps may well last for two, three, or four seconds and be associated with 'trouble' such as searching for a name. In what follows, I shall use the possibility of this metric to focus on a data set from broadcast talk where a pause lasting more than 1.2 seconds becomes hearable as a silence and may well attract very particular attention in the broadcast context.

Extract 3 is taken from a series of interviews conducted on British television by the Irish psychiatrist and broadcaster Dr. Anthony Clare. In this interview, broadcast in 1995, he is talking to the Irish Republican politician, Gerry Adams, at a time when the northern Irish peace talks were at a critical juncture. Extract 3 comes very near the beginning of the interview.

Extract 3: *The Anthony Clare Interview* with Gerry Adams (06/08/1995) (STV)

AC: Anthony Clare
GA: Gerry Adams
Link: http://www.youtube.com/watch?v=8CLWyGgU3xI (extract 01:23–03:05)

```
      1    AC:  er your personality (.) your traits (.) are indeed crucial (.)
      2          to: the: outcome of a quite elaborate political process
      3          that's going on that involves many other people of course
      4          I refer of course to the Northern Ireland peace process
      5          would you: comment on that
→     6          (1.0)
      7    GA:  well it's difficult (.) for me to give you er (.) an objective view
      8          of that the business I'm about is (.) er trying to empower people (.)
      9          and er I do understand the dynamics of the:: (.) personality
     10          and (.) the tendency in politics for a personality cult
     11          and I'm actually very very opposed to that (.)
     12          but I think all of us bring our own our own personal weaknesses and
     13          strengths (.) to whatever we do
     14    AC:  and when you look back (.) at your life
     15          and certainly the first years of it (.)
     16          what do you identify (.) as (.) key aspects of your personality
     17          that now indeed you draw on
→    18          (2.5)
     19    GA:  (hhh) well
→    20          (1.0)
     21          I actually find (.) in in trying to write about childhood and
→    22          (3.0)
     23          after childhood very difficult because there has been
     24          so much has happened
     25          and (.) it's it's difficult to focus (.)
     26          but I suppose it's the sense of belonging (.) er I (.)
```

27   I think because of the nature of colonialism

28   and in (the) sense the Irish are a colonised people

29   we suffered because of our relationship with er Britain (.)

30   not just in terms of (.) division (.) poverty and other (.) er

31   elements but also I think in terms of how we see ourselves

32   how we see the world

Anthony Clare's questions are a blend of the public and the private. The preface to his first question links the question of Adams's personality to the outcome of the peace process: "er your personality (.) your traits (.) are indeed crucial (.) to: the: outcome of a quite elaborate political process that's going on." Adams replies in general terms, acknowledging that "all of us bring our own our own personal weaknesses and strengths (.) to whatever we do." Clare reinstates the topic of personality: "what do you identify (.) as (.) key aspects of your personality that now indeed you draw on." And again Adams returns the discourse to an abstract level—almost politico-historical in its generality: "the Irish are a colonized people we suffered because of our relationship with er Britain (.)." The gap between the personal and political is negotiated through a complex set of pauses. Each of Clare's questions is met with a pause, of one second at line 6, and two and a half seconds at line 18. In both of Adams's replies, furthermore, he explicitly registers the difficulty posed by the question: "well it's difficult (.) for me to give you er (.) an objective view of that"; and "(2.5) (hhh) well (1.0) I actually find (.) in in trying to write about childhood and (3.0) after childhood very difficult."

It is not my purpose in this chapter to attribute particular meanings to these silences: it might be that Adams resents questions about his personality at a time when public events are poised as to their outcome; it might be simply that he finds it hard to talk about his childhood and upbringing, especially in front of a large audience. My point is simply that while pauses of a second or less are routine in most kinds of talk, pauses longer than a second 'sound' significant and become a hearable property of the talk.

It is hardly accidental, of course, that Dr. Clare asks Adams about his personality. Even in his role as a broadcaster, Clare was also well known as a psychiatrist. Indeed, an earlier BBC radio series was called *In the Psychiatrist's Chair* which drew audiences and pleased critics. Lynn Barber, for instance, has commented that Clare "elicited the most interesting radio interviews of my lifetime," while another critic, Gillian Reynolds, described the segment in Extract 4 as "a memorable moment" from "his most controversial encounter."

Extract 4: *In the Psychiatrist's Chair.* Anthony Clare interviews Claire Rayner, the British "agony aunt" (1988)

AC: Anthony Clare
CR: Claire Rayner
Link: http://www.bbc.co.uk/programmes/p0112lk7

	1	CR:	I know what it likes it's like to be a beaten child=
	2	AC:	=leaving aside the question of what's the point (.)
	3		put that aside for a second (.) a second (.)
	4		the point of looking at it (.)
	5		let's let's put aside the point
	6	CR:	mm
→	7		(1.0)
	8	AC	would it be painful
	9	CR:	YES
	10	AC:	I mean acutely painful
	11	CR:	probably
→	12		(1.0)
	13	AC:	you're not sure
→	14		(4.0)
	15	CR:	almost certainly yes
	16		almost certainly it would (.)
	17	AC:	you mean ti:::me hasn't dulled it
	18		or your er your method of coping with it
	19		hasn't defused it of its (0.5) agony
	20	CR:	NO
→	21		(5.0)
	22	AC:	it was that bad
	23	CR:	mm
→	24		(1.0)
	25	AC:	let me ask you something else (.)
	26		in what way d'you think it has shaped you
→	27		(1.5)
	28	CR:	I think it's made me reasonably resilient
	29		believe it or not
	30		I do bounce back

As well as a high incidence of pauses (e.g. at lines 7, 12, and 24), there are additional silences at lines 14, 21, and 27. Whilst Clare's questions are effectively polar questions (e.g. "would it be painful"), including declarative requests for confirmation (e.g. "it was that bad"), unusually for this context they receive only minimal responses: "yes," "probably," "no," "mm," and in the case of both "yes" and "no" (at lines 9 and 20), delivered with particular emphasis. In other words, although the responses suffice to meet minimally the requirements of the questions, they fall short of the normal expectations of an interview program, where even polar questions serve as an invitation to talk further and develop the topic embedded in the question. Thus, the question "would it be painful (to talk about)" does not simply ask for "yes" or "no" but prompts for talk on the topic of the pain—how would it be painful, or, more revealingly, why would it be painful? To answer only "yes" or "no" thus counts as an avoidance of the topic of pain.

It is in this context—of what might be considered 'non-compliant' answers—that the silences take on particular significance. They can, of course, be interpreted in a variety of ways—as willed resistance to inappropriate questions, as the inability to confront difficult areas of childhood experience, or as searching for the right words to articulate something not previously expressed, and so on. It would be a mistake, however, to attribute the silences simply to one party. In this respect, it is worth comparing the pause at line 7 with the silence at line 14

	5	AC:	let's let's put aside the point
	6	CR:	mm
→	7		(1.0)
	8	AC:	would it be painful
	13	AC:	you're not sure
→	14		(4.0)
	15	CR:	almost certainly yes

At line 7, although the pause follows a vocalization of assent from Rayner ("mm"), it is hearable as coming within Clare's turn—between his question preface ("let's put aside the point") and the question itself ("would it be painful"). The silence at line 14, however, follows a clear point of turn transition relevance. Unlike the pause at line 7, it belongs to Rayner rather than Clare. Each of these may usefully be compared with the silence at line 21.

	17	AC:	you mean ti: ::me hasn't dulled it
	18		or your er your method of coping with it
	19		hasn't defused it of its (0.5) agony
	20	CR:	NO
→	21		(5.0)
	22	AC:	it was that bad
	23	CR:	mm

This silence follows a minimal response by Rayner to Clare's question. In that sense, given the pre-allocated turn sequence of interviews, turn transition to Clare is relevant; and the silence, then, belongs to Clare who technically has the floor. If, however, the minimal response is taken as an insufficient answer to the question, then the silence may be heard as an invitation to CR to continue. In some sense, therefore, silences can be *co-produced*—especially if they belong clearly to neither party.

The ambiguity about this third case points to a crucial and dynamic property of broadcast silence that is impossible to capture in transcription: silences unfold, and they change in character or significance in the act of their unfolding. Here we must recognize the role of the participation framework for broadcast talk. It is not just that broadcast silence has significance—variable at that—which is interpretable to the co-participants to the talk. Silences, as they unfold, are also a hearable property of certain styles of talk for the broadcast audience.

Silence as a hearable property of certain styles of broadcast talk

Elsewhere (Montgomery 2007), I have argued that the incidence of pausing may provide an incidental indicator of generic differences between different types of broadcast journalistic interview, most particularly between those of the accountability type—where the emphasis falls on calling public figures to account—and those of the experiential kind where the focus falls more deliberately on exploring or rehearsing the personal experience of the interviewee in respect to some news event.

Accountability interviews tend to be adversarial and agonistic: they are about justifying to a public past actions performed, or words said, by the interviewee. Experiential interviews, by contrast, tend to rest on an assumption of cooperativeness. They rest on the assumption that the interviewee has undergone some experience that will be of interest to the audience. It is rare that the interviewer will hold an interviewee accountable for his or her experience. For this reason, the latter type tends to allow the interviewee more 'space' to develop answers than the former.

From this perspective, the incidental link between genre and pausing or silence may be better understood as operating indirectly, articulated in terms of style, in such a way that pausing and silence (or, alternatively, their relative absence) amount to a 'key' or performative setting ('liveliness,' for example, vs. 'earnestness') for doing particular genres and subgenres. The agonistic genres that depend upon forms of verbal display tend towards liveliness whereas the reflective genres which take personal experience as their focus tend toward earnestness.

Generic types of interview, of course, do not always occur in pure form; and, as others have argued (Ekström 2011; Hutchby 2011), hybrid examples of the types are not uncommon. In the following example from the prominent UK political discussion program *The Andrew Marr Show*, the interview seems to shift footing to move between accountability and experience at a crucial moment. The interview itself received much comment in the press at the time, some of it focusing on a lengthy pause by the interviewee, Alastair Campbell, the political aide well known for his close association with Tony Blair, the former British prime minister.

Extract 5: Andrew Marr interviews Alastair Campbell (2010)

AM: Andrew Marr
AC: Alastair Campbell
Link: https://www.youtube.com/watch?v=nFAkA2X_hN8 (Extract 03:58–05:29)

1	AM:	right so so (.) I come back to the original question then (.)
2		if:: (.) beyond doubt was not established (.) in the intelligence
3	AC:	[((cough))
4	AM:	when this inquiry looks at the intelligence
5		does it then follow (.)
6		yes or no (.)
7		that the prime minister misled parliament
8	AC:	the prime minister didn't mislead parliament
9	AM:	even (.) even if the:: (.) intelligence (.)
10		when it's looked at (.) does NOT confirm (.)
11		THAT assertion (.) that it was beyond reasonable doubt
12	AC:	yes because (.) (hhh)
13		look as I said (1.3) I mean forgive me for this I've
→ 14		(2.5) (hhhh)
15	AM:	because this is the question
16		I mean this is the thing
17		that people say you can't answer this question (.)
18	AC:	I've been through a lot of this Andrew (.)
19	AM:	mm
20	AC:	and I've been through a lot of that inquiry (.)
21	AM:	mm
22	AC:	and er
→ 23		(6.5)
24		Tony Blair (.) I think is a TOTally honourable man (1.0)
25		and I also think that what we've taken on this (.) is (.)
26		what I'VE taken on this (.)
27		CONstantly you did it again this morning
28		which is probably why I'm a bit upset
29		this constant sort of vilification (.)

30 AM: when did I vilify you
31 AC: [well you compared the novel to the dossier
32   and it's all fiction and all the rest of it
33   it's not (1.5)
34   and I I just think the way that this whole issue has developed now
35   where (.) I don't think people ARE interested in the truth anymore Andrew
36   (.) [I think you're all interested in setting in settling your scores=
37 AM: [well (.) let me let
38 AC: =and setting your own agenda.
39   an an I I'm sorry if I do get (.) upset about this
40   but I I (.) WAS there alongside Tony
41   I KNOW how that decision weighed on him (.)
42   I KNOW the care that we took (.)
43 AM: mm
44 AC: and (.) I just think it's
45 AM: [but you surely must under(stand)
46   six hundred thousand people (1.0) died (.) after that

There are in fact two lengthy pauses, one of 2.5 seconds at line 14 and one of 6.5 seconds at line 23. In each case they are 'within turn' for Alastair Campbell; that is, in neither case is Campbell's turn syntactically, semantically, or prosodically complete at the point where the pause begins.

In the first case, however, the interviewer, Marr, reinstates the question that led to Campbell's turn: effectively, he treats the developing pause as a relevant turn transition point. In the second case he does not; and the pause develops into a 6.5-second silence before Campbell resumes his turn. In both cases the pause is heard as belonging to Campbell; and, indeed, they were treated as such in newspaper commentaries, as well as in the BBC's own transcript of the interview made available on its website:

ALASTAIR CAMPBELL
Yes because . . . Look, as I said . . . I mean forgive me for this. (sighs/hesitates)
ANDREW MARR:
Because this is the question. I mean this is the thing; that people say you can't answer this question.
ALASTAIR CAMPBELL
I've been through a lot of this, Andrew, and I've been through a lot of that inquiry. And er . . . (hesitates) Tony Blair, I think is a totally honourable man,

—BBC transcript of *The Andrew Marr Show*
(http://news.bbc.co.uk/2/hi/uk_news/politics/8502824.stm)

The Daily Mail's account attributes a more emotive quality to the exchange. In an item headlined "Emotional Campbell cracks up in a TV interview" it is claimed that:

> During several lengthy pauses, one lasting 15 seconds, the former Labour spin chief took a series of deep breaths while trying to compose himself.

The Daily Mail further suggests that

> Alastair Campbell suddenly stops during the interview and closes his eyes . . .
> . . . he exhales and looks away from interviewer Andrew Marr . . .
> . . . he goes silent for a while and then says "I've been through a lot of this, Andrew . . ."
>
> (http://www.dailymail.co.uk/news/article-1249152/Emotional-Alastair-Campbell-cracks-TV-interview-Iraq-war.html)

In fact the two extended pauses (or silences) at lines 14 and 23 bear comparison with the shorter pauses at lines 18 and 20:

18   AC: I've been through a lot of this Andrew (.)

19   AM: mm

20   AC: and I've been through a lot of that inquiry (.)

21   AM: mm

Here, in each case, the pause occurs at a point where the turn—on syntactic grounds at least—could be considered complete; and, although in each case the pause lasts for less than half a second, it is met each time with a low-key "mm" from the interviewer. In neither case, in other words, does the pause develop; and that it does not do so is the outcome of joint work by both parties.

Indeed, the extended, 6.5-second silence at line 23 is interpretable in various ways—from *The Daily Mail's* assertion that Campbell "cracks up" with emotion, to comments at the time on *Digital Spy* claiming that it was a "staged" silence—"the act was worthy of an Oscar." Whatever the truth of such claims (and it is worth noting that some of them at least—such as those above—are mutually exclusive), this silence is first of all a hearable phenomenon in the talk. As a post on *Digital Spy* commented during the broadcast:

> Anyone watching this? Alastair Campbell just had to take a moment to compose himself after coming over all tearful when Marr asked him about the Iraq inquiry . . . *I wasn't paying attention until he stopped talking*, so I missed the question that triggered it.
> (http://forums.digitalspy.co.uk/showthread.php?t=1212878; my italics for emphasis)

And, second, the silence is susceptible to interpretation: indeed it seems to demand or invite interpretation.

Discussion

On any one occasion of broadcast talk, of course, a particular silence may be interpretable in a variety of ways, where notions of utterance planning, on the one hand, and extreme emotion, on the other, offer perhaps the most favored alternatives. The examples of broadcast silence in this chapter suggest, however, that a broader interpretation is possible. As a general rule, these silences take place along the boundary between public and the private, between what might be described as the publically available persona and the private individual. In the case of Alastair Campbell and Andrew Marr, the silence coincides with a shift between doing (public) accountability:

> 8   AC: the prime minister didn't mislead parliament

and invoking (personal) experience:

> 18   AC: I've been through a lot of this Andrew (.)
>
> 19   AM: mm
>
> 20   AC: and I've been through a lot of that inquiry (.)
>
> 21   AM: mm
>
> 22   AC: and er
>
> → 23   (6.5)
>
> 24   Tony Blair (.) I think is a TOTally honourable man (1.0)
>
> 25   and I also think that what we've taken on this (.) is (.)
>
> 26   what I'VE taken on this (.)
>
> 27   CONstantly you did it again this morning
>
> 28   which is probably why I'm a bit upset

In this sense the pauses or silences are part of the negotiation of the shifts of footing between the two domains—indeed, in Goffman's terms they may be said to 'key' those shifts. Or perhaps it would be better to say that they are part of doing boundary work between the two domains. In the case of Anthony Clare's interview with Claire Rayner, Clare himself subsequently wrote that he wished to probe behind her public persona, justifying this on the grounds that, given her occupation as an agony aunt "to purvey advice, reassurance, solace, sympathy and support to the thousands who seek it from her, it was important to discover whether she really was the composed, controlled superwoman she occasionally personified" (Clare 1993: 209). Elsewhere in the interview he suggests "as long as you are outwardly what you are no-one really knows you," to which she responds: "What does it matter? I don't necessarily want everyone to know me." Against this background, Rayner's clipped responses about her childhood and her silences are part of boundary maintenance work that effectively dramatizes the division between public and private. Much the same could be said about the lengthy silence from Whitney Houston before she commits to the claim that Bobby Brown was jealous of her:

```
      15   OW:    was he jealous (.) of you
→     16   WH:    (7.0) hhhh (4.0)
      17          he's not going to like this but yes
```

The case of Gerry Adams might be considered the inverse of that involving Alastair Campbell. In Campbell's case he shifts from the domain of public affairs to that of private experience. In the case of Gerry Adams, on the other hand, Anthony Clare is asking explicitly about aspects of Adams's personality as they might relate to the peace process.

```
      14   AC:    and when you look back (.) at your life
      15          and certainly the first years of it (.)
      16          what do you identify (.) as (.) key aspects of your personality
      17          that now indeed you draw on
→     18          (2.5)
      19   GA:    (hhh) well
→     20          (1.0)
      21          I actually find (.) in in trying to write about childhood and
→     22          (3.0)
      23          after childhood very difficult because there has been
      24          so much has happened
      25          and (.) it's it's difficult to focus (.)
      26          but I suppose it's the sense of belonging (.) er I (.)
      27          I think because of the nature of colonialism
```

Here Adams deflects a question about the private domain of personal traits to the politico-historical realities of colonialism. In general, therefore, what we find at stake in these examples of silence in broadcast talk is not a simple resistance to talking about something private in public but rather complex work around the exact boundaries between the two and a problematic negotiation of a shift from one footing to another.

Conclusions

It is important to note that the transcription of pauses/silences does scant justice to their dynamic, changing properties. They unfold in real time between one stretch of talk or item and another; and only when they are complete, with the resumption of talk, is it possible for participants (including the broadcast audience) to come to an assessment of their significance. The analyst's account struggles, indeed, to capture the phenomenology of silence. However, there seems to be warrant in the data for regarding a gap in talk of up to 1.2 seconds as equivalent to a momentary pause, and therefore as hardly noticeable in the normal course of events (unless they are repetitive). In the broadcast setting, however, a gap longer than 1.2 seconds becomes distinctly noticeable, and all the more so as it extends toward five, six, or seven seconds, thereby counting as a notable silence. Gaps of such duration in the broadcast setting, especially on radio, may begin to qualify for assessment as dead air, provoking thoughts that it might be brought about by technical failure. More likely, however, they will attract the kind of attention expressed by the blogger:

> *I wasn't paying attention until he (Campbell) stopped talking*, so I missed the question that triggered it.

Silences in broadcast talk, therefore, do not share in the ethos of liveliness. Rather they are a property of what I have called talking in earnest—*viz.* talk with a 'serious' purpose. An underlying and not much noted character of broadcast talk is the presumption of its interest to a large overhearing audience: that is, there must be a warrant for broadcasting it; it is presumed to be shaped to embody certain qualities of 'listenability' or 'viewability' that will sustain the interests of the broadcast audience. The most obvious way of achieving this is through liveliness. This kind of talk flourishes as fast and fluent, sometimes funny, sometimes antagonistic; and it could be argued that it is highly performative in its character, relying on forms of verbal display. Its nature, however, can be usefully measured against another kind of talk which engages the interest of audiences precisely because it seems to be 'for real' and where the talk is devoted to exploring or extracting the hitherto 'unsaid.' Here the silence, with its unfolding, uncertain, and inconclusive character, plays a striking and risky role. It invites interest but of a very different kind than lively talk.

Nonetheless, inasmuch as they attract attention, they may well do so in terms of an element of presumed performativity. As the blogger comments of Alastair Campbell's silence: "the act was worthy of an Oscar." On the contrary, however, I hope I have shown that it is difficult for such silences—even Houston's seven seconds, followed after an intake of breath by four seconds—to be in any simple way performed or staged by one or other party. Undoubtedly they are events in the talk; but in all of these cases of silence in broadcast talk-in-interaction there is an element of complicity and co-production. They may be owned in different degrees by one or other speaker, but their unfolding duration draws both interlocutor and audience into their drama. For this very reason they seem best understood not as a feature of personal style per se but rather as imbricated within and part of a generically appropriate style of talking—where styles of talking are adopted as a kind of performative set or key for particular genres. Of course, styles, as performances of a genre, will always carry an individual element, even as part of the rubric for a particular genre. Indeed, it is precisely in this way that innovation can enter into the generic field. For genres are always in process; they are always work in progress.

In conclusion, however, silence in broadcasting—as the concept of dead air implies—goes to the very heart of the styling of broadcast talk and of its interest to audiences. The possibility of silence—and its uncertainty and undecidability when it occurs—is the void over which broadcast talk is maintained and which gives it its interest.

Acknowledgements

I would like to thank the following who contributed to the preparation of this chapter: the Research Committee of the University of Macau, who approved research leave of one semester during 2015, and the University of Strathclyde who made me welcome during that period of leave, particularly Dr Michael Higgins and Maureen McDonald. I would also like to note my appreciation of the lively and informed responses of the members of three seminars where early versions of this material were presented: in particular *The Ross Priory International Seminar for the Study of Broadcast Talk; Media Talk*, Griffith University, Australia; and the University of Copenhagen *Round Table on Sociolinguistics and the Talking Media: Style, Mediation and Change*. I would also like to thank the Hebrew University of Jerusalem and Professor Richard Kulka and his family for inviting me to give the 1st Shoshana Blum Kulka Memorial Lecture, where some of this material formed the basis of my talk. Finally, I would like to express my heartfelt thanks to Nik Coupland and Janus Mortensen whose penetrating and insightful comments did much to improve an earlier draft. Its faults, of course, remain my own.

Transcription conventions

The transcripts are divided into lines which, for ease of readability, correspond as much as possible to major syntactic units—usually the clause. Each line of the transcript is numbered on the left-hand side and the speaker is identified by initial letters of his or her name (e.g. AM = Andrew Marr) at the beginning of his or her turn or stretch of speech.

Since punctuation in speech is performed prosodically, standard written punctuation marks such as commas, full stops, and colons are not applied in the normal way. Other conventions:

(.)	pause of half a second or less
(1.5)	pause timed in seconds
(only partly intelligible)	uncertain transcription
((fast))	contextual gloss—usually manner of speech

[	beginning of overlapping stretch of speech
=	introduces latched turn
:	extended syllable
hhhh	inhalation
(hhhh)	aspiration
[greeting]	discourse coding
→	indicates line which is the focus of comment or discussion
CAPITALS	indicate emphasis

References

Basso, Keith H. 1970. "To give up on words": Silence in Western Apache culture. *South Western Journal of Anthropology* 26, 3: 213–230.

Bauman, Richard. 1983. *Let Your Words Be Few: Symbolism of Speaking and Silence Among Seventeenth-Century Quakers*. New York: Cambridge University Press.

Clare, Anthony. 1993. *In the Psychiatrist's Chair*. London: Mandarin.

Ekström, Matts. 2011. Hybridity as resource and challenge in the political interview. In Matts Ekström and Marianna Patrona (eds.) *Talking Politics in the Mass Media*. Amsterdam: John Benjamins. 135–156.

Hutchby, Ian. 2011. Doing non-neutral: Belligerent interaction in the hybrid political interview. In Matts Ekström and Marianna Patrona (eds.) *Talking Politics in the Mass Media*. Amsterdam: John Benjamins. 115–134.

Jaworski, Adam. 1993. *The Power of Silence*. London: Sage.

Jefferson, Gail. 1988. Notes on a possible metric which provides for a 'standard maximum' silence of approximately one second in conversation. In Derek Roger and Peter Bull (eds.) *Conversation: An Interdisciplinary Perspective*. Clevedon: Multilingual Matters. 166–196.

Marriott, Stephanie. 2007. *Live Television: Time, Space and the Broadcast Event*. London: Sage.

Montgomery, Martin. 2007. *The Discourse of Broadcast News: A Linguistic Approach*. London: Routledge.

Myers, Greg. 2000. Entitlement and sincerity in broadcast interviews about Princess Diana. *Media, Culture & Society* 22, 2: 167–185.

Scannell, Paddy. 2013. *Television and the Meaning of* Live: *An Enquiry into the Human Situation*. Oxford: Blackwell.

Tannen, Deborah & Muriel Saville-Troike (eds.). 1985. *Perspectives on Silence*. Norwood: Ablex.

Tolson, Andrew. 2005. *Media Talk: Spoken Discourse on TV and Radio*. Edinburgh: Edinburgh University Press.

Wikipedia. 2014. Dead air. https://en.wikipedia.org/wiki/Dead_air. (Last accessed June 26, 2014).

10

The meaning of manner: Change and continuity in the vocal style of news reading and information announcements

Theo van Leeuwen

Introduction

This chapter is a reflection on change and continuity in a key aspect of the style of news reading, and, more generally, information announcements: intonation and rhythm. I will suggest that this style, with its emphasis on conveying urgency, objectivity, impartiality, and authority, has in some respects remained remarkably constant since at least the early 1980s, while in other respects it is now undergoing the influence of the 'marketization of public discourse' (Fairclough 1993) and the diversification entailed by branding. More generally I argue that in researching style we should look for continuity as well as change, and that in researching change we should look for the specific factors that drive change rather than treat change as some kind of natural process.

News reading speech

In a study of intonation in news reading I conducted in the early 1980s (van Leeuwen 1982, 1983, 1992), I drew attention to a range of characteristic features of news reading which I interpreted as ritualized expressions of key news values.

The study was based on recordings of three news items by 21 news readers in three Sydney AM radio stations. I also conducted interviews with the announcers and analyzed their use of intonation and rhythm in these interviews for comparison. This brought out, among other things, that, when reading the news, the news readers used a significantly lower pitch register than when answering my questions in the interviews.

223

Style, Mediation, and Change. Edited by Janus Mortensen, Nikolas Coupland, and Jacob Thøgersen
© Oxford University Press 2017. Published 2017 by Oxford University Press

In my transcriptions of these recordings I focused on four aspects of intonation and rhythm.

- *Stress*

This I indicated by bolding and italicizing. The rhythmic feet which stress creates as a result of the isochronous spacing of the stressed syllables, I indicated by a slash arbitrarily placed before each stressed syllable (e.g. a/*slash* is/*placed* be/*fore* the/*stressed*/*syl*lables)

- *Phrasing*

This I indicated by a double slash at the end of each phrase and by placing the phrase between square brackets (for instance, [a/*slash* is/*placed* be/*fore* the/*stressed*/*syl*lables//])

- *Relative prominence of the stressed syllables*

This I indicated by superscript numbers (for instance [a/[1]*slash* is/[4]*placed* be/[5]*fore* the/[2]*stressed*/[3]*syl*lables//]). It should be noted that these are *relative* levels. The question is not whether a given syllable *is* 'level 1' or 'level 2' or how many levels there are in general. The question is whether it is more or less prominent than other syllables in the same phrase, with superscript 1 being the most prominent.

- *Pitch direction of phrase-final syllable(s)*

Phrase-final pitch direction is either 'continuing,' indicated by an acute accent (´) or final, indicated by a grave accent (`) (for instance, [a/[1]*slash* is/[4]*placed* be/[5]*fore* the/[2]*stressed*/[3]*syl*làbles//])

It is not possible to explain here in detail why I developed this approach instead of using one of the many approaches already in existence. My key motivations were (1) the discovery that the structuring of speech is primarily a matter of rhythm rather than of intonation as proposed, for example, in Halliday's work on intonation (1967), (2) that prominence is caused by a complex interaction of pitch, intensity, duration, and vowel color, rather than by pitch alone, so that, for instance, the structure is preserved also in whispered speech, where tone is absent, and (3) that the functionalities of grammar on the one hand, and intonation and rhythm on the other, are usually quite independent of one another (cf. van Leeuwen 1982, 1999). My transcription focused on the *functional* elements of intonation and rhythm— its function of 'framing' the moves in the ongoing speech act by creating phrase boundaries (short pauses, lengthening of a final syllable, or a change of gait); its function of creating relative salience, through the distinction between stressed and unstressed syllables and through endowing stressed syllables with different degrees of prominence on the basis of their importance for the message; and its function of indicating whether a turn, or a significant section of a monologue, is complete ('finality') or incomplete ('continuity'), thereby creating units larger than the phrase. As mentioned, in everyday speech, as in poetry, the boundaries of phrases often do not coincide with the boundaries of grammatical units, and phrases may contain hesitation noises and other nonlinguistic utterances, even gestures, rather than words.

The functionalities on which this analytical approach focuses are not unique to speech and can be found in other time-based modes of communication as well. Salience and framing, in particular, are necessary textual functions in any mode of communication, and in spatial modes such as images or printed or electronic pages framing is realized by frame lines, empty space between elements, and so on, and salience by boldness, relative size, foregrounding, eye-catching tonal or color contrasts, and so on (cf. Kress and van Leeuwen 2006; van Leeuwen 1999, 2005). Analyzing salience can therefore reveal what speakers (or the institutions that produce and maintain certain styles of professional speech) judge to be important in communicating their message. And analyzing phrasing can reveal what speakers or institutions want listeners to understand as discrete moves in the ongoing speech event (e.g. discrete items of information).

I observed four key features of news reading.

- *High rate of utterance and the urgency of the news*

The mean rate of utterance was 4.69 syllables per second, as opposed to 4.1 in radio commercials, 3.93 in classical music announcing (both of which were also read from scripts), and 3.89 in the interviews I conducted with the (same) news readers. I interpreted this as conveying the urgency and recency of the news. I am by no means the only one to have observed this. In his book *Television, Technology and Cultural Form*, Raymond Williams (1974: 116) had noted:

> Over much of the actual news reporting there is a sense of hurried blur. The pace and the style of the newscast takes precedence over the items in it . . . The flow of hurried items establishes a sense of the world: of surprising and miscellaneous events coming in, tumbling over each other from all sides.

- *Non-final finality and the authority of the news*

The news readers I recorded often used a terminal, 'final-sounding' downward pitch glide in the middle of sentences—hence at moments which were not final in the sense of concluding a particular news item or section of it. Sometimes this produced a kind of 'headline' effect, as with the finality intonation on "Renown" in:

[the con/¹*tai*nership//] [²*A*sian Re/¹*Nòwn*//] [is /¹*due* to leave/²*Bris*báne//] . . .

Sometimes it occurred at the end of apparently randomly chosen phrases, as with "push" in the following example:

[re/¹*pórts*//] [are con/¹*ti*nuing to/²*come* ín//] [of a/²*big* Is/¹**raeli**/³*pùsh*//] [over the/
¹*bor*dér//] . . .

226 Styles of Technologically Mediated Talk: What's New Anyway?

I interpreted this as an 'authoritative' intonation. Finality, I reasoned, is assertive, the tone of definitive statements and commands. If it occurs mid-sentence finality becomes assertiveness, definiteness for its own sake, a ritualized display of authority—and news readers can of course use final intonation and pauses without fear of being interrupted.

- *Disjunction and the factuality of the news*

The news readers tended to make the grammatical subject (as well as other elements of the sentence) into separate phrases, for instance:

[¹*Life*savérs//] [¹*úsed*//] [²spe cial tech/¹*níques*//] [to/¹*keep* Larkin a/²*flóat*//] [in the/ ¹*wa*tèr//]

This kind of disjunction I interpreted as a ritual expression of factuality, as it makes the 'who,' the 'what,' the 'where,' the 'why,' and the 'when' into separate informa- tion units. Doing this was in fact explicitly recommended in a 1976 textbook of 'announcing techniques':

> Careful grouping of words can help you say exactly what you want to say. For example read the following sentences, pausing at the spaces:
>
> He   won the right to vote
> He   won the right   to vote
> He   won   the   right   to   vote
>
> ... [the first one] reads well if the intention is to distinguish the victor. It tells two things: who and what. Number two reads even better if the intention is to identify three things: the person, the victory, and the nature of the victory. Three sounds choppy and singalong. (Herbert 1976: 94)

When questioned about this, one of the news readers I interviewed in fact used this intonation pattern to illustrate the factuality of the news:

[but with/¹*néws*//] [²*you* are/¹*sim*plý//][re/¹*la*tíng//] [eh/¹*fácts*//] [¹*to* peoplè//]

- *Regularity and the impartiality of the news*

The news readers I recorded read in an even tempo and tended to regularize the number of syllables per rhythmic foot, preferring rhythmic feet of three or even four syllables, which, at times, caused them to de-stress what might be considered impor- tant content words (e.g. "get" in the first example that follows, and "thousand" and "hundred" in the second example):

[²*are* to get/¹*sa*lary/³*in*creasés//]

[forty/¹*one* thousánd//] [¹*eight* hundred/²*do*llàrs//]

This I interpreted as a ritual of impartiality. As one news reader explained it to me: "Everything has to have equal mechanical emphasis so you don't editorialize."

Perhaps this is the reason for the frequent complaint that news readers 'stress the wrong words.' In an article in *The Listener* (1979) Alvar Liddell, a prominent BBC radio newsreader during the Second World War, blamed a particular announcer for introducing the habit:

> The indefinite and definite articles were more often than not pronounced in their stressed form; the auxiliary verbs ... were often abnormally aggressive rather than normally neutral ... It had nothing to do with sound news reading, which is an official rendering of official writing. (478)

It may also be the reason for the complaint that news readers sound monotonous. In 1977, in *Radio: A Guide to Broadcasting Techniques*, Evans said "Newscasters sound monotonous simply because their speech rhythms are too regular" (Evans 1977: 50).

It may finally also be the reason for the frequent comment that news readers place more stresses than is normal. This is in fact not the case. The mean percentage of stressed syllables in news reading was 40.91, and in Australian Broadcasting Corporation (ABC) news reading it was even as low as 37.78, as opposed to 41.79 in the interview material. But the impression might have arisen because of the unusual stresses, and because the writing frequently does not use anaphoric reference, repeating the full lexical item over and over, and stressing it every time it occurs, as if it is, each time, a new item of information.

News reading today

The data for this study are now more than 30 years old, but although I have not replicated the whole of my earlier study, surveying a number of recent radio and television news programs from the United States (Bloomberg), the United Kingdom (BBC), Australia (ABC), and the Netherlands (NOS), I immediately observed that all these features, so familiar to me from my earlier study, are still very much in evidence. The following Dutch example, for instance, displays regularity as well as disjunction (I provide a 'literal' translation):

[de/²*Fran*se po/¹*li*tie//] [heeft een ver/²*dach*te ge arres/¹*téerd*//] [voor de/⁴*aan*slag in het/ ³*Joods* Mu/²seum in/¹*Brus*sèl//]

([the/²*French* po/¹*lice*//] [has a/²*sus*pect ar/¹*res*ted//] [of the at/⁴**tack** on the/ ³Jewish Mu/²seum in/¹*Brus*sels//])

This example from the BBC has strong disjunction:

[an A/²*me*rican/¹**sol**diér//] [held/²*pri*soner by the/¹*Ta*libán//] [for nearly/¹*five*/ ²*yéars*//] [has been re/¹*léased*//] [in/¹*Eas*tern Af/²*gha*nistàn//]

This example from the ABC has non-final finality and disjunction, as well as regularity:

[²*Spea*king in/¹*Syd*ney this/*mor*níng//] [¹*Tony*/²*A*bbòtt//] [¹*in*di/²*cat*éd//] [he is²/ *wi*lling to ne/*go*tiate/*as*pects of the/¹*Bud*gét//] [*but* he re/*mains*/¹*firm*ly com/ ²*mi*ttéd// [to/ *in*tro/*du*cing/²*Me*dicare/ ¹*co*-paymènt//

And this example, from Bloomberg, has strong regularity, destressing "hundred" in "three hundred million," and even destressing "Lucas" the first time he is mentioned. It also has extra strong 'excited' stresses on "three" and "per," which I have indicated by means of capitalization—I will return to this in the following, as it in fact represents a change from earlier practice:

[The pro/²*posed* Lucas/ *Cul*tural/ ¹*Arts* Muséum//] [*would* be a/¹*THREE* hundred/²*mi*llion dollar/ *show*cáse//] [for/*Lu*cas's/¹*PER*sonal co/²*llec*tion of//] [²*art* and memora/¹*bi*lià//]

All examples, incidentally, have a high rate of utterance similar to that of the recordings I made more than 30 years ago.

Manner and its history

In my work on social practices (van Leeuwen 2008), 'manner' (or, as I called it in that book, 'performance mode') is a key aspect of social practices, often as strongly regulated by normative discourses of one kind or another as other aspects of social practices. In including it in my account of social practices, I was inspired by Hymes's concept of 'key,' which he defined as "the tone, manner or spirit in which an act is done," and which, he said, is related to ritual, and may be "in conflict with the overt content of the act" and "override" it (1972: 62), as indeed happens in news reading when ritualized intonation patterns hinder the informative function of the news, despite news readers' professed belief in clarity.[1]

Thanks to the historical studies of Cardiff (1980), Leitner (1980), and others, it is possible to reconstruct something of the history of manner in radio speech and observe that it shows three distinct, though overlapping, stages. These same stages can be seen in the history of other media practices, as described for instance in a study of film lighting (Boeriis and van Leeuwen 2016).

- *Genesis*

The first phase is characterized by local experimentation, trial, and error. David Cardiff (1980) has documented how the BBC, in the late 1920s, became aware that the new medium of radio should adapt public speech to its reception in the listeners' living rooms, and began to experiment with scripts that contained deliberate hesitations, and with fully scripted vox pops which, for a small remuneration, were read in the studio by London taxi drivers. Leitner (1980) described how, in Nazi Germany, Goebbels told radio announcers to use local dialects and "sound like the listener's best friend"—all in the name of developing a 'conversational' style. Barnouw (1966) describes similar experiments in the United States. News reading, however, had to remain 'official' and in the early days of television, the BBC even refrained from showing the news readers, using a picture of Big Ben (conventionally referring to the famous bell tower of the Palace of Westminster in London) instead, but eventually an element of conversationality, or what Fairclough (1993) called 'synthetic personalization,' would enter here, at first in commercial radio and television, but gradually also in public radio and television, albeit sometimes reluctantly.

- *Consolidation*

In the second phase, the practice is no longer learned 'on the job' but taught formally. Textbooks and courses create explicit normative discourses, generalizing where previously each new situation was seen as specific. This began in the late 1960s and broke through more fully in the 1970s, with textbooks such as those by Herbert (1976), and Evans (1977), from which I quoted earlier, and before them Lewis (1966).

Today such normative discourses receive even wider distribution through online courses such as *WikiHow* (http://www.wikihow.com/Read-and-Speak-Like-a-TV-News-Reporter), *Howcast* (http://www.howcast.com/videos/42641-how-to-talk-like-a-newscaster), and *LiveScience* (http://www.livescience.com/33532-tv-announcers-voice.html), which purport to teach "how to read and speak like a news reporter" (WikiHow). Globally distributed through the Internet, they consolidate the ritualized manner of news speech and promote its use beyond broadcast news, into announcements of all kinds (in public transport, airports, etc.). The global speech style promoted by sites such as WikiHow and Howcast is marketed as conveying confidence, conviction, and authority as well as friendliness ("use a conversational but authoritative voice," WikiHow), and as applicable to any subject matter (what is important "is not what you are saying, but how you are saying it," WikiHow).

More than 20 years ago, Fairclough (1993) drew attention to the "marketization of public discourse," the use of the language of advertising and promotion in domains where hitherto they had not been used, such as university job advertisements and bureaucratic documents. He spoke of the "colonization of the public domain by the practices of advertising" and the concomitant "appropriation of private domain practices by the public domain" (1993: 140) which causes personal communication to become infected with the language of promotion and makes self-promotion a key part of identity building. A similar argument can be made with regard to journalistic writing. Pioneered by news agencies such as Reuters (cf. Machin and van Leeuwen 2008), news became reduced to small, self-contained 'items' that can be edited, topped-and-tailed, and rearranged in multiple ways, at the expense of larger cohesive structures. This fragmentation of information eventually became central in technical processes such as information searching and assembling announcements from small pieces of information (e.g. in public transport announcements) (cf. Mooney 2014) which have, today, contributed to the commodification and quantifiability of information.

- *Automatization*

In the third phase, which is only just beginning, the formulation of rules has developed to the point that automatization can be attempted, initially in short, public announcements, and now, for instance, in Mac OS X ('Operating System Ten'), which "flawlessly converts text to clear, easy to understand speech" (Acapela, http:// www.acapela-group.com). Like all digital technologies, such technologies are global, homogenizing the delivery of information in many languages, yet also allowing customization, as explained on the website of the *Acapela Group*, a company which provides synthesized voices for announcements and 'product enhancement': "Use your own exclusive voice, perform your voice charter, enhance your brand identity and differentiate your services with your own exclusive synthetic voice." This emphasis on branding takes its inspiration from Hollywood where accents and dialects had long been used for purposes of dramatic characterization (cf. van Leeuwen 2009) and includes, among other things: "voices with accents, voices of celebrities, voices that surprise you by their naturalness and custom-made voices" (Acapela).

Analyzing contemporary 'automatized' announcements shows that they use some of the key functional characteristics of news reading speech as I have described it above, for instance disjunction (e.g. in the next example, the gaps between "the gap," "between the train," and "and the platform"!) and 'non-final finality' (e.g. in "mind the gap," "the next station is," and "to New York" in the examples that follow). At the same time they mix in elements of the manner of live radio commercials (cf. van Leeuwen 1982, 1984) in which emphatic monosyllabic meter seeks to imprint brand names, telephone numbers, and so on in listeners' memories, and exaggerated stresses seek to convey excitement. In public announcements such excitement can become spurious and unrelated to the content, as with the exaggerated stresses on "and" and "Farringdon" in the examples that follow.

[¹*Pléase*//] [¹*mind* the/²*gàp*//] [be/²*twee*n the/ ¹*tráin*//] [¹*AND* the/²*plat*fòrm//] [¹*thís*//] [is/ ²*Chis*wick/ ¹*Pàrk*//]

[the/ ¹*next*/³*sta*tion/²*ìs*//] [¹*FA R*ringdòn//] [¹*change*/²*fór*// [¹*Na*tional/ ²*Rail*/³*ser*vicès//]

[*All*/¹*pas*sengers/²*tra*velling//] [on/⁵*flight*/ ¹*six*/ ⁴*one*/ ³*five*/ ²*fóur*//] [to New/ ¹*Yòrk*//] [there is a de/³*par*ture/¹*hall*/²*chànge*//]

The meaning of manner

Styles developed in the media have increasingly become models that influence many other genres. The hyperbolic style of advertising now informs many other genres, and the information style that was developed by news agencies such as Reuters is now widely applied beyond journalism itself. What are, according to the normative discourses of contemporary media courses and Internet tutorials, the key characteristics of news reading and its wider application to other kinds of announcements?

- *Conversational, yet authoritative*

You must sound "like somebody's friend, keeping them company as they drive to work," yet be credible, a trustworthy source of information, "a voice they can trust" (LiveScience, http://www.livescience.com/33531-tv-announcers-voice.html)—'confident,' 'authoritative,' 'engaged,' 'powerful.'

This comes with suggestions that echo those of the textbooks from which I quoted earlier. Stress relates to meaning—"Stress the words that best communicate what you are talking about" (LiveScience, ibid). Intonation ('inflection,' 'cadence') should be 'even,' 'calm,' 'balanced.' The voice should be 'loud,' 'powerful.' Tempo should be slow: "Speak slowly and enunciate carefully," "know when to slow down" (LiveScience, ibid). Using a low pitch register is recommended: "lower pitch sounds more authoritative so that the audience member feels confident in their ability and credibility" (WikiHow, http://www.wikihow.com/Read-and-Speak-Like-a-TV-News-Reporter). Non-final finality is also mentioned: "a downwards inflection when saying a key word stresses certainty", whereas "raising your voice or using an upwards inflection when saying a keyword conveys doubt, uncertainty" (LiveScience, http://www.livescience.com/33531-tv-announcers-voice.html). How to realize a 'conversational' voice, however, is never technically explained. It must, apparently, somehow emerge from auto-suggestion: the speaker should 'sound engaged.'

- *Neutral and global*

The more large media corporations globalize, and the more reliance is placed on globally distributed technologies, the more media styles become global styles (cf. Machin and van Leeuwen 2008, who discuss the pressures this puts on languages other than English). The same performance of authority is now to be accepted across the globe, which, paradoxically, means that, as an announcer, you have to "sound like you're from nowhere," according to Amy Caples, a "former news anchor teaching voice classes at Temple University" (LiveScience, http://www.livescience.com/33532-tv-announcers-voice.html).

In *Outline of a Theory of Practice*, Bourdieu suggested that explicit normative discourses do not always reflect everything that practitioners do, and it is certainly true that the suggestions in textbooks and Internet tutorials are fragmentary and leave much to be picked up by osmosis:

> The master must bring to a state of explicitness, for the purposes of transmission, the unconscious schemes of his practice ... But the subtlest pitfall doubtless lies in the fact that such descriptions freely draw on the highly ambiguous

> vocabulary of *rules* ... to express a practice that in fact obeys quite different principles. The explanation agents may provide of their practice ... conceals, even from their own eyes, the true nature of their practical mastery, i.e. that it is *learned ignorance* (*docta ignorantia*), a mode of practical knowledge not comprising knowledge of its own principles. (Bourdieu 1977: 18–19)

In the age of automatization, however, this is changing. To convert text into speech, detailed algorithms need to be written. Everything must be made explicit. And once it is explicit it is written in the modern equivalent of 'being written in stone.' Natural evolution is no longer possible and only technical intervention can bring change, as new versions of the relevant software are introduced. All this brings a risk of over-ritualization, and, indeed, of ossification.

That this risk is real can be gleaned from the comments of ordinary people, who, sometimes hiding behind names like Sailor, Star Power, Boco Dragon, and Kuppoppo, comment on the manner of news readers in blogs, chatrooms, and message boards such as Straight Dope and NeoGaf, and on sites such as Yahoo! Answers. And although some comments echo the normative discourses, many are critical. Here I provide some common examples.

- *News readers all sound the same*

News reading speech is thought to be "unconversational" and "unnatural." News readers "sound like robots" and do not differentiate between stories: "It could be a cop shot, or a story of a kitten in a tree. Same delivery" (http://boards.straight-dope.com/sdmb/archive/index.php/t-204946.html)—this despite the fact that the normative discourses recommend the opposite—"Talking quickly portrays an excited tone," while "talking slowly portrays a more serious tone": "Pace reflects the mood of the story" so you can tell "what is sad, what is exciting, all with the voice" (WikiHow, http://www.wikihow.com/Read-and-Speak-Like-a-TV-News-Reporter).

- *Wrong stress patterns*

Despite the recommendation to "stress the words that best communicate what you are talking about"), commentators feel that announcers stress "little words that are normally unstressed," "overemphasize certain words and syllables," and go for "vocal cliff hangers." "They want to make the news sound more important, but now that everybody does it, it has no effect." Similar critiques are leveled, for instance, at announcements on public transport:

> I have often noticed that announcers tend to emphasise prepositions, conjunctions, and auxiliary verbs rather than nouns and main verbs. Examples: First Capital Connect WOULD like to apologise FOR this delay, and for ANY inconvenience this may cause. Compensation forms CAN be found at www. dotfirstcapitalconnect, DOT co, DOT uk. (user comment on www.phonetic-blog.blogspot.co.uk)

- *Disjunction*

Disjunction, too, does not go unnoticed. Announcers are thought to sound 'choppy' and 'staccato.' Public transport announcements "seem to be cut and pasted from short clips—like the Speaking Clock, but less plausible" (user comment on www. phonetic-blog.blogspot.co.uk)

- *Announcements have "odd intonation patterns"*

Announcing intonation is 'freakish,' 'weird,' 'odd,' bizarre,' 'singsong,' 'an exaggerated lilt.' "It's like up and down and up and down and it sounds very matter of fact". "I hear just cadence." Or this more detailed evaluation:

> I have the impression that (commercial, news, sports, weather, etc.) announcers speak to us as if we were small children in desperate need of great surprises, hence their absurd melodies. Some correspondents of the BBC World Service, for example, are a bit irritating because of this. News readers here in Spain are equally insufferable. (user comment on www.phonetic-blog.blogspot.co.uk)

Conclusion

I have two points by way of conclusion. First, we have seen that intonation and rhythm in news reading have remained remarkably constant since at least the early 1980s. The literature on orality (e.g. Ong 2002) suggests that in traditional societies practices *do* change over time, but without this being consciously noticed—people think they do things the way they have always been done. Today we tend to focus on innovation and do not always notice the tenacity of certain traditions, even when they are being challenged by new developments. In the field of media, practices tend to change as the result of major changes in the media landscape—for example in the case of radio where the introduction of television led to the development of 'music radio' programming, and introduced the new role of the radio disc jockey. But during the intervening periods, many media practices tend to stay relatively stable—both advertising and news writing and reading are a case in point. Durand's (1970) account of visual rhetoric in advertising, for instance, written 45 years ago, is as valid today as it was then, as is Goffman's (1979) account of gendered poses in advertisements. As for the style of news reading and related announcing practices, the Internet has brought many changes in the visual presentation of information, but few if any in the presentation of authoritative information through the spoken word, particularly as far as intonation and rhythm are concerned.

However, this does not mean that no change is happening at all. In an era that can be characterized as the information age as well as the age of the rule of the market, advertising and news reading have both become dominant practices whose influence is felt well beyond the domains of advertising and news reading as such. As we have seen, there are signs that in some contexts the two begin to intertwine, as friendliness is stressed and the excited tones and emphatic monosyllabic meter of advertising infiltrate information announcements, while other characteristics, such as disjunction and non-final finality, remain. Other changes include accents and dialects being used for branding, when versions of accents and dialects which have long been used in entertainment media to characterize dramatic personae are employed for purposes of characterizing companies through branding.

Despite their contemporary dominance, however, neither advertising nor news reading in the end achieves what it sets out to do. Trust and credibility are lacking. True conversationality and engagement are not achieved, despite all attempts. As we have seen, this has been noted and commented on (and often satirized) by professional as well as lay commentators for a long time, but with little effect on the relevant practices.

Stuart Hall put his finger on it many years ago:

> In one event after another ... the same informal theories—supported by the same ideological commitments and functioning as an 'objective' set of technical-professional routines—produce the same mysterious product with systematic regularity. (Hall 1970: 1058)

Note

1. The term *manner*, as used here, is entirely compatible with the concept of style as it is used in this book. As I have used 'style' somewhat differently in earlier work (van Leeuwen 2005), I will for the moment continue to use 'manner' and leave the similarities and differences between the ways I have used these two concepts for another occasion.

References

Barnouw, Erik. 1966. *A Tower in Babel: A History of Broadcasting in the United States to 1933*. New York: Oxford University Press.

Boeriis, Morten and Theo van Leeuwen. 2016. Towards a semiotics of film lighting. In John A. Bateman and Janina Wildfeur (eds.) *Film Text Analysis: New perspectives on the analysis of filmic meaning*. London: Routledge. 24–46.

Bourdieu, Pierre. 1977. *Outline of a Theory of Practice*. Cambridge: Cambridge University Press.

Cardiff, David. 1980. The serious and the popular: Aspects of the evolution of style in the radio talk 1928–1939. *Media, Culture & Society* 2: 29–66.

Durand, Jacques. 1970. Rhétorique et image publicitaire. *Communications* 15: 70–93.

Evans, Elwyn. 1977. *Radio: A Guide to Broadcasting Techniques*. London: Barrie and Jenkins.

Fairclough, Norman. 1993. Critical discourse analysis and the marketization of public discourse: The universities. *Discourse & Society* 4, 2: 133–159.

Goffman, Erving. 1979. *Gender Advertisements*. London: Allen Lane.

Hall, Stuart. 1970. A world at one with itself. *New Society* 18, 6: 1056–1058.

Halliday, M. A. K. 1967. *Intonation and Grammar in British English*. The Hague: Mouton.

Herbert, John. 1976. *The Technique of Radio Journalism*. Melbourne: Edward Arnold.

Hymes, Dell. 1972. Models of the interaction of language and social life. In John J. Gumperz and Dell Hymes (eds.) *Directions in Sociolinguistics: The Ethnography of Communication*. New York: Holt, Rinehart and Winston. 35–71.

Kress, Gunther and Theo van Leeuwen. 2006. *Reading images: The Grammar of Visual Design* (2nd ed.). London: Routledge.

Leitner, G. 1980. BBC English and Deutsche Rundfunksprache: A comparative and historical analysis of the language of the radio. *International Journal of the Sociology of Language* 26: 75–100.

Lewis, Bruce. 1966. *The Technique of Television Announcing*. London: Focal Press.

Liddell, Alvar. 1979. Newsweeding. *The Listener* (April 5, 1979): 478.

Machin, David and Theo van Leeuwen. 2008. *Global Media Discourse: A (Critical) Introduction*. London: Routledge.

Mooney, Annabelle. 2014. Spoken signs and literal hailing: Public announcements in public transport. *Empirical Language Research* 8: 22–44.

Ong, W. 2002. *Orality and Literacy: The Technologizing of the Word* (2nd ed.). London: Routledge.

van Leeuwen, Theo. 1982. *Professional Speech: Accentual and Junctural Style in Radio Announcing*. MA Thesis, Macquarie University.

van Leeuwen, Theo. 1983. The intonation of radio news readers. *Australian Journal of Cultural Studies* 2, 1: 84–98.

van Leeuwen, Theo. 1984. Persuasive speech: The intonation of the live radio commercial. *Australian Journal of Communication* 7: 25–35.

van Leeuwen, Theo. 1992. Rhythm and social context. In Paul Tench (ed.) *Studies in Systemic Phonology*. London: Frances Pinter. 231–262.

van Leeuwen, Theo. 1999. *Speech, Music, Sound*. London: Palgrave Macmillan.

van Leeuwen, Theo. 2005. *Introducing Social Semiotics*. London: Routledge.

van Leeuwen, Theo. 2008. *Discourse and Practice: New Tools for Critical Discourse Analysis*. New York: Oxford University Press.

van Leeuwen, Theo. 2009. Parametric systems: The case of voice quality. In Carey Jewitt (ed.) *The Routledge Handbook of Multimodal Analysis*. London: Routledge. 68–78.

Williams, Raymond. 1974. *Television, Technology and Cultural Form*. London: Fontana.

PART V

Postscripts and Prospects

11

Style, change, and media: A postscript

Jannis Androutsopoulos

My following comments on the volume's nine main chapters (Chapters 2–10) proceed in four steps: I address 'talking media' as a space to study sociolinguistic change; then draw on an example to illustrate how different layers of sociolinguistic change can be read off a single multimodal text; then outline three ways of linking style, change, and media as they emerge from these chapters; and conclude by discussing the relation of mediatized representations to audience uptakes and its implications for future research in a sociolinguistic change paradigm.

'Talking media' as spaces of sociolinguistic change

When it comes to elaborating the notion of sociolinguistic change, this volume's main focus on spoken language in broadcast media—'talking media'—is spot on. Relating spoken language to (socio)linguistic change inevitably brings to mind the dominant understanding of language change in sociolinguistics (see the editors' Introduction, Chapter 1). It is of course possible to examine language change in broadcast language from a variationist perspective, and adequate archives of broadcast language can even provide data for a real-time study of language change (Van de Velde, Van Hout and Gerritsen 1997). By and large, however, sociolinguistic studies of broadcast language have focused less on linguistic change than on language style, and hardly ever on the interaction between the two. Studies of language style in broadcast media mainly follow the audience design paradigm (Bell 1984), whereby stylistic variation in media language is theorized as an index of a speaker's orientation to an imagined audience and their assumed sociolinguistic norms, or to specific referees who are indexed in media talk (see Hay, Jannedy and Mendoza-Denton 1999 and chapters in Hernández-Campoy and Cutillas-Espinosa 2012).

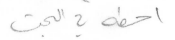

Style, Mediation, and Change. Edited by Janus Mortensen, Nikolas Coupland, and Jacob Thøgersen
© Oxford University Press 2017. Published 2017 by Oxford University Press

This volume examines the relation of linguistic style and sociolinguistic change in broadcast language off these beaten tracks. Its contribution therefore seems easier to capture at first sight in terms of what it isn't: it is not about quantitatively defined stylistic variation in broadcast media language. It does not address language change in a systemic, feature-specific sense. It does not construct 'language in the media' as an opposite to 'language in the community,' nor does it legitimize the study of media language by its potential influence on spoken vernaculars. Rather, the volume attempts to carve out a theoretical space for the sociolinguistic study of broadcast media language with particular focus on various types of style, particularly language style.

Compared to the established concept of language change, the notion of sociolinguistic change appears less streamlined, more heterogeneous, and messy. I believe this is due not only to the novelty of its conception but also to the diversity of its referents, and its programmatic aim of covering a broad set of sociolinguistic processes that go beyond feature-based linguistic change within a single linguistic system. In my own understanding (Androutsopoulos 2014), which overlaps with and was initially inspired by Coupland's conception (Coupland 2009, 2014), a sociolinguistic change approach aims to extend the levels of patterning at which changes in language-in-society relations may be observed, including, among others, change in the configuration of linguistic repertoires, change in language practices and genres, and change in language ideologies. A sociolinguistic change approach therefore detaches the notion of change from a structuralist and monolingual bias and reinterprets the tension between vernacular (spontaneous, unmonitored, informal) and standardized speech as resources for performance rather than features of linguistic behavior (cf. Coupland 2001). Moreover, a sociolinguistic change approach problematizes the rigid divide between linguistic elements ('dependent variables') and socio-situational contexts of communication ('independent variables') that has been customary in most sociolinguistic studies of language change hitherto. This has implications for the understanding of media itself in the study of linguistic change. Rather than setting media as an external variable, a sociolinguistic change approach, as I understand it, would seek to deconstruct the apparently monolithic notion of 'the media' and ask how specific contexts, representations, and actors of media discourse draw on linguistic resources in ways that may be relevant for change in language/society relations (see discussion in Androutsopoulos 2016).

Indeed, one thing this volume demonstrates is how 'the media' and media language can be deconstructed by looking closely at mediatized genres, performers, and contexts of speech, on the one hand, and uptakes of media language fragments in mediatized and mediated conversational speech, on the other (see the final section of this chapter, *Beyond 'talking media': Uptake and circulation*). This is not to deny the radical, ongoing changes which technologies of mediation and institutions of mediatization[1] are currently undergoing. Several chapters in this volume emphasize how large-scale processes of social and cultural change, such as globalization, are contingent on innovations in technologies of mediation and their social use. These changes matter when it comes to reminding ourselves that the social life of language is not structured the same way today as it was in the past, and that the Uniformitarian Principle does not apply to social and cultural conditions of language (Bergs 2012). It is just as important to remember that the term *media* references a broad range of discursive means and spaces, each with distinct affordances of representation, interaction, dissemination, and circulation.

When it comes to broadcast language, then, a sociolinguistic change approach operates on quite different premises than variationist approaches to language change. Broadcast language is not just viewed as exerting direct influence on nonmediated language. All evidence available today suggests that such influence can be indirect, generically variable, and ideologically driven.[2] Rather, the premise is broader, and could perhaps be worded as asking how representations in media discourse, and the speech forms that occur in these representations, relate to linguistic variation and metalinguistic discourses in a speech community. Media are thereby viewed as spaces of sociolinguistic change in their own right, in which processes of enregisterment are carried out, new linguistic forms circulate, and metalinguistic discourses originate and unfold. The aim is to develop new perspectives on how language in the media contributes to the (re)production of language ideologies, how it interacts with mediated uptakes, and how it changes in the context of swiftly changing mediascapes.

An example: *Ich hab Polizei*

As I write this, the latest hype in Germany's pop culture is a video clip called "I have police" (*Ich hab Polizei*), released in the last week of November 2015. Published by Jan Böhmermann, a popular comedian with his own show on public television, the clip is intended and understood as a parody of German gangsta rap. The clip is published under the pseudonym *POL1Z1STENS0HN* ('son of a policeman') whose spelling indexes a subcultural spelling convention (substituting digits for letters) and at the same time embeds the German emergency call number (110).[3] The song became an instant hit, first aired on Böhmermann's own television show, then reaching more than seven million views on YouTube in the first two weeks after its broadcast (and more than eight million views in a span of four weeks), and giving rise to a critical debate.

The video's multimodal narrative begins with Böhmermann impersonating a man who is threatened by gang members and calls the police for protection. As the narrative unfolds, the police are positioned in an ambivalent way as an institution that both protects citizens from violence and itself enforces violence in an excessive way. Much of the visual parody consists in policemen and women adopting the pose of gangsta rappers, styled in a manner that is familiar from US and German rap video clips. The boundary between gangsta rappers and the police force is blurred as the clip features the police gaining power over gang members, thereby embodying gang practices and aesthetics. Böhmermann's lyrical voice addresses the gang and represents the police viewpoint, all by parodying the demeanor and style of a gangsta rapper. Parody is constituted by music style, visual narrative, video aesthetics, dress, and body posture, and not least the linguistic content and form of the lyrics.

Böhmermann's lyrical voice, while fluent and idiomatic, is immediately heard as 'ethnic' by virtue of features in prosody, phonology, and grammar that are widely perceived as indexing 'ethnic' or 'immigrant' German. Most conspicuous are a few supra-segmental features (such as unusual word stress, e.g. *POlizei*), the palatalized articulation of the *ich* sound (e.g. in the first person singular pronoun, *isch*), the categorical omission of definite articles (as in *Ich hab Polizei*), and the dropping of case markers.

Both the video performance and its readings in media commentaries make it clear that Böhmermann is mocking the lyrics and visual style of gangsta rap that is associated with immigrant-background artists such as Frankfurt-based *Haftbefehl* and Berlin-based *Kay One*. These and other artists tell stories of ethnic alterity, discrimination experience, and subcultural milieux populated by migrant-background youth types. In media commentaries, some by authors who are themselves affiliated with the German rap scene, Böhmermann was accused of mocking immigrant speech. For example, a commentary dated November 27 (Engelhardt 2015) is titled *Wenn der Biodeutsche wie ein Kanake spricht* ('When a bio German speaks like a wog')[4] and concludes by saying:

> Alle reden gerade von der Integration mindestens einer Million Flüchtlinge. Viele von ihnen werden erstmal genau die Sprache sprechen, die Böhmermann veralbert.

> 'Everybody is talking about the integration of at least one million refugees. Many of them will start by speaking precisely the language that Böhmermann makes fun of.'[5]

I bring up this example because it shows how a particular mediatized representation is premised on certain processes of sociolinguistic change, in particular genre and language-ideological change, and at the same time drives these processes forward. The clip obviously presupposes an awareness of German gangsta rap, a local take on a globally familiar sub-genre of rap music that evolved in the course of the last 15 years. As mentioned earlier, Böhmermann's performance is specifically modeled on Haftbefehl, an artist who became popular in 2012. Haftbefehl was drawing on the multiethnic urban style of German currently known as *Kiezdeutsch*, 'hood German,' and his lyrics were celebrated for their dense mixture of lexical elements from several immigrant languages.

The bottom line for both Haftbefehl's lyrics and Böhmermann's parody is the enregisterment of 'ethnic' styles of German, a process that has been developing since the mid-1990s (Androutsopoulos 2011; Wiese 2015). This is a process largely driven by mainstream entertainment and news organizations, alongside German academia and pedagogy, and thereby shaped to a large extent by linguistic othering and stereotyping. An outcome of this enregisterment is the increased social awareness of a new 'ethnic' variety of German with its stereotypical speakers, typical linguistic features, and a rank in present-day Germany's orders of indexicality. In this process, empirically attested linguistic variation and innovation among immigrant-background speakers in urban areas, as described, for example, by Keim (2007) and Wiese (2012), became ideologically structured from the viewpoint of dominant, standard language ideology brokers.

It is only against the backdrop of this enregisterment that Böhmermann's lyrics can be heard as mocking 'ethnic' German. In empirical fact, Böhmermann avoids any direct 'ethnicizing' of the clip's characters, and the lyrics themselves feature only a few features enregistered as *Kiezdeutsch*, most notably the omission of determiners and the palatalized variant of the *ich Laut* plus an 'ethnic'-sounding prosody. The song's lyrics refrain from using Turkish or Arabic-origin words, a strategy otherwise widely associated with the German gangsta rappers mentioned above. Still, the critique immediately linked this video to older, discriminatory representations of migration-induced ethnolinguistic differentiation in Germany. A commenter closely associated with the German hip-hop scene (Staiger 2015), sums up the video's main point by mimicking Böhmermann's voice (hence the quotation marks):

> "Rap, das ist doch diese Musik, wo die Kanacken nicht richtig Deutsch können, die Präpositionen weglassen und die ganze Zeit 'isch' statt 'ich' sagen. Voll lustig, wenn man das nachäfft. Isch mach disch Krankenhaus. Muhahahahahaha."

> "Rap, this is that music by wogs who don't speak correct German, omit their prepositions and say 'isch' instead of 'ich'. Quite funny, mimicking that. I make you hospital. Ahahahaha."

Like Engelhardt above, Staiger also uses the social label *Kanacke* to index a deprecatory stance toward immigrants and their speech forms in German, and additionally mentions two iconic features of German ethnolects, which also occur in the video lyrics. Staiger also quotes a well-known stylized ethnolectal phrase (*Isch mach disch Krankenhaus*), which embeds the *isch* variant twice and also includes a further enregistered feature of ethnolectal German, the creation of new dummy verb constructions with *machen*, 'make.' This particular construction is easily understood as 'to make fit for hospital' and ties in well with the assumption that (uneducated) second-language speakers of German are likely to use simplifying constructions of this sort. In effect, then, Staiger criticizes Böhmermann for having a naïve and stereotypical view of immigrants and their language. Staiger then continues by directly addressing Böhmermann:

> Ehrlich gesagt habe ich gedacht, dass diese Art des Humors nach dem Tod von Stefan und Erkan ein für allemal ausgestorben ist. Dank dir kommen jetzt die lebenden Toten zurück.

> 'I frankly thought this kind of humor had died once and for all with the demise of Stefan and Erkan. Thanks to you, the living dead are now back.'

So, Staiger contextualizes his critique by referencing two mediatized moments in the enregisterment of ethnic German: a popular ethnic comedy duo of the late 1990s (Stefan und Erkan) and one of the most popular 'ethnic' catchphrases of the 2000s (*Isch mach disch Krankenhaus*).

In sum, the video clip only gains its meaning in the context of a double enregisterment, viz. the gangsta rap genre and an 'ethnic' variety of German. Both lines of enregisterment are, in turn, contingent on social and cultural mediatization. That is, they can only occur in a media culture where specific uses of linguistic heterogeneity are valorized through association with particular cultural models of speech (such as the figure of the immigrant-background gangsta rapper), thereby reinforcing these models even further (cf. Spilioti, Chapter 3; Coupland, Chapter 4; Kelly-Holmes, Chapter 5).

The example is also instructive with regard to processes of dissemination and uptake. It can be viewed as part of a broader process of repertoire change to the extent that it, together with many other clips, shows and advertisements, extends the presence and 'visibility' of nonstandard speech forms in media discourse, thereby making broadcast language more heterogeneous or, in Bakhtinian terms, more centrifugal. Second, there are various processes of uptake radiating from this video clip. There is conversational update, not empirically attested but discursively anticipated by some critics, notably related to the potential impact of this video in reinforcing stereotypes of 'ethnic' German. Engelhardt (2015) assumes that many viewers will respond to this video by "holding their bellies while laughing at these funny phrases," while other commentators expect the video to be popular at police station Christmas parties. There is also mediated uptake, both in the commentaries and in remix versions, which take up the key phrase, *Ich hab Polizei*, and recontextualize it in new, notably political, contexts.

Linking style, change, and media

Style has evolved in sociolinguistics as a set of theoretical understandings with different methodological and analytical implications (cf. Coupland 2007; Gadet 2005; Schilling-Estes 2002). Which notions of style are useful in studying sociolinguistic change in broadcast language? This is a question dealt with by most chapters in this volume, drawing on a range of style concepts. This conceptual diversity is made explicit by Thornborrow (Chapter 7), who distinguishes between style in rhetorical performance, the social style of particular actors, and the style of media production. In my reading, three ways of linking style, change, and media, not necessarily mutually exclusive but rather overlapping and interacting in complex ways, stand out across the chapters.

The first is *genre style*, in the sense of a typified way of accomplishing a communicative act. Genre styles in broadcast media change over time, examples being the (arguably) changing styles of news reading throughout history (van Leeuwen, Chapter 10), but also changes in advertising style, the style of weather reports or that of talk shows (see also Thornborrow, Chapter 7, and Montgomery, Chapter 9). Note that this understanding of change in genre style is cast at quite a high level of generalization, abstracting away from variation by media organization, audience, or individual speaker. In this sense, genre style backgrounds, or erases, individual authorship and agency, foregrounding instead culturally typified ways of accomplishing communicative tasks. In Chapter 10, van Leeuwen offers a 'phase model' of style change in broadcast news speech—experimentation, consolidation, automatization—which could be useful for modeling style change in other media genres as well.

The analysis of change in genre style is complicated by the fact that genres are not just static containers, which can be kept invariant for the purposes of variation analysis, but rather themselves evolving in terms of structure and norms. Several chapters in this volume reference Luginbühl's (2014) approach to genre change in television news shows, where change is operationalized as the composition of a news show by functionally defined components, or building blocks. Luginbühl shows how this composition changes over time in US and Swiss news shows and argues that genre change facilitates the conversationalization of news presenters' speech. Thornborrow's analysis of interactional style in reality television demonstrates how innovative television formats incorporate specific communicative acts, which require the typification of interactional styles, an example being the style of dialogic voice-over comments. Again, changes in the production design of genres and formats can be seen as facilitating a change of speech styles toward increased informalization and hybridization. By extending lay participation, new formats of reality TV extend the repertoire of voices heard on TV. In this sense, understanding how new speech styles find their way into media representations entails understanding how media genres change.

A second relevant understanding of style is *individual style*, especially the linguistic and interactional style of highly visible media speakers, such as journalists and artists, as discussed by Lorenzo-Dus (Chapter 2), Spilioti (Chapter 3), Coupland (Chapter 4), and Jaworski (Chapter 8). Individual styles are examined there in terms of (1) how they make apparent broader tensions of language and society, (2) how they provide orientation points for audiences in their own practices, and (3) how they may impact on genre change. The interplay of individual style and genre style is exemplified by Lorenzo-Dus's case study of the Spanish journalist Jordi Évole who differentiates himself from conventional styles of broadcast interviews by drawing on pragmatic stances such as "mock naïvety" and also on informality. Evole's style is seen by the analyst and audience members alike as reshaping the genre of political interviews in Spain. This finding resonates with other evidence for the impact of individual linguistic practices on aspects of sociolinguistic change: individuals (e.g. language activists or popular performers) act as agents of change to the extent that their (mediatized) language practices are widely responded to and recontextualized by audiences (see e.g. Moriarty 2014 on the case of an Irish-language rapper). It also resonates with a conceptual tenet of sociolinguistic change—that is, the need to examine the interplay of institutional policies and individual practices in understanding large-scale processes of change such as standardization, vernacularization or revitalization (see Androutsopoulos 2014; Coupland 2014).

The third dimension of style discussed in this volume is *stylization-in-performance*, more specifically the way broadcast performers enact semiotically dense articulations of enregistered features in the process of impersonating culturally familiar characters. Examples discussed in the volume are stylization in radio pranks in Greece (Spilioti, Chapter 3), the performance of a female rugby interviewer in Wales (Coupland, Chapter 4), and the use of French in the *Stella Artois* advertisement examined by Kelly-Holmes (Chapter 5). Though they differ in the tensions between fictionality and factuality they articulate, these examples share a departure from conventional, standardized monolingual language practices and an orientation to practices of language mixing and switching in ways which are contingent on the specific sociolinguistic histories of the respective nation-states (or regions) as much as on the sociolinguistic stereotypes they endorse. We see here performances that go against such stereotypes (as with *Madamrygbi* discussed by Coupland) or reinforce, but at the same time expose, stereotypes (as with the stylized French-accented English by Kelly-Holmes).

Media performances are relevant moments of sociolinguistic change in that they reinforce processes of enregisterment (Johnstone 2011). They index a certain stage of enregisterment, crystalize certain sociolinguistic conditions (such as the translanguaging practices in Wales, or the status of English in Greece), and invite audiences to reflect on typified speakers as much as on these sociolinguistic conditions themselves. As Kelly-Holmes points out in Chapter 5, the use of socially marked features in an advertisement presupposes the enregisterment of these features, and at the same time reinforces their enregisterment. As Spilioti (Chapter 3) puts it, "stylizations consolidate sociocultural profiles [...] and increase people's awareness of ideological values associated with particular ways of speaking and acting" (p. 70).

While this echoes the long-familiar assumption that broadcast media can influence language attitudes, especially by reinforcing standard language consciousness (Milroy and Milroy 1999: 31), the present discussion takes the focus off standard-language ideologies and toward the discursive formation of a wider range of registers. It addresses language-ideological change as change in its own right, rather than as something peripheral or epiphenomenal to language change itself. It also places the interaction between mediatized stylizations and their uptake by audiences high on the agenda.

[handwritten annotation: T-shirt example ← parade]

Beyond 'talking media': Uptake and circulation

While the analytical focus on 'talking media' as broadcast language seems straightforward at first sight, it becomes less so in the analytical process. This is not only due to transmodal instantiations of 'talk,' as, for example, interactive written discourse goes to show, but also to processes by which media talk is linked to its transmedia surroundings by being taken up, revoiced, recontextualized, and normatively evaluated by audiences. Language practices involving the recontextualization of media talk feature prominently in several chapters, notably Chapters 2 (Lorenzo-Dus), 5 (Kelly-Holmes), 6 (Bednarek), and 9 (Montgomery).

One pattern emerging here, I suggest, is what I have elsewhere identified as an audience-centered dimension in the study of mediatization and sociolinguistic change. It is the opposite to a media effects view, a 'what media do to language' line of thinking, which predominates in the variationist approach to media and language change (see discussion in Androutsopoulos 2014). By asking instead 'what audiences do with media language,' this line of work orients to practices of uptake, which can (but do not always) lead to a social circulation of media language fragments. In Agha's terms, this is the relation between mediatized representations and mediated uptakes (Agha 2011; Androutsopoulos 2016). This is a new way of thinking about the connection between media language and audiences. Rather than examining how media language might influence audience speech at a structural level, the aim is to examine the uptake of media language fragments in people's own linguistic practices (face-to-face and digitally mediated ones) and the potential role of this uptake in the spread of linguistic innovations. Practices of uptake may eventually lead to indexical bleaching, by which the mass-media origin of a feature is no longer indexed in its uptake (see Androutsopoulos 2016; Squires 2014; and Bednarek, Chapter 6, in this volume).

Rather than isolating broadcast speech, then, several chapters seek to explore its connections to transmedia contexts, and one thing we learn is how varied these connections are, and in how many different ways broadcast speech can be reframed in its uptake. In Chapter 9, Montgomery's analysis of silence in talk shows is enriched by the analysis of mediatized uptakes (notably newspaper reports) in which silence in the performance of politicians is reframed in various ways, echoing a range of political orientations. Kelly-Holmes (Chapter 5) shows how audience members respond to a commercial with stylized French-accented English. YouTube becomes a site of creative stylization through playful echoing of the advertisement, but also a site for critical reflexivity through comments on its perceived (strategic) artificiality.

This interest in the recontextualization of mediatized discourse fragments is closely linked to an interest in circulation—a still under-theorized notion, by which we could attempt to understand trajectories of fragments from mediatized representations as they move around and across various speakers, chains of texts, media, and discourses. In Chapter 6, Bednarek moves in this direction by distinguishing different types of (re)circulation on the example of the ever-popular *Big Bang Theory*. Bednarek's typology relies on the circulated item's referent (i.e. the narrative, the production, or dialogue) and its performative impersonation (or voicing) in a new context. In addition, Bednarek and also Kelly-Holmes raise the issue of circulation sites. Even though material artifacts such as fan T-shirts can act as means of circulation, it is digital media, especially participatory (or 'social') media platforms such as Twitter and YouTube, which seem to be currently revolutionizing the large-scale circulation of media fragments. Circulation often involves repeated acts of resemiotization (Idema 2003)—that is, change in the semiotic modality of language (e.g. from spoken to written) and change in the semiotic composition of the relevant artifacts (e.g. from a broadcast series to multimodal textual units, such as 'meme' series that evolve in social media). Circulation can also involve chains of remediation—that is, shifts in the media spaces through which fragments can be observed to circulate. As a result, professional media content, amateur content, and audience conversations become interconnected in the circulation process.

In conclusion, this volume contributes to developing a nuanced perspective of 'media' as spaces of sociolinguistic change and of 'media language' as a set of language practices that interact in diverse ways with non-mediatized language. Once the view of media as unidirectional influence on spoken-language variation and change is overcome, new research questions on the interplay between mediatized and mediated language practices can be put forward. Understanding the (digital) circulation and recontextualization of linguistic fragments across genres and media, in particular, is likely to become an important item on the agenda of sociolinguistic change research.

Notes

1. For particular ways of establishing distinctions between mediation and mediatization see Chapter 1, *Introduction: Conceptualizing style, mediation, and change*, in this volume, but also Agha (2011) and Androutsopoulos (in press).

2. See discussion in Androutsopoulos (2014) and chapters in the same volume, but also the debate on "Media and language change" in *Journal of Sociolinguistics* 18(2). 2014.

3. See Böhmermann (2015) and the relevant Wikipedia (2015) entry.

4. The label used in the original, *Kanake* (sometimes spelt *Kanacke*) is a highly offensive derogatory term for immigrants from the Mediterranean and Middle East. It has been

appropriated by immigrant-background Germans, notably artists and cultural activists, as a positive in-group label (see Pfaff 2005). In the present context, its use presumably aims at indexing a conservative German view of immigrants.

5. All English translations in the chapter are mine.

References

Agha, Asif. 2011. Large and small scale forms of personhood. *Language & Communication* 31, 3: 171–180.

Androutsopoulos, Jannis. 2011. Die Erfindung ›des‹ Ethnolekts. *Zeitschrift für Literaturwissenschaft und Linguistik* 164: 93–120.

Androutsopoulos, Jannis. 2014. Mediatization and sociolinguistic change: Key concepts, research traditions, open issues. In Jannis Androutsopoulos (ed.) *Mediatization and Sociolinguistic Change*. Berlin: De Gruyter. 3–48.

Androutsopoulos, Jannis. In press. Theorising media, mediation, and mediatisation. In Nikolas Coupland (ed.) *Sociolinguistics: Theoretical Debates*. Cambridge: Cambridge University Press.

Bell, Allan. 1984. Language style as audience design. *Language in Society* 13, 2: 145–204.

Bergs, Alexander. 2012. The Uniformitarian Principle and the risk of anachronisms in language and social history. In Juan Manuel Hernández-Campoy and Juan Camilo Conde-Silvestre (eds.) *The Handbook of Historical Sociolinguistics*. Malden: Wiley-Blackwell. 80–98.

Böhmermann, Jan. 2015. POL1Z1STENS0HN a.k.a. Jan Böhmermann—Ich hab Polizei. https://www.youtube.com/watch?v=PNjG22Gbo6U.

Coupland, Nikolas. 2001. Dialect stylization in radio talk. *Language in Society* 30, 3: 345–375.

Coupland, Nikolas. 2007. *Style: Language Variation and Identity*. Cambridge: Cambridge University Press.

Coupland, Nikolas. 2009. Dialects, standards and social change. In Marie Maegaard, Frans Gregersen, Pia Quist and Jens Normann Jørgensen (eds.) *Language Attitudes, Standardization and Language Change*. Oslo: Novus. 27–50.

Coupland, Nikolas. 2014. Sociolinguistic change, vernacularization and broadcast British media. In Jannis Androutsopoulos (ed.) *Mediatization and Sociolinguistic Change*. Berlin: De Gruyter. 67–96.

Engelhardt, Katja. 2015. Wenn der Biodeutsche wie ein Kanake spricht. http://www.br.de/radio/bayern2/sendungen/zuendfunk/netz-kultur/netz/boehmermann-isch-hab-polizei-100.html.

Gadet, Françoise. 2005. Research on sociolinguistic style [Soziolinguistische Stilforschung]. In Ulrich Ammon, Norbert Dittmar, Klaus J. Mattheier and Peter Trudgill, Peter (eds.) *Sociolinguistics [Soziolinguistik]* (2nd ed.), Vol. 2. Berlin: De Gruyter. 1353–1361.

Hay, Jennifer, Stefanie Jannedy and Norma Mendoza-Denton. 1999. Oprah and /ay/: Lexical frequency, referee design, and style. In John J. Ohala, Yoko Hasegawa, Manjari Ohala, Daniel Granville and Ashlee C. Bailey (eds.) *Proceedings of the 14th International Congress of Phonetic Sciences*. The Regents of the University of California. http://www.internationalphoneticassociation.org/icphs/icphs1999. 1389–1392.

Hernández-Campoy, Juan Manuel and Juan Antonio Cutillas-Espinosa (eds.). 2012. *Style-Shifting in Public. New Perspectives on Stylistic Variation.* Amsterdam: John Benjamins.

Idema, Rick. 2003. Multimodality, resemiotization: Extending the analysis of discourse as multi-semiotic practice. *Visual Communication* 2, 1: 29–57.

Johnstone, Barbara. 2011. Dialect enregisterment in performance. *Journal of Sociolinguistics,* 15, 5: 657–679.

Keim, Inken. 2007. *Die "türkischen Powergirls": Lebenswelt und kommunikativer Stil einer Migrantinnengruppe in Mannheim.* Tübingen: Narr.

Luginbühl, Martin. 2014. Genre profiles and genre change. The case of TV news. In Jannis Androutsopoulos (ed.) *Mediatization and Sociolinguistic Change.* Berlin: De Gruyter. 305–330.

Milroy, James and Lesley Milroy. 1999. *Authority in Language: Investigating Language Prescription and Standardisation* (3rd ed.). London: Routledge.

Moriarty, Mairéad. 2014. Súil Eile. Media, sociolinguistic change and the Irish language. In Jannis Androutsopoulos (ed.) *Mediatization and Sociolinguistic Change.* Berlin: De Gruyter. 463–486.

Pfaff, Carol W. 2005. "Kanaken im Alemannistan": Feridun Zaimoglu's representation of migrant language. In Volker Hinnenkamp and Katharina Meng (eds.) *Sprachgrenzen überspringen.* Tübingen: Narr. 195–222.

Schilling-Estes, Natalie. 2002. Investigating stylistic variation. In Jack Chambers and Natalie Schilling (eds.) *The Handbook of Language Variation and Change.* Oxford: Blackwell. 375–401.

Squires, Lauren. 2014. From TV personality to fans and beyond: Indexical bleaching and the diffusion of a media innovation. *Journal of Linguistic Anthropology* 24, 1: 42–62.

Staiger, Markus. 2015. Lieber Jan Böhmermann, dein ‚POL1Z1STENS0HN' ist einfach nur standesgemäße Überheblichkeit. *Noisey.* http://noisey.vice.com/de/blog/ein-offener-brief-an-jan-bohmermann-von-marcus-staiger-341.

Van de Velde, Hans Roeland van Hout and Marinel Gerritsen. 1997. Watching Dutch change: A real time study of variation and change in standard Dutch pronunciation. *Journal of Sociolinguistics* 1, 3: 361–391.

Wiese, Heike. 2012. *Kiezdeutsch. Ein neuer Dialekt entsteht.* München: C. H. Beck.

Wiese, Heike. 2015. "This migrants' babble is not a German dialect!": The interaction of standard language ideology and 'us'/'them' dichotomies in the public discourse on a multiethnolect. *Language in Society* 44, 3: 341–368.

Wikipedia. 2015. Ich hab Polizei. https://de.wikipedia.org/wiki/Ich_hab_Polizei.

12

Style as a unifying perspective for the sociolinguistics of talking media

Nikolas Coupland and Janus Mortensen

In the Introduction we suggested that style, in the sense that we that we overviewed there, could serve as a unifying perspective for our main concerns in this book, and possibly for sociolinguistics more generally. In this brief concluding chapter we want to elaborate on this theme, partly by retrospecting (as Jannis Androutsopoulos has already done, in Chapter 11) on the analyses offered by the main chapters in earlier parts of the book. We want to develop the idea that although style offers a coherent theoretical and empirical framework for analyzing social meaning making in any context of talk and social interaction, it has particular relevance and distinctive nuances in the analysis of talking media. This is because technologically mediated (TM) talk, while being highly differentiated in itself, is (as we have noted) quintessentially a styling and stylizing medium, richly active in many aspects of style. It is able to deploy particular contextualization devices that are not generally available in face-to-face interaction. Correspondingly, as the historical process of mediatization progresses, the production and uptake of TM talk proceed against changing background assumptions about the meanings of sociolinguistic diversity, while also continuously contributing to diverse processes of sociolinguistic change.

We have already pointed to several potential polarities that are unified in the style perspective:

- The holistic conception of style maintains focus on multiple semiotic modalities, particularly linguistic and visual dimensions of meaning and their interplay.
- Style has developed on the basis of fusing descriptively detailed accounts of data with critical insights and agenda.
- Style integrates the analysis of local discursive/pragmatic processes with more abstract and less obvious metapragmatic processes, including ideological processes that accompany ways of speaking.

251

Style, Mediation, and Change. Edited by Janus Mortensen, Nikolas Coupland, and Jacob Thøgersen
© Oxford University Press 2017. Published 2017 by Oxford University Press

- Styling relates not only to the articulation of personas or individual identities but also to the (re)construction of relationships and communicative genres.

These unifying attributes will resurface in the following discussion. But we want to focus mainly on the attribute that we made prominent in the Introduction—the fact that style sensitizes us to the dialectical relationship between what is stable and what is dynamically unstable in relation to social meaning. That is, we want to focus further on the relationship between social/sociolinguistic styles (which can have a reasonably durable constitution as metacultural objects) and styling (a process which can never perfectly fill out a known style, and in which there is inherent potential for sociolinguistic change, including the development of new consolidated styles).

What examples of consolidated social/sociolinguistic styles do we find in the earlier chapters? In fact they are far too many to mention in turn, because each analytic chapter in its own way takes multiple such styles to be key points of reference for the styling activities that are documented. It is, nevertheless, possible to identify certain broader categories. As Androutsopoulos[1] points out, one recurrent dimension of style in the foregoing chapters pertains to genre and genre change. Van Leeuwen's analysis of radio news reading style focuses on what has settled into being normative in that genre, particularly in terms of prosody. Van Leeuwen emphasizes the considerable continuity that exists over time and across multiple national broadcasting contexts of news reading. Yet the investigation presupposes the existence of a conflicting set of prosodic norms—those that tend to be realized by the same speakers outside the news reading genre (as evidenced, for example, in background interviews). Van Leeuwen makes the prediction that the consolidated prosodic style of news reading, indexing order, control, neutrality, and so on, may diffuse into other contexts of 'public announcement'—a consolidated style that might expand its generic reach. But as and when this happens, the style of news reading and its associated meanings are unlikely to be left unchanged. Even if a style has become consolidated to such an extent that it can be exported to other contexts as a sort of commercial product, the style still has to be brought off in that new context, and this process will invariably entail the generation of new meanings, both in the immediate context and, by implication, in the context where the style originates. In other words, van Leeuwen's stage of automatization is probably unlikely to be the final stage in the 'history' of a style.

Montgomery similarly examines what have already become technologically mediated genre conventions, exploring varying tolerances of silence in different subgenres of on-screen interviewing. He points out that the most immediately relevant consolidated style is a very general one in broadcasting, the principle of avoiding 'dead air,' relative to which moments of silence (contrasting with routine pausing) powerfully index a speaker's reticence or troubled speech, which may further suggest states of stressful self-examination and high emotion. In this case, then, the analysis directly explores what is stylistically consolidated across most TM genres—avoiding silence, where 'speaking for fun' in an entertainment-focused chat show is taken to be the paradigmatic case of 'no silence'—and what is stylistically 'deviant' from that norm—'speaking in earnest,' which can occur, inter alia, in confessional moments of what Montgomery calls accountability interviews. We should note that in each of these subgenres we are dealing specifically with relational styles, interpersonal designs that are played out between an interviewer and an interviewee. Each participant's contribution is unique in the evolving context of talk, but the relevant design template for the relationship is maintained. Montgomery characterizes the 'earnest,' silence-encompassing subgenre as being occasioned (e.g. in the Alastair Campbell case) by a blurring of the personal and the political, triggered by the interviewer's line of questioning. Although accountability interviews have some established presence in television mediascapes, expressive silences of this sort could also be seen as TM discourse managing to escape from its own normatively dominant convention of avoiding dead air.

However, if we spread the genre net a little wider, then the principle of dead air is arguably not so entrenched, and different meanings for silence are apparent. In the United Kingdom Radio 3 is the BBC's classical music channel, and here tolerance of lengthy silences between orchestral sequences is commonplace and quite widely commented on. Silence in this context seems to imply orderliness and dignifying restraint. 'Pregnant silences' have also become a trope in announcing the results of competitive game shows, as competitors are made to wait to hear their fate. This sometimes seems to be a stylization of dead air, constructing moments of not-so-profound tension and anxiety as if they were profound. More genuine-seeming constructions of high-emotion-silence (like those in Mongomery's data) are also to be found outside accountability interviews (e.g. in 'reveal' segments of lifestyle-transformation programs). Overall, we might think that it is surprising that it is possible to locate *any* long-lasting normative styles for *any* genres of talking media, when innovation is so powerfully demanded on marketing grounds. That is to say that the shelf life of a talking media style is liable to be shorter than in non-technologically mediated contexts.

Both van Leeuwen and Montgomery analyze what they take to be already consolidated genre-styles, and specifically styles that have been normalized within TM discourse, even though their meanings are established partly in contrast to non-TM norms. Most chapters, however, do not focus primarily on the consolidated styles that are most salient for the speakers and for the data being analyzed. Instead, they focus on how local acts of TM styling rework or subvert existing normative styles, whether these originate within or outside TM discourse. In the chapters in Part I, the principal points of reference for innovative styling are TM-normalized styles. Lorenzo-Dus argues that the journalist Jordi Évole is leading a potential change in the style of journalistic interviewing in Spain, so that current norms for that genre are clearly a stylistic point of reference, and indeed a point of departure, both for Évole himself and for the viewing public. His constructed naïvety and ordinariness are innovative and unsettling for interviewees who are being held to account precisely because the existing norm for journalistic practice can be considered 'weak,' compliant, and inadequately interrogative. Popular online commentaries on Évole's 'incisive' style recognize the potential for it to lead to a wholesale shift in journalistic practice, one that is better attuned to the contemporary sociopolitical climate in Spain.

Lorenzo-Dus's study is particularly suggestive about how we should theorize stylistic stability and dynamism in the context of talking media. Specific styling innovations (which in this case involve constructions of self and of stance in interpersonal relations) in highly localized contexts (the *Salvados* show and the Twitter exchanges under the hashtag *olvidados*) can attract ideological significance relative to pre-existing stylistic media norms whose currency is acknowledged by at least a segment of the targeted audience. These local acts of construction can then start to become consolidated, not least through iterative processes of remediation, which offer the potential for more concerted sociolinguistic change. A reconfigured norm for accountability interviewing in the Spanish public sphere would certainly stand as a sociolinguistic change—a politically and culturally consequential language-implicating change, and indeed an emancipating change, occasioned by and responding to social change.

The *Madamrygbi* instance that Coupland considers shares all these elements. *Madamrygbi*'s transgressive incursions in the relational styling of her interviews with rugby celebrities locally undermine the normative ideological frameworks of both Welsh-language broadcasting and national sport in Wales. She voices her interpersonal transgressions, as she tries to wrong-foot her interviewees, using English-framed stock phrases, contravening the Welsh-only requirement of the TV channel on which she appears; she sexualizes the fan-rugby star relationship, challenging the reverence that, at least for some, continues to define the status of rugby as Wales's 'national game.' *Madamrygbi* embodies innovative critical stances toward each of these Welsh cultural 'sacred cows.' In their own very different ways, then, both *Madamrygbi* (Eirlys Bellin) and Évole function as metacultural agents. Their local performances critically oppose dominant norms and implicitly propose alternatives which, on the available evidence, have already started to come into wider circulation. In both the Spanish and the Welsh cases, the styling initiatives are far from being the first small acts of resistance to dominant ideologies. Rather, they exploit critical stances that have already begun to open up. The Spanish national 'crisis' that Lorenzo-Dus describes has created instability and brought many social and sociolinguistic norms into question. Similarly in Wales, the nationalist agenda that has driven the revitalization of the Welsh language has run up against the increasingly insistent forces of globalization and cultural hybridization.

Sociocultural change again forms the backdrop to Spilioti's analysis of the Greek satirical radio show Ελληνοφρένεια, where the presenter/prankster *Apostolis* confounds callers with his style play, particularly with the style that comes to be known as '*Apostolis*'s English.' As in the Welsh case, issues of anti-syncretic (language purity) ideology and what it means to be a speaker of Greek are in the air, alongside shifting and inconsistently held ideological views about the value of English as a global language. The relational chaos that *Apostolis* engenders with his unsuspecting callers brings competing language-ideological values to the surface, with *Apostolis* himself sometimes explicitly using evaluative labels (such as 'peasant Greek') and voicing evaluative, though often ambiguous, stances. A further characteristic shared by the Welsh and Greek cases is that 'normal standard language' features in each of the data sets. Both *Madamrygbi* and *Apostolis* can and do deploy 'standard' versions of their national languages, alongside the syncretic and counternormative stylings. Stylistic difference is therefore highlighted in the counterpoint between 'standard' ways of speaking and the 'deviant' patterns that they break into (in a process strikingly similar to that described by Montgomery under completely different conditions), at marked points of disjunction in the discourse. Audiences get a real-time sense of stylistic deconstruction and reframing in the discourse, implying managed movement out of normative sociolinguistic regimes into far looser and more engaging metalinguistic frames.

In his review Androutsopoulos sees 'personal style' as a second general styling dimension being enacted across the data instances studied in the book, and the high level of individuation achieved in almost every case study is indeed striking. Note how we have already, in the main, been referring to named individuals (real names or character names) in discussing the data, and pointing to their known profiles in particular mediascapes. But the important observation here is that these individuals have carefully and reflexively styled personas, made recognizable to audiences through very particular semiotic resources which are repeatedly woven into iterative performances. In semiotic terms these resources are person-indexes which, over time, tend to become iconized as co-referential with the personas. The semiotic fragments become indistinguishable from the constructed personas, which themselves become indistinguishable from the persons; they define their individual distinctiveness. In short, this personal styling process is the construction of *celebrity* (see references to Rojek, Couldry, and Turner in the Introduction).

Celebrities are constructed on the simple basis of identifiability (*famous for being famous* is the popular phrase), and the work of persona styling in its most abstract sense is the creation of personal difference. To this extent styling is fundamental to 'celebritization,' whereby the value of any individual who achieves celebrity is *not* dependent on any conventional cultural metric. In relation to talking media, celebrities certainly need to be 'watchable' and 'listenable,' but not according to any conventional sociolinguistic criteria of, say, social status or social attractiveness. In the cases studied in this book we see many different, and even incompatible, ways in which individuals achieve celebrity status in talking media. Évole and *Apostolis* have some status as celebrities in their respective professional fields, if only in the sense that each has become a focus of evaluative comment in the public sphere. Similarly for the case of *Madamrygbi*, although Eirlys Bellin, as a character actor, probably meets more conventional criteria for celebrity-hood (she performs a wider range of characterological types, has clearly demarcated public and performance identities, engages in a wider range of self-promotional activities, and so on). The characters that Montgomery analyzes are all fully accredited celebrities, for example, Paul O'Grady/*Lily Savage* and Oprah Winfrey on the one hand (both are very well known 'television personalities') and Gerry Adams and Alastair Campbell on the other hand (both have featured prominently in the mediation of British politics). Van Leeuwen depersonalizes his news readers, although he mentions Alvar Lidell as the prototypical British news reader who first focused the normative style of British news reading during World War II.

Chapters in Part III directly extend the book's coverage of styled celebrity. Jaworski's performers are all either international celebrity artists (Laurie Anderson, William Wegman, Barbara Kruger) or international celebrities in other regards (Steve Martin, John McEnroe), and much of the initial interest in the design of the TV episodes that Jaworski studies hinges on the subtle interplay between individuals with different fields of acknowledged expertise and interest (McEnroe functioning as art lover, etc.). The semiotic resources that iconize these celebrities tend to be more visual, material and body-kinetic than linguistic—for example, when Wegman's famous Weimaraner dogs appear in the visual frame while his art is being introduced, or when viewers recognize Anderson's chairs as familiar elements of her performance art. These visual tropes can be thought of as features of pre-existing and relatively stable semiotic styles, specific to individual celebrities. They are both further consolidated and subtly reconfigured in the current performances, in many ways paralleling the linguistic tropes or 'catchphrases' through which *Madamrygbi*, or for that matter *Lily Savage, Apostolis*, or even Évole, style their individual personas.

As this implies, what is being styled in the name of celebrity person-hood in these instances is not reducible to 'personal identity' in the conventional sociolinguistic sense. Sociolinguistics has tended to view personal identities as intersectional complexes of social identity categories, so that an individual speaker might be defined as being a female of a particular age, class, and ethnicity with a particular regional provenance, and so on. Such categorizations maintain something of their general relevance in the TM representations and performances, but the process of celebritization tends to elide the social meanings that normatively attach to each conventional social dimension. Celebrities tend *not* to be defined on the basis of conventional demographics but on the basis of difference itself and on the basis of how difference plays into the priorities of symbolic markets relevant to mediatized practices. A celebrity is a marketably styled persona, and technological mediation makes individuals marketable in complex and unpredictable ways.

This is very clearly evident in Thornborrow's chapter. Thornborrow introduces her study by endorsing the view that, in some tele-factual ('reality TV') genres, private selves are transformed into public selves-in-performance. This is the transition in which, as the analysis demonstrates, ordinary selves are transformed into celebrities, at least according to criteria of watchability. The class-based polarities that have led to the selection of some key participants, who observe out-of-class others through the filter of their own class-based expectations, provide the main point of dramatic articulation in, for example, the *WifeSwap* sequences that Thornborrow analyzes. Class disparities between 'haves' and 'have nots' are pervasively referenced in the data, but personas defined on this basis are also pervasively performed. Class-linked indexicalities of voice (phonological 'accent,' which Thornborrow comments on in passing) confirm what are, by sociolinguistic convention, sharply hierarchized relations between participants. Yet in *WifeSwap* individuals are equally privileged as legitimate judges of others' lifestyles, and those sharply differentiated lifestyles become equally objectionable and risible through the eyes of their critics. Class-based taste and style are the focal concerns of such episodes, but the ultimate value of class is subordinated to the value of watchable difference. Conventional socio-linguistic/indexical values tend to be leveled and to be overtaken by more media-salient priorities.

Contemporary talking media in the United Kingdom are notable for how the much-mentioned earlier regime of 'talking proper,' particularly associated with the BBC and its first director, John Reith, has, in a socio-structural sense, been overtaken by new priorities. The language ideology of 'talking proper,' in one account, has been reconfigured as 'talking posh' (see Mugglestone, discussed in the Introduction, and discussions in Coupland's earlier publications). *Posh* labels a way of speaking that is viewed from a critical, non-ideologically compliant standpoint, although the phrase *talking proper*, with its knowingly 'non-standard' syntax, carries a similarly critical nuance. From a style perspective, it is entirely predictable that, as the sociopolitical centripetalism of the British Establishment and indeed the British Empire has progressively collapsed, the sociolinguistic centripetalism of Received Pronunciation as the preferred voice of talking media should also collapse, amounting to a process of mediated vernacularization. As the *WifeSwap* example shows, class-based semiosis has not simply vanished from talking media, but it tends to be repositioned in a much more open and multiply centered semiotic economy where the sheer difference of vernacular speech styles (because 'standard' by definition excludes diversity) is itself marketable. In Montgomery's data, note how comedian Paul O'Grady styles *Lily Savage*'s persona on the basis of (what would conventionally be called) crass, tasteless, and vulgar observations and expressions, also through a broad Liverpudlian accent, as well as through her exuberance and silence-avoidance.

It is in the two chapters of Part II that marketized values for style come most clearly into prominence—in Kelly-Holmes's analysis of *C'est Cidre*, a promotional advertisement for a cider product made by *Stella Artois*, and in Bednarek's analysis of how diverse traits and narratives from *The Big Bang Theory* come into wide transnational circulation, e.g. via fans' T-shirts. Kelly-Holmes's chapter is also cited by Androutsopoulos as an example of 'stylization-in-performance,' which he sees as the third main way in which style is thematized in the book. Androutsopoulos defines stylization as "performers enact[ing] semiotically dense articulations of enregistered features in the process of impersonating culturally familiar characters"

(p. 246). Let us first follow through on the theme of markets and martketization and then, finally, pick up Androutsopoulos's point about style as stylization.

The styling of a celebrity persona through talking media overlaps quite directly with the styling of a commercial product as a distinctive brand. As we saw previously, Kelly-Holmes argues that a brand has to be styled on the basis of a selective set of semiotic characteristics, which can then be associated with a specific 'place' (which might be best interpreted as a distinctive space or niche in a specific marketized economy). We might say that *Stella Artois*'s cider is, in its own way, a 'celebrity,' or conversely that the human celebrities we have already considered are, in their own ways, commercial brands, notwithstanding the fact that people who perform personas-as-brands are generally able to exercise control over their own styling and circulation. Kelly-Holmes's point that symbolic attributes of styled brands take precedence over any referential communicative function (e.g. when the use of French in branding a product services symbolic objectives more than being understood by French speakers) in fact confirms our point, above, about conventional indexical values tending to be leveled under celebritization. Of course, in the case of *C'est Cidre*, the brand itself is voiced by a supposedly human celebrity, in the person of the company's fictional president, *Le Président*.

The *C'est Cidre* ad clearly shows how styling in talking media can function against radically different assumptions from those that have dominated in sociolinguistics, for example as regards multilingualism. In the most banal terms, we might say that the ad blends French and English language codes in the marketing of a putatively French (more factually, Belgian) product to an English-speaking market. But Kelly-Holmes points out that it is not 'French' that is in question here. It is mock or fake French, and primarily (in *Le Président*'s utterances) English pronounced not only in a 'French accent' but in a phonological style that is recognizably associated with how English speakers mock French speech. As Kelly-Holmes also notes, this style has, in Agha's term, been enregistered, at least in the sense that many non-French-speakers can perform a version of this style (as in the online uptakes analyzed in the chapter). At some level these performers know that it indexes a not fully serious but also not fully playful transcultural orientation—it plays into the long history of antagonism between the English and the French, and reciprocal stylizing resources are available to French speakers for parallel symbolic purposes (the English are *les rosbifs*, and they can be parodied via an enregistered fake-English phonological style). Fake French is also a trope of talking media, featuring in several prominent shows (including the 85 episodes of the BBC television sitcom *Allo Allo*). In any event, fake French as it features in the ad is a metacultural stance-bearing resource, rather than a 'variety' or a 'language code.'

Fakeness is a basic constructional principle of the ad's design. As noted in the chapter, the ad is visually styled to evoke the 1960s and the stage-set against which *Le Président* performs is itself styled to be visible *as* a stage-set. His eulogistic comments about the product are themselves transparently hyperbolic, echoing an earlier *Stella Artois* advertising campaign which referred to its beer as an *inimitable chef d'oeuvre*, an 'inimitable masterpiece.' Why does fakeness sell? An answer starts to emerge if we recognize the densely reflexive environment in which talking media operate. As Bauman and others have established (see relevant sources cited in the Introduction), performance in general involves an intensification of meaning which relates directly to the richness of contextualisation that supports performances. This is true of 'ordinary performance' (e.g. the telling of an anecdote to a group of face-to-face associates), but it is far more obviously true of those institutional-ized and technologized modes of performance that we can call 'high' performance events. Reflexivity refers to awareness, including degrees of awareness by consum-ers (audiences) of the entextualization processes that have shaped a performance. It also refers to degrees of awareness by producers and performers of the probable awareness of consumers, implying that reflexivity is a matter of complex lamina-tions of awareness being structured into certain types of communicative event.

Styling always implies a degree of awareness and strategic functioning in the light of metapragmatic awareness. As we have seen earlier, styling can be a matter of creating semiotic congruence with pre-existing normative expectations, or creat-ing dissonance with them by confounding or reinterpreting norms. But consumers are always crucially implicated in these processes, in the sense that stylistic meaning is a matter of uptake, which is itself conditioned by consumers' particular condi-tions of reflexive awareness. If we now come back to fakeness, we can see that what is knowingly styled to appear fake, if it is also perceived by consumers to be a knowing construction, can actually provide an attractive semiotic infrastructure for the delivery of social reality. The knowing construction of inauthentic mean-ing can provide a 'shell' that is able to part-conceal and part-reveal fragmentary authenticities, and this process is likely to appeal to audiences and customers who have acquired a taste or a tolerance for semiotic double entendres of this sort. That group might be said to already include all of us who participate in mediated culture.

This perspective may help us to understand how, and perhaps even why, fans of some popular TV sitcoms choose to recirculate images, slogans, dialogue frag-ments, and selective plot lines (e.g. via T-shirt displays), as in Bednarek's analysis of the widespread recirculation of elements of *The Big Bang Theory*. This activity is, as Bednarek points out, commercially embedded—it is an example of 'global' merchandising around a media product. But it is also a fascinating case study of how semiotic features of fictionally mediated worlds migrate into wider circula-tion where their significance arguably becomes even less determinate. *The Big Bang Theory* is a sustained evocation of US nerd culture, and wearing a T-shirt that knowingly references this culture and its talking media celebrities appears to align the wearer, albeit often in a highly cryptic way, with this cultural stance. All the same, as Bednarek observes, when the T-shirt text is a salient slogan from the show, it remains unclear whether the 'voice' in question is the wearer's or the source char-acter's, or a mixture of the two. It could presumably also be neither.

This sort of ambiguity is productive, perhaps particularly in the recreational dimensions of informal clothing wearing and sitcom watching. Bednarek argues (following Johnstone and Androutsopoulos) that the wearing of a *Big Bang Theory* T-shirt indexes membership of a *Big Bang Theory* watching community, which must be true in a general sense. But precisely how the wearer is positioning herself or himself in relation to that community remains interestingly opaque. To claim that wearers are 'endorsing' nerdism, or displaying their 'inheritance' in some sense of a mediated persona and that persona's world view, would seem to be premature, although endorsement of the show's entertainment value seems less controversial. On the other hand, if we see the displaying of a *Big Bang Theory* slogan on a T-shirt as an act of stylization (as Bednarek does), then we can say that it is in fact precisely the indeterminacy of the wearer's stance that is important.

Competing definitions of stylization exist, and recourse to Bakhtin does not resolve them. Androutsopoulos's definition in terms of "impersonating culturally familiar characters" (quoted earlier) raises the question of how we should interpret "impersonation." The voicing of others' voices can be done as simple referential accounting (reporting what was said), but alternatively in an act of celebration, in parody or in metaparody (where a speaker parodies his or her own stance as a parodist), and these are all crucially distinct in their pragmatic effects. Coupland has defined stylization more specifically, as a mode of performance whereby a stylizer knowingly holds back from signaling full ownership of a voiced utterance. In other words, stylization is a strategic exploitation of multilayered reflexivity, when the stylizer leaves traces of his or her own styling devices and leaves recipients to activate their own resources of reflexive interpretation in order to infer potential stances and intentions on behalf of the speaker. Stylizing is doing social meaning on the basis of provisionality. The wearing of a sloganizing T-shirt could easily fall within the remit of stylization in this sense, but so could many of the other styling processes that have been analyzed in this book.

Historical mediatization lies at the heart of a much broader process of 'reflexivization'—a social change that has been theorized to be one of the defining traits of globalizing late modernity, but a change that is also fundamentally semiotic. Technologically mediated communication (obviously, to different degrees in different contexts) has both exploited and accelerated this general tendency for meaning to be couched in provisional and conditional terms, even though it also has the resources to multiply and to intensify our experience of diversity. Talking media discourse is managed into existence through complex, multilayered design processes and editorial procedures entertained in reflexive awareness of what consumers and markets desire and demand. That discourse is consumed against complementary assumptions on behalf of increasingly discerning and active consumers. Social meaning, in its various sociolinguistic senses, cannot avoid being caught up in these relativizing webs in the context of talking media. Talking media and their derivatives are, as we have noted on several occasions, in some senses the home base for style and styling, but they are also active in leading a gradual shift into the mediated stylization of everything.

Note

1. Unattributed citations in this chapter refer to those authors' chapters in this book (to avoid tedious repetition of "in this volume"). We hold back from introducing new references in this chapter, in the interests of clarity and in our attempt at consolidating and extending previously introduced ideas and arguments here.

INDEX

Made in the USA
San Bernardino, CA
15 August 2017